HOW TO MAKE SLIME

35 DIY SLIME RECIPES

KUKI SHAMUS

iMasterLife.com

Copyright © 2017 by Kuki Shamus

All rights reserved. No part of this publication may be produced, transmitted, transcribed, stored in a retrieval system, or translated into any language, in any form, by any means, without written permission of the author. Understand that the information contained in this book is an opinion, and should be used for personal entertainment purposes only. You are responsible for your own behavior, and this book is not to be considered medical, legal, or personal advice. Nor is this book to be understood as putting forth any cure for any type of acute or chronic psychological illness. The programs and information expressed within this book are not medical or psychological advice, but rather represent the author's opinions and are solely for informational and educational purposes only. The Author and the publisher do not hold any responsibility for errors, omissions or contrary interpretation of the subject matter herein.

Edited by:

Silvia Shamus & Marc Shamus

Published by:

i Master Life Publishing

How to Make Slime / Kuki Shamus
ISBN-13: 978-1-945719-05-9

CONTENTS

Personal Message from Kuki Shamus 1

Introduction 2

Download Your Slime Tips And Tricks Resource Guide 3

Note from the Publisher 4

SECTION I SLIME BASICS 5

1. What is Slime 6
2. Supplies 7
3. Tools 9
4. Metric Conversion 17
5. Activators 18
6. Borax Solution 14
7. Safety 17
8. Storage & Care 18
9. Fun 19

SECTION II 100% BORAX FREE SLIME RECIPES 21

Recipe 1. Cherry Gum Slime 22

Recipe 2. Twinkle Galaxy Slime 25

Recipe 3. Crunchy Ball Slime 29

Recipe 4. Alicorn Slime 32

Recipe 5. Googly Monster Slime 35

Recipe 6. Fish Bowl Slime 38

Recipe 7. Pearly Whites Slime 42

Recipe 8. Glow in the Dark Slime 45

Recipe 9. Sunny Foam Slime 48
Recipe 10. 1-2 Simple Slime 51
Recipe 11. Fruity Edible Slime 53
Recipe 12. Nacho Cheesy Slime 56
Recipe 13. Hydra Slime 59
Recipe 14. Gold Rush Slime 62
Recipe 15. Abracadabra Slime 65
Recipe 16. Bubbly Slime 69
Recipe 17. Kuki Cookie Slime 72
Recipe 18. Cotton Candy Slime 76
Recipe 19. Jack O' Slime 79
Recipe 20. Snowy Christmas Slime 84

SECTION III   BORAX SLIME RECIPES 89

Recipe 21. Glitzy Slime 90
Recipe 22. Easy Glitter Slime 92
Recipe 23. Cherry Jiggly Slime 95
Recipe 24. Simple Crunch Slime 98
Recipe 25. Tie Dye Bubbly Slime 101
Recipe 26. Choco Nutella Slime 105
Recipe 27. Purplelicious Slime 108
Recipe 28. Sassy Glossy Slime 111
Recipe 29. Dark Matter Slime 115
Recipe 30. Blue Jelly Slime 119
Recipe 31. Cherry Slushy Slime 121
Recipe 32. Holographic Slime 125

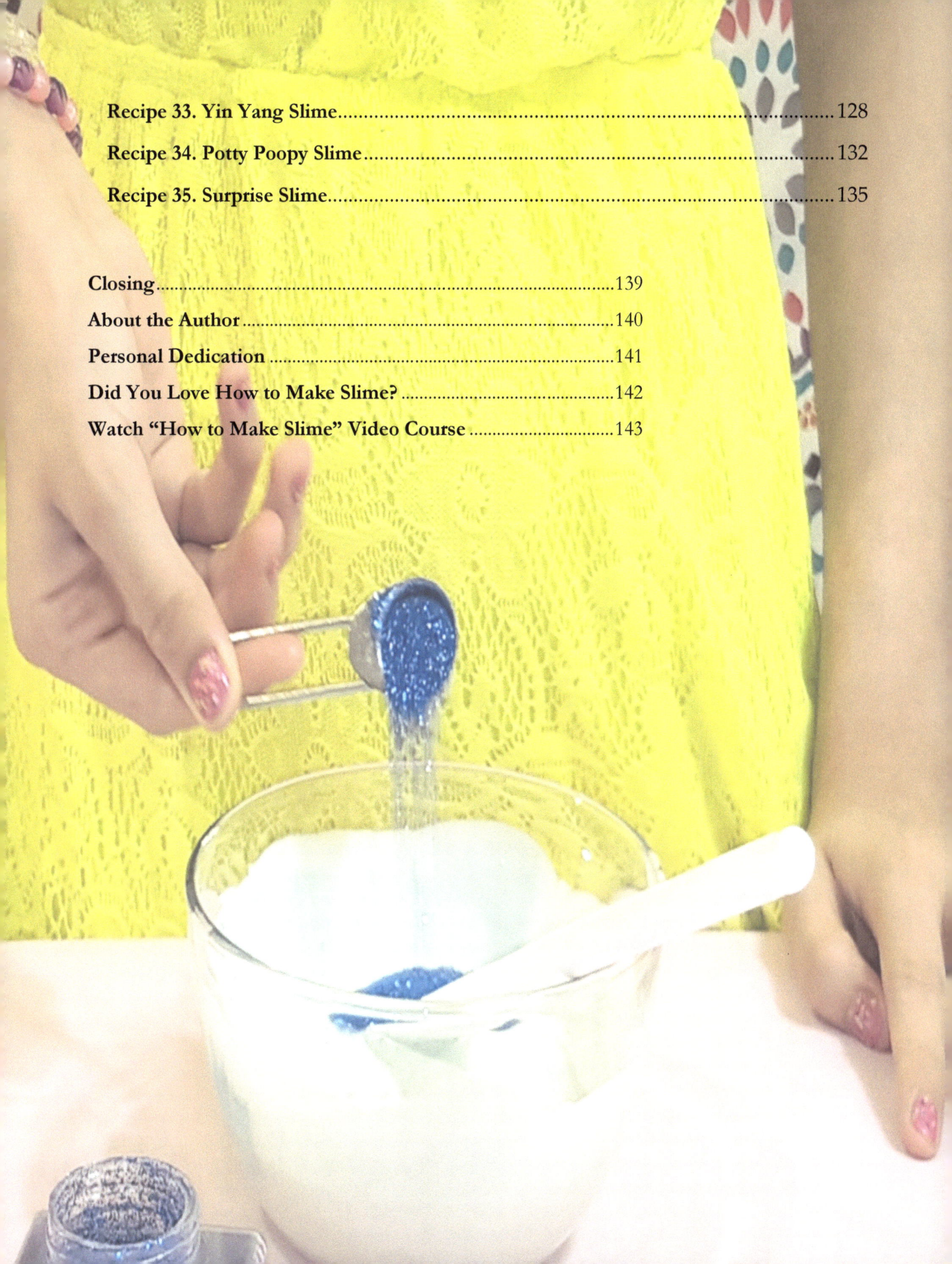

Recipe 33. Yin Yang Slime...128

Recipe 34. Potty Poopy Slime...132

Recipe 35. Surprise Slime...135

Closing..139
About the Author................................140
Personal Dedication............................141
Did You Love How to Make Slime?........142
Watch "How to Make Slime" Video Course................143

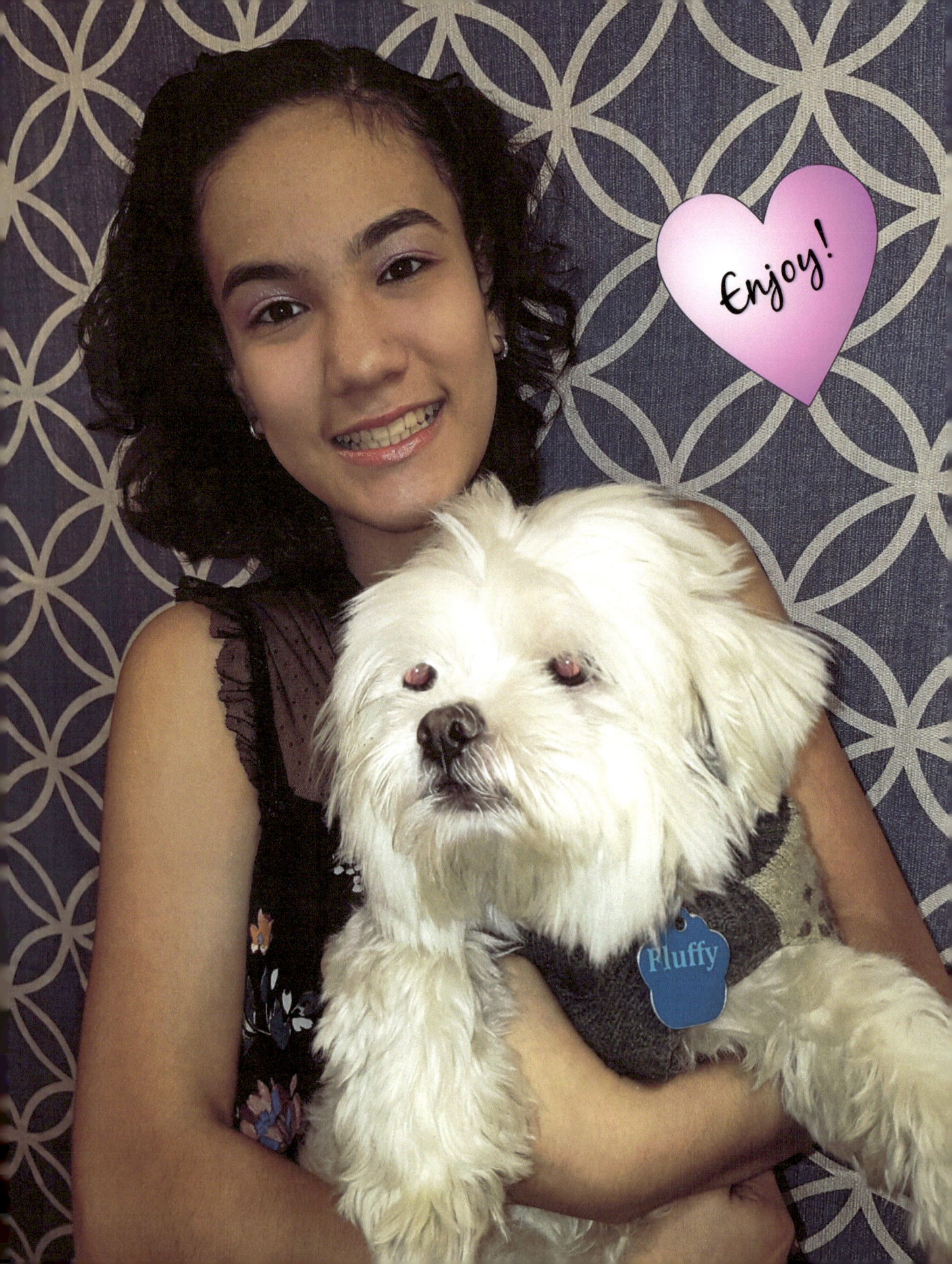

Personal Message from Kuki Shamus

Hi. Thank you so much for buying my book. I'm very proud of the final product. All profits from this book go directly towards funding my education costs and all the projects which I develop.

I'm Kuki Shamus. I'm a home schooled 12 years old. I love creativity and making things myself. My passions are music, art and dogs; especially Cavalier King Charles Spaniels. I, like most kids my age, enjoy spending time with friends, surfing the internet for funny videos and making videos to post on social media sites.

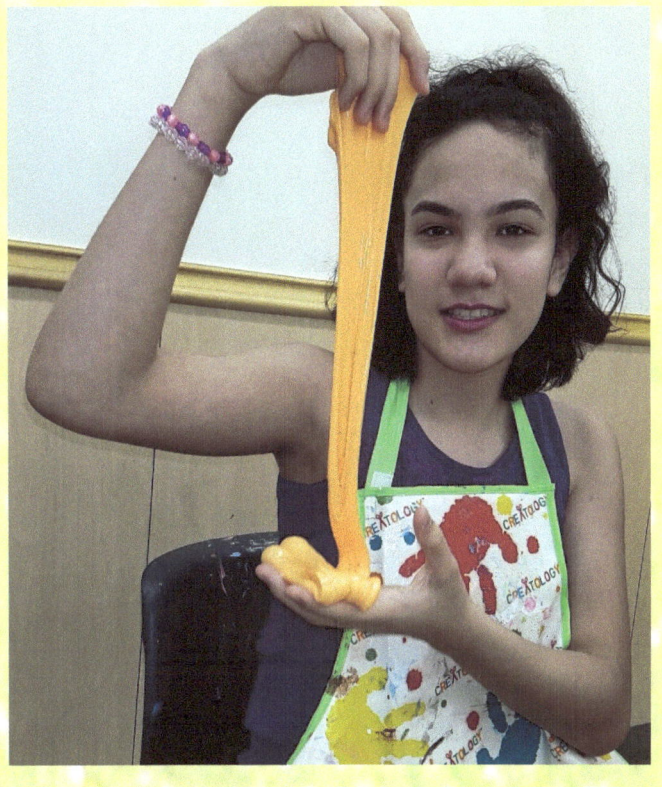

Slime is currently a popular trend. Although it is not a new idea, it has had a great amount of interest from kids this year. I'm in love with slime. I really am. What I love the most about slime is the texture as I poke it, the satisfying sound it makes as you squeeze it and the overall messy process of making it.

This slime book, **How to Make Slime**, is written by me, a kid, and made for kids as well as anyone else who wants to make their own slime to play with. It has been super important for me to share my tips and knowledge of slime with everyone after making tons of batches and learning what works and what doesn't.

I will teach you how to make 35 different types of slime. I know this might be way too much information for some of you as my book is super detailed, but take it slow and have a parent help you go through it. Make all the slimes that draw your interest.

All you need to know about making slime is written in this easy to follow book. Each recipe has a full ingredient list so you know what your parents need to buy. Each recipe also has step by step picture directions so even a novice can have fun making slime.

Introduction

I love slime so much. I watched hundreds of videos when I first started to make slime. However, most videos were not correct. They didn't provide needed measurements. Most of the time, the recipes were dead wrong. The slime did not come out as shown. I would waste all my time and supplies. The result was a mess. It was very frustrating when this happens since parents may feel you were wasting money.

I wrote this slime book and related slime video course (http://iMasterLife.com/SlimeCourse) because I want to help people like me to have fun making slime without all of this headaches. I believe this book can assist you and your parents understand how valuable slime making can be. After all, making slime is both a chemistry lesson and arts and crafts class.

To me, making slime is not just about having fun and being messy. As a kid, it is about learning too. Learning to read, learning to follow instructions, learning math when it comes to amounts of ingredients, and spending good quality time with your family and friends. I just wanted a good healthy way for you to learn and have fun while making better quality slime.

That is why I put this slime publication together for you!! This whole book is about slime. It includes cool recipes resulting in satisfying slime. This book will help you understand the science behind making slime and it will educate parents about slime. This book helps any beginner soon become a master of slime.

This book has 35 proven slime recipes All recipes have been fully tested by me and my "TESTING TEAM" aka sisters. Each of them gives the 35 recipes 1 thumb up for being fun and 1 thumb up for being satisfying. That's a lot of thumbs up!

My mom has always taught me to be thrifty and buy things without spending too much money. I share a few tips for people with low budgets. Your parents will be most likely to buy you ingredients for your slime "IF" it doesn't cost them too much money. In this book, I recommend ideas as to where to buy and find ingredients very cheap so your parents can buy you the ingredients you need.

So, do not worry if you never made slime before. There are very easy recipes that any person can make and have fun doing. I think that it will be a great way for you to spend time with your loved ones. Enjoy this book and have lots of fun creating slime.

DOWNLOAD YOUR SLIME TIPS AND TRICKS RESOURCE GUIDE

Get access to your FREE slime resource reference guide by going to

http://iMasterLife.com/SlimeBonus

Inside the bonus guide, you'll discover...

• How to be super Safe when handling slime

• What is the best way to Clean Up slime spills

• Cool Hacks to make the best slime ever

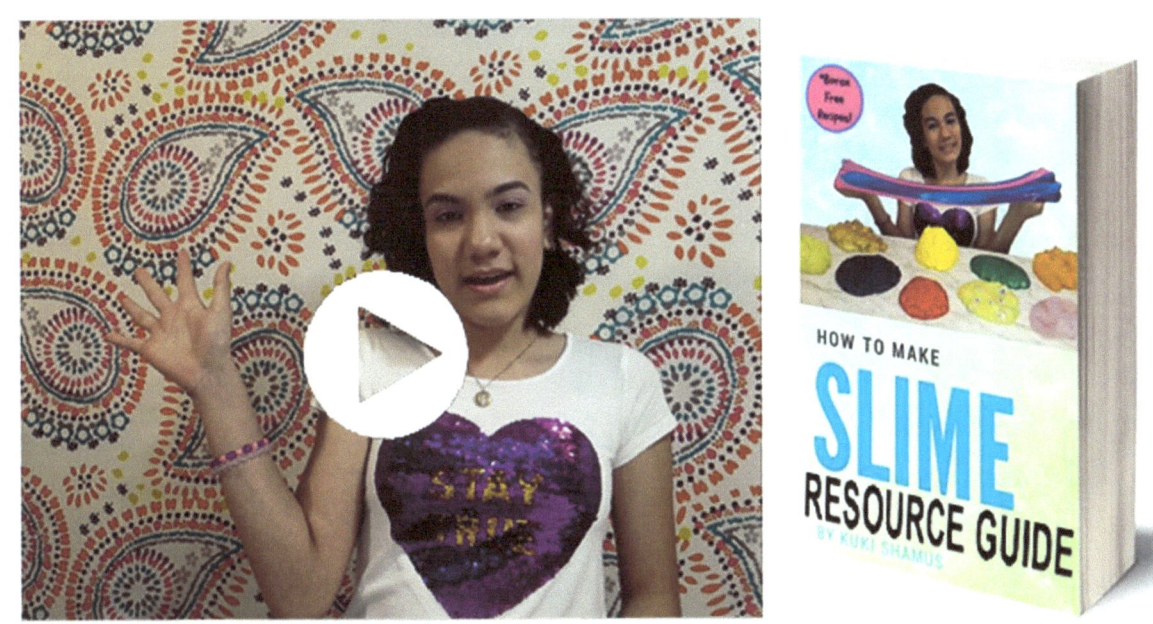

Note from the Publisher

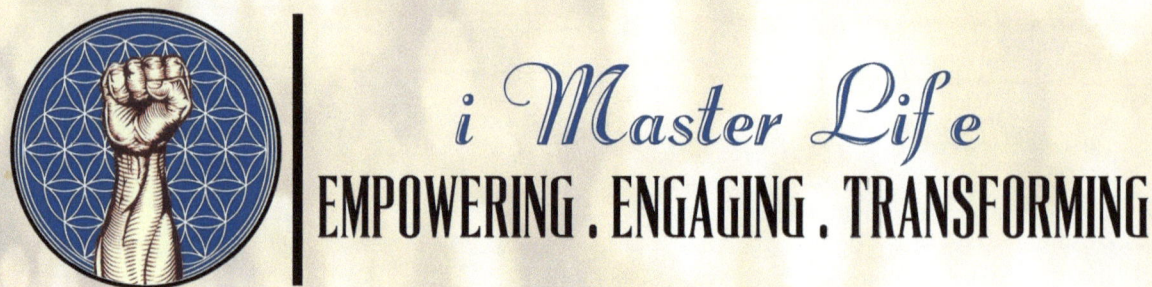

Thank you for purchasing this **i Master Life Publishing** book. Our goal is to get high quality Life Mastery materials and other worthwhile media into the hands of incredible people like you.

FOLLOW US:

Join our mailing list and get updates on new releases, deals, bonus content and other great publications from **i Master Life Publishing**.

iMasterLife.com/fan

SUPPORT US:

If you enjoyed this or any of our other books, would you please help support **I Master Life**. The sustainable revenue you provide ensures we can continue to provide publishing the very best media possible for you.

Just go to this link:

iMasterLife.com/fund

Thank You!

Marc A. Shamus
Founder

KUKI SHAMUS

SECTION I
SLIME BASICS

Summary

In this section, I go into details about all you need to know about creating slime. Be sure to read this section because doing things correctly will give you success in making the best slime ever.

Slime basics I will discuss include:
• I will cover supplies (ingredients), tools and activators you need to buy.
• I also explain what an activator is, which activators to use and why.
• Learn how to make the cheapest and easiest activator to have in hand when you want to make slime quick.
• I provide a metric conversion cheat sheet I created to make this book user friendly world-wide.
• I show you safety tips to protect yourself as well as recommendations on how to store and care for your slimes, thus preserving your slimes longer, enabling long term slime fun.

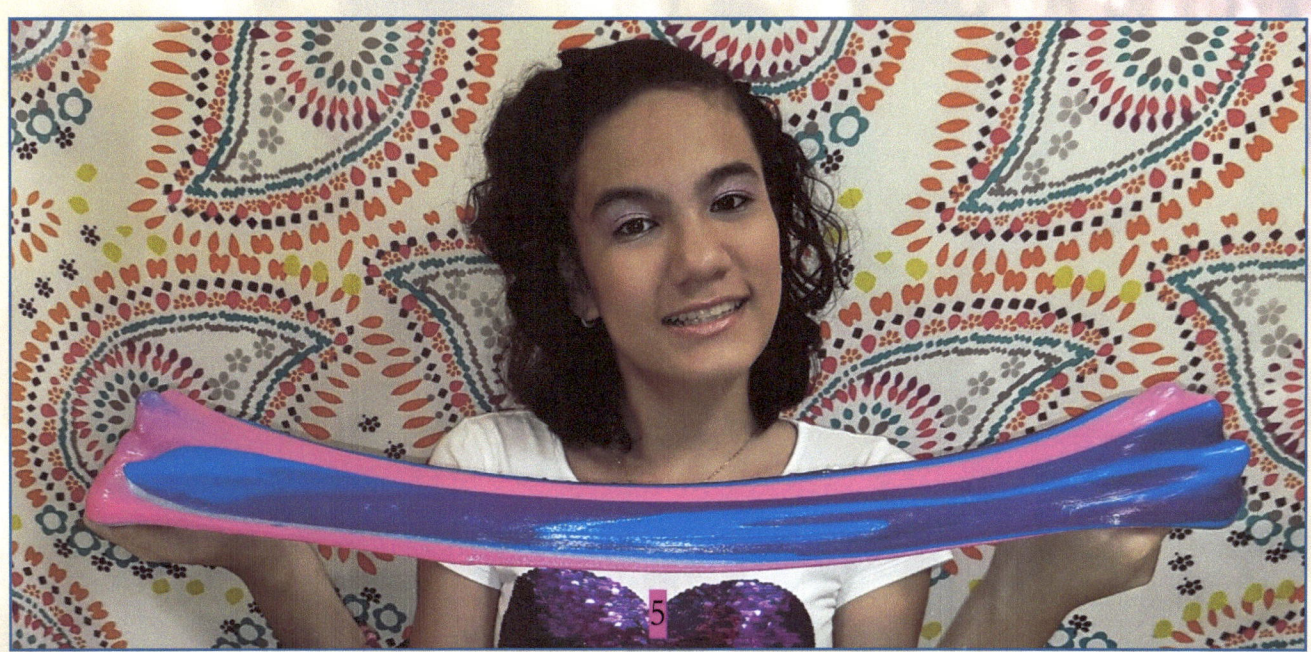

1. WHAT IS SLIME

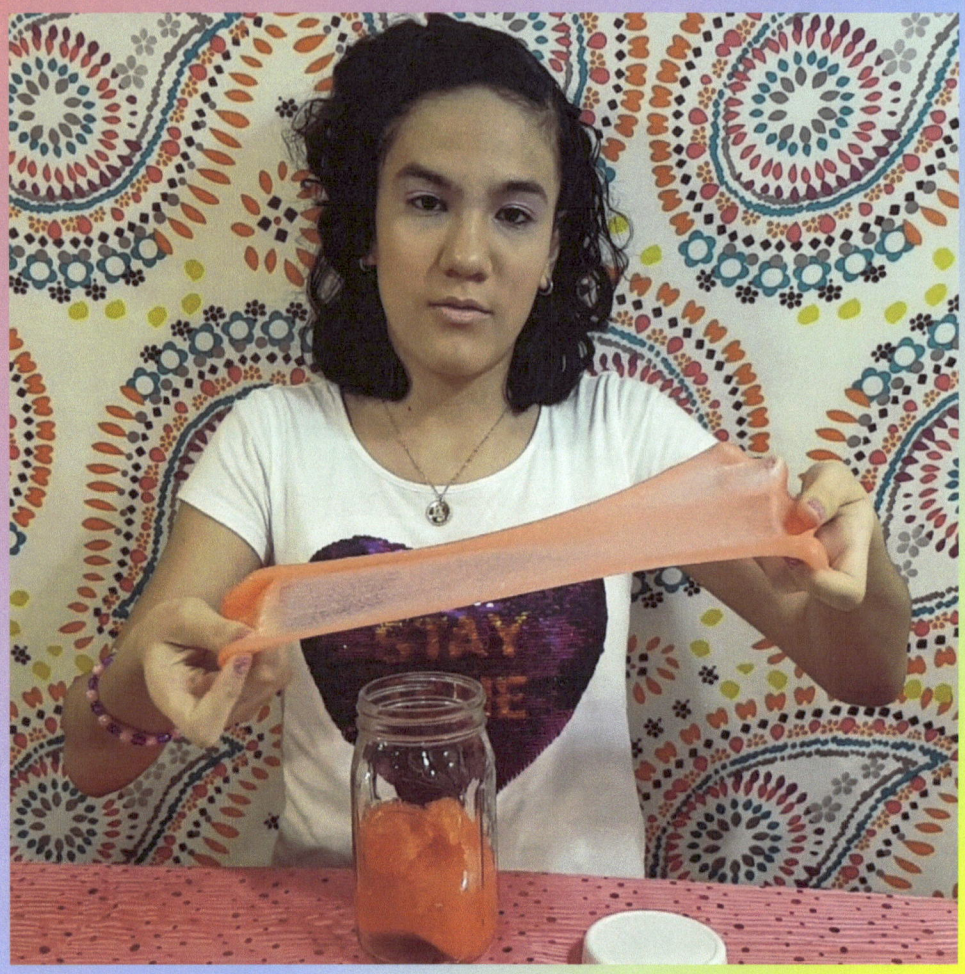

I love, love, love slime. I love making it, poking it, stretching it, squishing it through my fingers. Most everyone loves it. I think slime is so cool because when you think about it, slime is science, more specifically chemistry.

Chemistry is the science of mixing chemicals together. I just love how some simple ingredients that you have at home can make such a fun thing like slime.

But what is slime exactly? Slime is a gooey stress toy that is made primarily with PVA glue, borax and water. Slime can be created as any color you can dream up. There are many variations of slime and lots of toppings you can add to it.

There is no set rule how slime should look. This is why it is so much fun creating it, since you are adding your own creativity into each batch you make.

2. Supplies

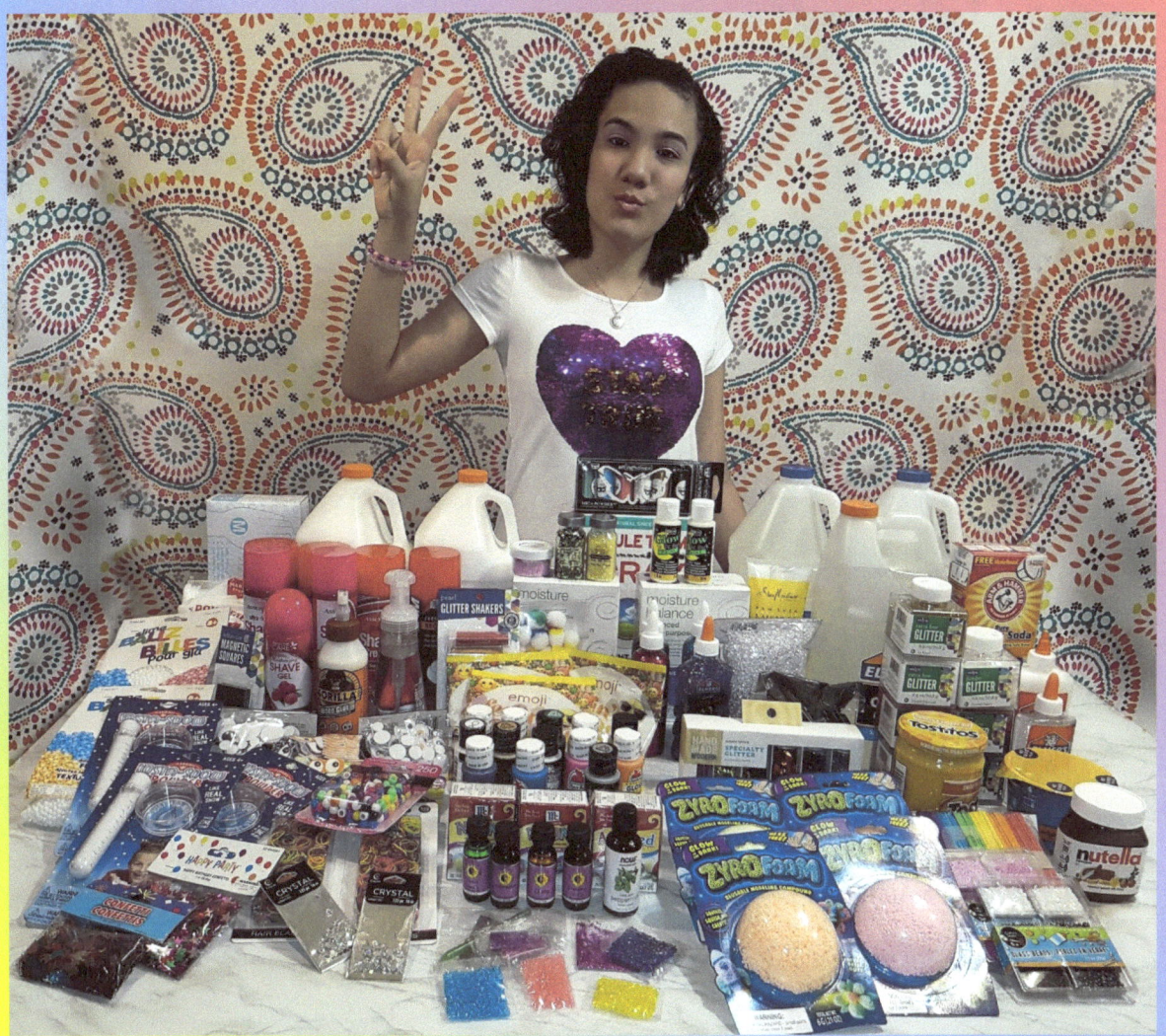

Supplies are going to be all of the ingredients needed to make your slimes. Please make sure you have these ready to go before beginning to make any given slime. A few main key ingredients you really need include:

1) Base – This would be the foundation core to your slime. One of the most popular bases that people use is PVA glue. For the best quality batches of slime, I suggest that you use Elmer's glue since this glue is not watered down. It's thicker in consistency than other glues and is a non-toxic product. Any PVA glue will work just fine even if it isn't Elmer's glue.

In edible slimes, your base could be something like gummy candies. You can see this base being used in my **Fruity Edible Slime** recipe on page 91.

HOW TO MAKE SLIME

2) Activator - In most slimes, your activator is a liquid that brings the "Base" together to form the slime. Some activators you could use include Borax Solution, Liquid Starch, Laundry Detergent and Contact Lens Solution. The exception to this rule would be the use of Shaving Gel being used to activate a wood glue base in my **1-2 Simple Slime** recipe on page 87.

In edible slimes, your activator is a powder that brings the food "Base" together to form the slime. Some edible activators you could use include Corn Starch and Powdered Sugar, both of which together are used to activate the gummy candy base in my **Fruity Edible Slime** recipe on page 91. Flour is an alternative edible activator.

For more details on activators, go to **Chapter 5 Activators** on page 13.

3) Texture Ingredients – Items that will give your slime a better feel and texture. Some of these are baby oil, hand lotion, baby powder, corn starch, shaving cream, shaving gel and foaming hand wash.

4) Toppings. - Things you add to a slime recipe to give it color, texture, or scent and make it fun. Ideas for toppings are sequins, glitter, rubber bands, coloring, scent, glow in the dark paint, styrofoam beads, jewels and any other decorative items that are small.

I recommend buying toppings at dollar store type of shops where you can get a lot of items for a small amount of money. Another great place to purchase items at is Walmart and Target. Both of these stores have their own craft section where you can find a good selection of these things.

Note: When you add your toppings during the slime making process, never add more in total amount of dry ingredients (toppings) than an amount equal to that of your wet ingredients (slime) in that recipe. So, for example, if you have 1 cup of wet ingredients, the maximum amount of toppings you could use would also be 1 cup.

3. TOOLS

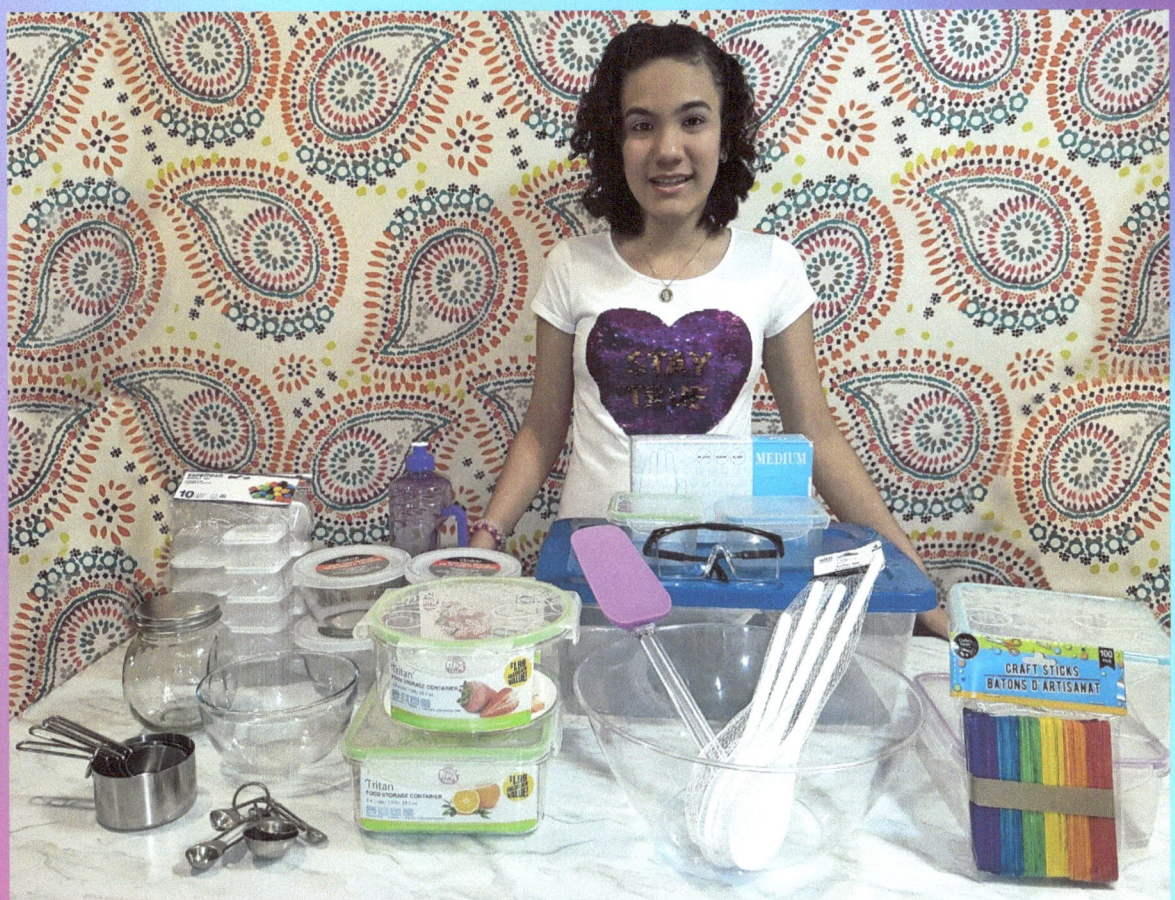

There are a few tools you will need when making slime. Some are very important, while others are optional. Your parents probably already have most, if not all of these in the kitchen already. If your mom and dad prefer you did not use theirs with making slime, you can buy these items at the dollar store.

Slime is usually easy to clean and can come off most tools. Tools can be washed in the dishwasher. It is important that you obey your mom and dad and do what they think is best.

Note: When making recipes, don't mix wood glue with wooden tools or it will get stuck to it.

HOW TO MAKE SLIME

- **1 Large Mixing Bowl.** Glass or metal is best, but you can still use plastic.

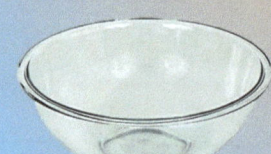

- **Measuring Cups.** I like the stainless-steel best, but you can use plastic

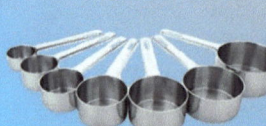

- **Measuring Spoons** Either metal or plastic is fine.

- **1 Large Measuring Cup (2-Cup size).** I like glass, but plastic is fine as long as you can use it in the microwave.

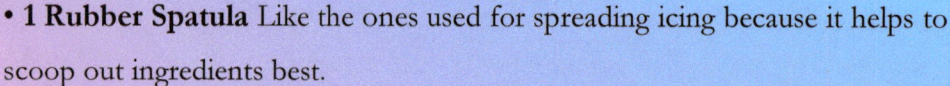

- **1 Rubber Spatula** Like the ones used for spreading icing because it helps to scoop out ingredients best.

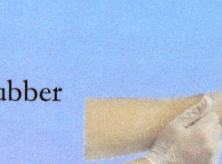

- **Disposable Gloves.** You can find these at the Dollar Tree. I like the rubber ones, not the plastic ones, because they end up being too loose.

- **Mixing Sticks** Like the ones for popsicles. Natural color is best.

- **Protective Eye Glasses.** Again, found at most dollar stores. A $1 item to make sure nothing accidentally goes inside your eye.

- **Airtight Containers** Use to store your slime. Ziploc bags don't contain slime well. I found out the hard way when I ruined my mom's canvas storage bins because the slime dripped out of the plastic bag. So please buy airtight containers. Besides, it helps your slime last longer You can buy them any size almost anywhere. I found some awesome BPA free rubber lid containers at my local 99 Cent stores.

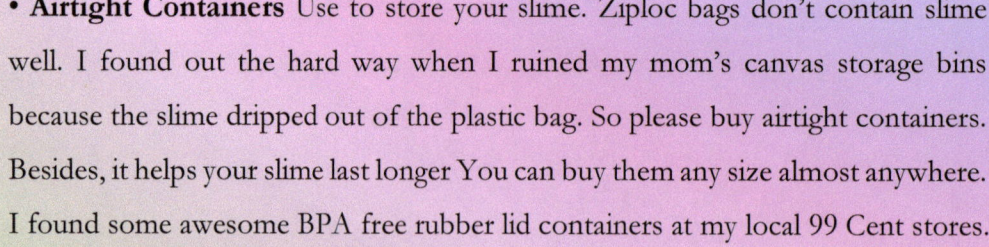
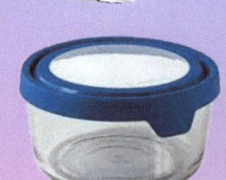

4. Metric Conversion

I believe everyone will enjoy making the slime recipes in this book, no matter where you live. The country I live in, the United States of America, bases its measurements from the old Imperial system. These are the type of measurements I will refer to in all of the recipes I provide.

However, much of the rest of the world prefers to use the Metric system. Therefore, I wanted to make sure there is an easy way to convert the recipe measurements, so all people can enjoy this book. Below are simple conversions of the most common measurements I will use in this book.

$1/8$ Teaspoon = 0.5 Milliliter

$1/4$ Teaspoon = 1 Milliliter

$1/2$ Teaspoon = 2 Milliliters

1 Teaspoon = 5 Milliliters

1 Tablespoon = 15 Milliliters

1 Ounce = 29.57 Milliliters

$1/4$ Cup = 60 Milliliters

$1/2$ Cup = 120 Milliliters

1 Cup = 240 Milliliters

5. ACTIVATORS

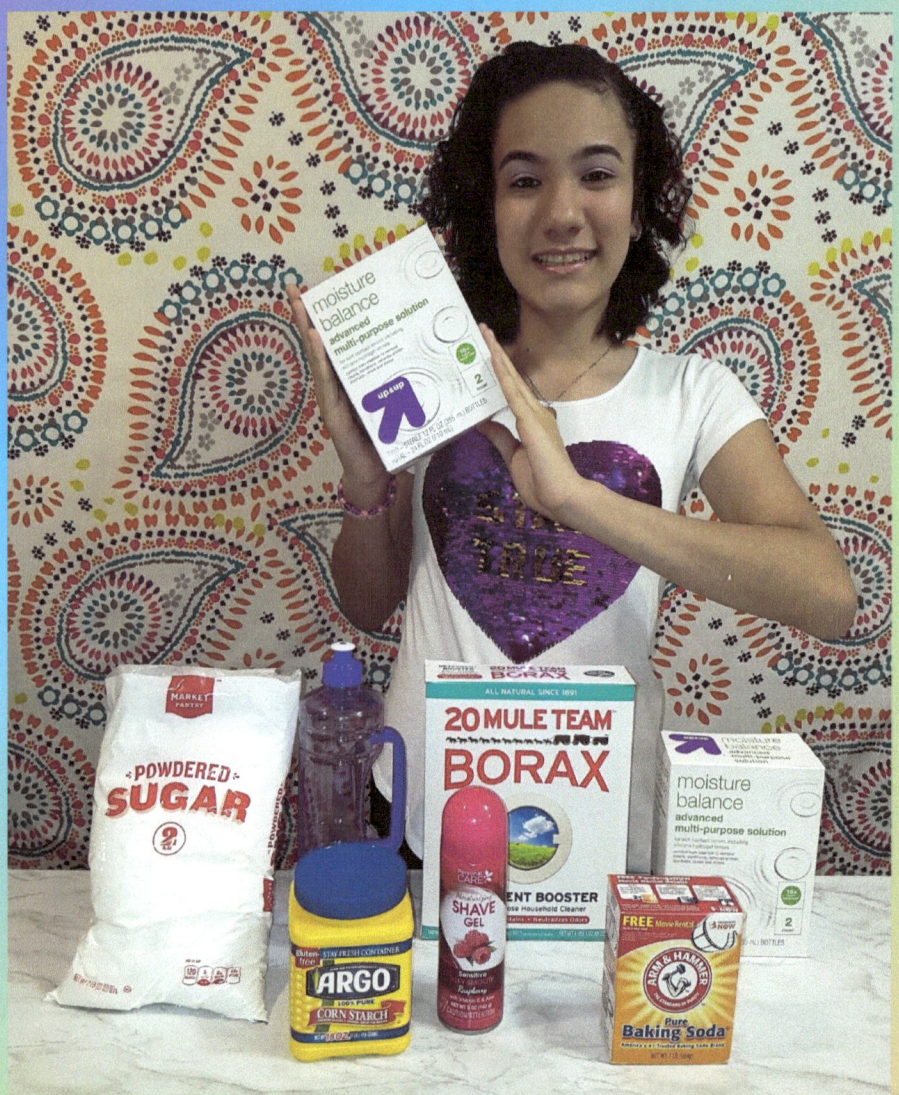

As I said before, slime making is science. When we mix the glue with another chemical, slime is the result. In order to get slime, you need what is called an activator. There are a few options for activators:

1) **Borax solution** – Cheapest to buy at about $4 for a four-pound box.

2) **Liquid Starch** – Like Sta-Flo

3) **Laundry Detergent** – Liquid detergent like Tide

4) **Contact Lens Solution** – Most expensive to buy at $3 for a generic brand 4-ounce bottle.

There are some parents who are concerned with using borax. I personally don't think borax is dangerous, yet I do think some kids are not supervised and equally do not know how to handle this very natural and old ingredient.

The MSDS (Material Safety Data Sheet) for borax gives it a same rating as Baking Soda and Salt. So, it is not very dangerous. My mom and I looked up this information just to make sure we do not expose kids to anything dangerous.

Dipping your bare hands into any chemical and not washing them afterwards is not safe. Even when you touch liquid hand soap and do not rinse your hands off, it can cause a rash and itching.

Some kids are more sensitive than others, so I always suggest you should wear gloves and eye protection while mixing your slime. If you prefer to not use borax, do not worry, you can safely use contact lens solution no different than the borax solution.

In this book, I will mostly focus on borax solution and contact lens solution for 2 reasons:

1) I believe that slime making should be as Non-Toxic as possible. Therefore, handling borax liquid solution and contact lens solutions are much better than liquid starch.

2) Liquid starch and detergents tend to have very strong scents. I have tried making a recipe that contained a very popular laundry detergent and after making it and playing with it just for a few hours gave me a big headache. I don't want kids making ANY slime with any potential dangerous ingredient.

Because of these two reasons, I focus only on borax solution and contact lens solution. So, have fun choosing which ever makes sense for you and your parents budget. If you see any recipe and it has listed borax as the activator and you prefer not to use borax, just switch it over to the same quantity of contact lens solution.

Recipes with contact lens solution, also need baking soda to activate the slime. In these recipes, add a pinch of baking soda (baking powder will not work) to glue mixture. Then slowly add contact lens solution (MUST HAVE BORIC ACID).

*Note about eye drops/saline solution: Make sure that you see either Boric Acid or Sodium Borate in the ingredients. If not, check for the words "Buffered Saline" on the package. If it says this, you can make slime!

6. BORAX SOLUTION

Everything should be quick and easy when making slime. Here is a very simple way to always have an activator solution in a borax recipe without having to make borax solution every single time you want to make slime. This solution will last 2 weeks so make smaller batches at a time.

Buy the following:
1) 16-ounce Plastic Water Bottle with Pull Top spout. You can buy one at dollar stores.
2) 20 Mule Team Borax Box - usually sold as a 4-pound box for a little more than $4

I like to make this borax solution because once is made I can just keep making more as I need and it only cost me the borax box and the bottle cost just the one time. Literally, a little more than a **$5** investment can give a person more than **56 Gallons** of borax solution.

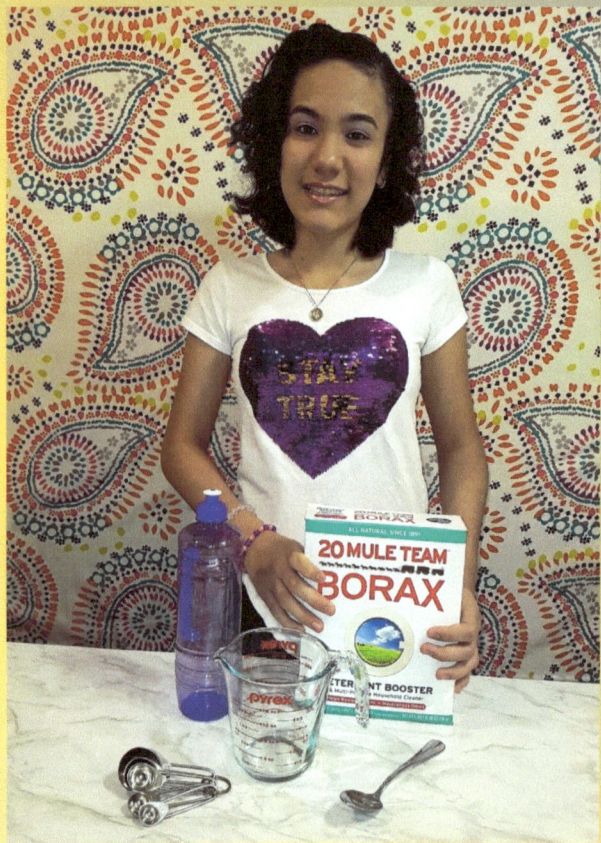

Ingredients
- 2 Cups Warm Water
- 1 Teaspoon Borax Powder

Directions

1) With the help of your parent, heat up **2 Cups Warm Water**. Do not make the water too hot; just warm enough to help dissolve the borax powder.

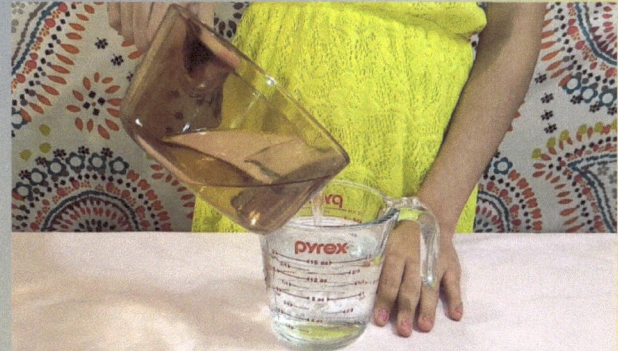

2) Then add 1 teaspoon of **Borax Powder**.

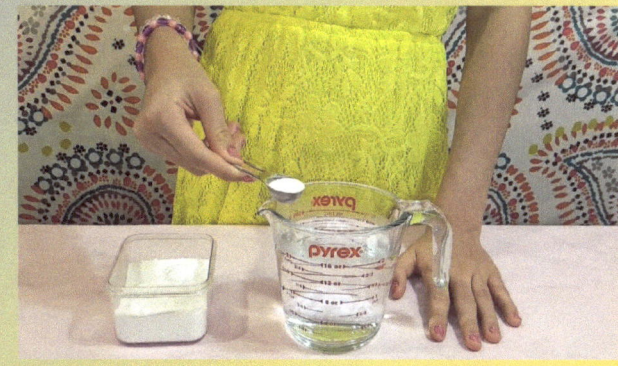

3) Use a **Spatula** to mix powder well until it fully dissolves.

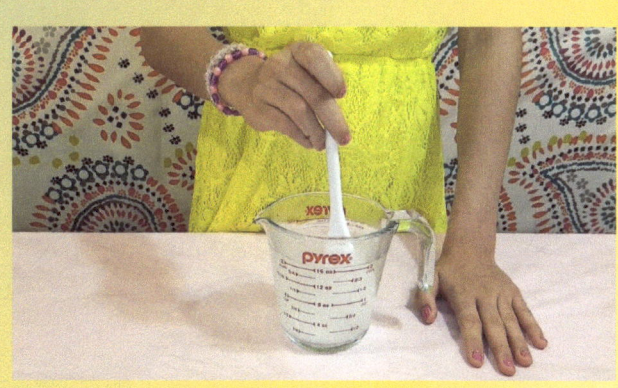

4) Pour this Borax Solution into the bottle water. Use a funnel to avoid spilling.

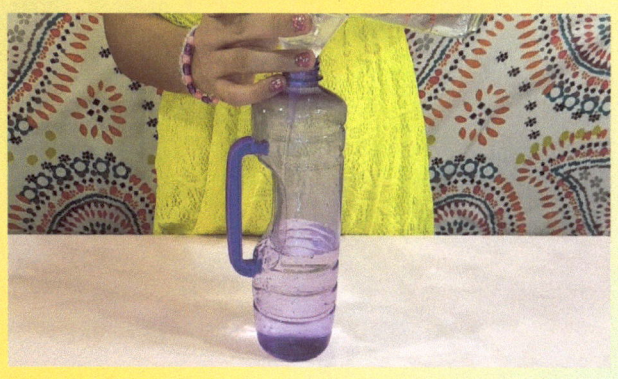

HOW TO MAKE SLIME

5) <u>Close</u> <u>the</u> <u>Bottle</u> with the pull top spout.

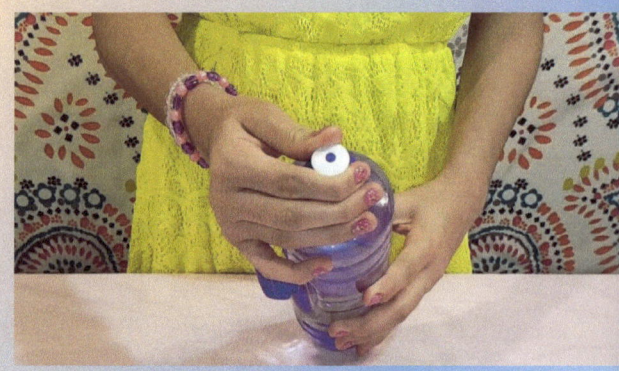

6) <u>Label</u> your Borax Solution bottle so no one accidentally drinks from the bottle. (optional)

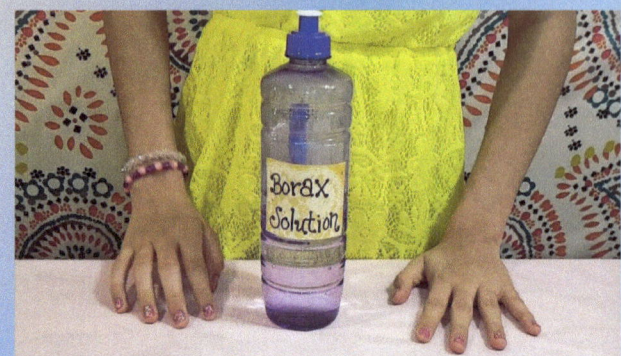

Store somewhere at room temperature. This solution only lasts 1 week. If you do not use all empty out your bottle and make a fresh batch again. The reason why we buy the pull top spout type of water bottle is because it will be easier to squirt directly into the measuring cup or directly into the glue as we are making our slime.

7. SAFETY

I want parents and kids to be aware that Safety is very important. Always be safe and ask a parent permission before making or mixing ANYTHING at home. This is VERY important, not just when making slime, but with everything. Slime making is a fun process when we are smart with safety. So be careful while having fun.

Safety Tips:

1) Always play at a table or hard surface that will not get stained or get slime stuck to it. Slime will stick to any fabric surface. Many of my friends have gotten slime stuck to their bed sheets, clothes and hair.

2) Never touch your eyes while making slime as you will cause for major eye irritation. If you do this by accident, be sure to flush out your eyes with cold water as the initial treatment.

3) Always wash your hands thoroughly, but gently with soap and water after slime play so there is less chance for itching or rashes.

4) Play nice with slime. Never throw slime around the room or at other people. Most likely, it will lead to something or someone having an issue as discussed in Safety Tips numbers 2 and 3.

5) Get help from an adult when heating up water for any recipe.

6) Don't go to sleep when playing with slime, for obvious reasons.

7) Wear protective eye glasses and disposable gloves as needed to protect you.

8) Clean up whatever mess you make after making or playing with slime.

8. STORAGE & CARE

Have fun with your slime. It does not have to be a one or two-time use after you make it. Keep slime stored in **Airtight Containers** to keep it from drying out and decaying too fast. If stored correctly, your slime may last about one month before it falls apart. Take good care of it so you can play with it for a long time.

I have friends who chose to store their slime in plastic sandwich bags, which became a big accident. These type of bags rip easy and don't close too well. Slime will leak out and may ruin things it spills on. Shelf life of slime stored this way is short lived, since it dries out super quick too.

Storage container size is also a consideration. You would not want a large container if you only made a really small batch of slime. It would be better to use a tiny storage container instead, so less air is in the container and it will be easy for storage space.

Even when using sturdy airtight storage containers, be sure to always put your lids on correctly. These containers, while much better than the plastic sandwich bags, still can spill and slime will dry out fast if the lids are not secured right. A moment of care to double check the lid is on correctly will make a big difference.

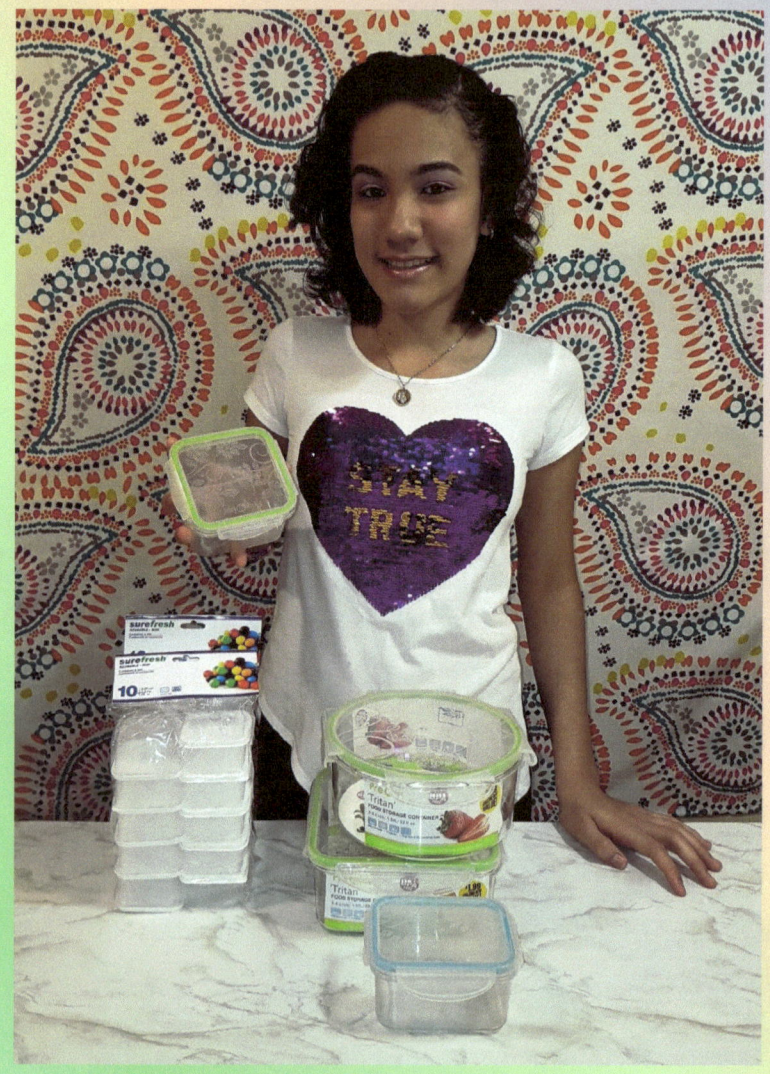

9. FUN

Sometimes, you have to change the recipe. Some companies have products that are not 100% the same chemistry as another product. Take these recipes I provide and follow them, but if you have to improvise, then do so. Making slime is about **fun**. So have a blast while making all these wacky and cool recipes. Now let's get to making some slime!

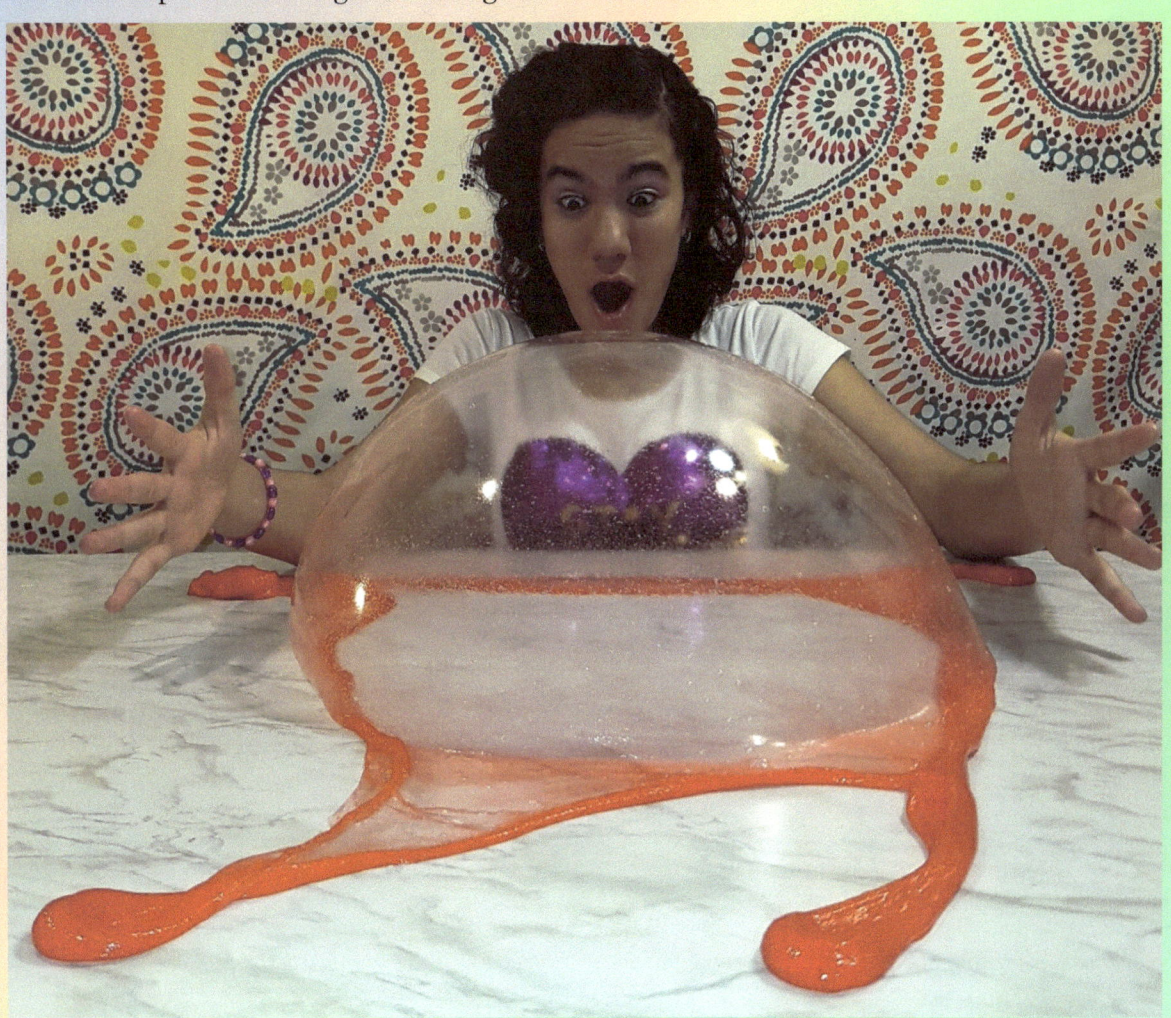

HOW TO MAKE SLIME

> Remember:
>
> Be Safe & Have Fun!

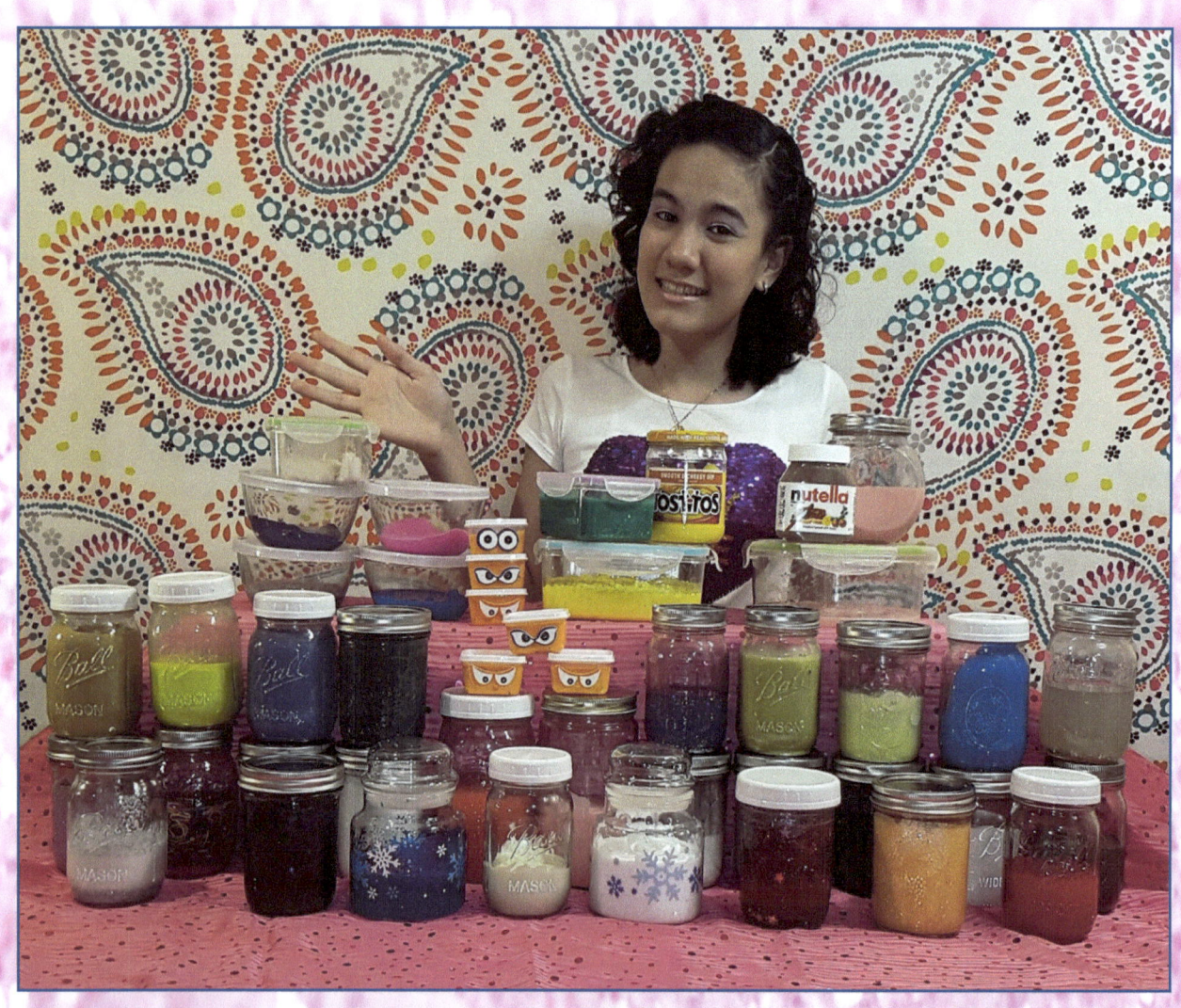

SECTION II
100% BORAX FREE SLIME RECIPES

All of the recipes in this section DO NOT contain borax.

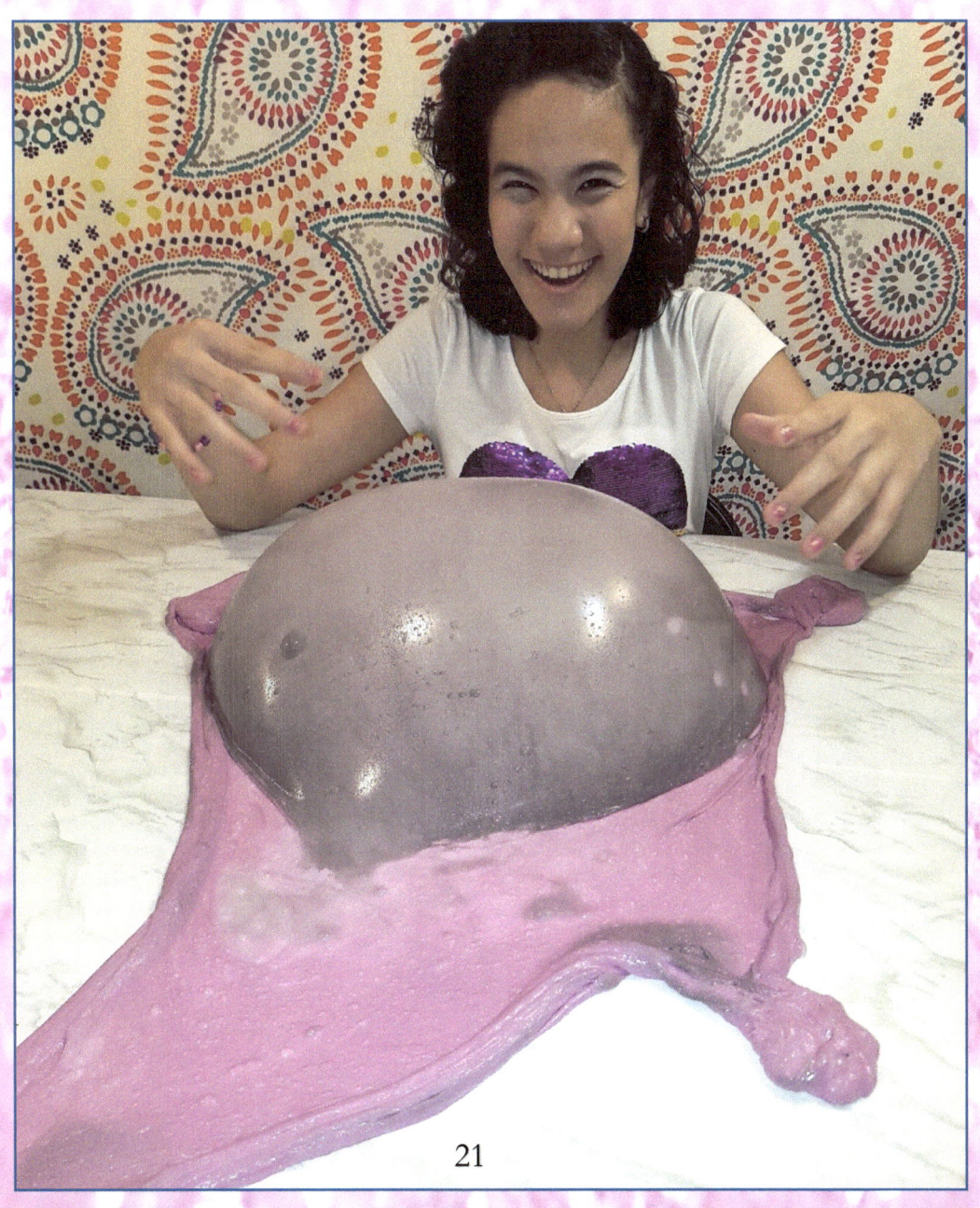

HOW TO MAKE SLIME

Recipe 1. Cherry Gum Slime

This recipe is call Cherry Gum because its smells and looks like Cherry flavored gum. We add red color and cherry scent so it resembles bubble gum. This slime is very light and fluffy to the touch. Now you have a reason to play with your dads shaving cream. This is by far one of my top 3 favorite slime recipe's.

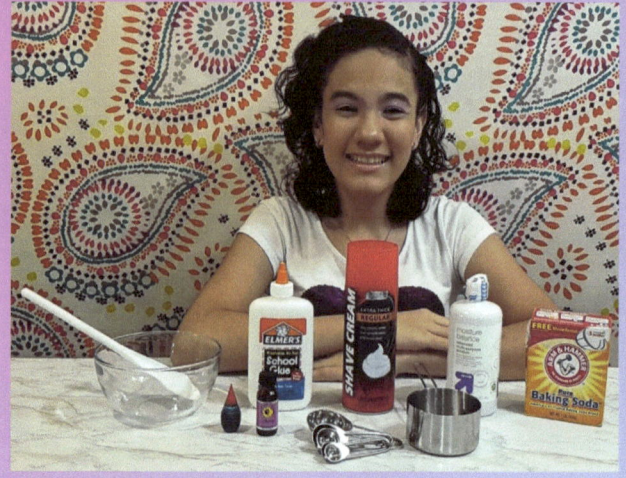

Ingredients

- 1 Cup White PVA Glue
- 8 Drops Red Food Coloring
- 3 Cups Unscented Shaving Cream
- $1/2$ Teaspoon Cherry Scent
- 1 Teaspoon Baking Soda
- 4 Tablespoons Contact Lens Solution

Directions

1) Pour **White Glue** into your mixing bowl.

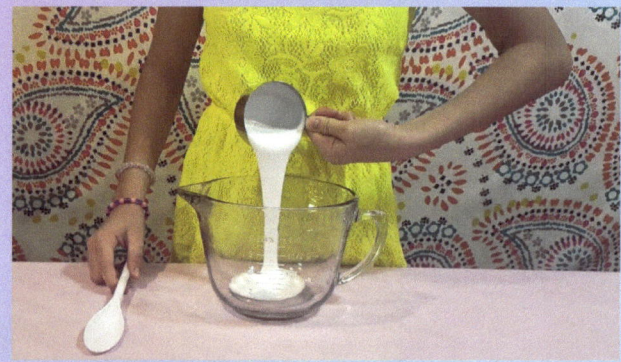

2) Add **Red Food Coloring** and mix well.

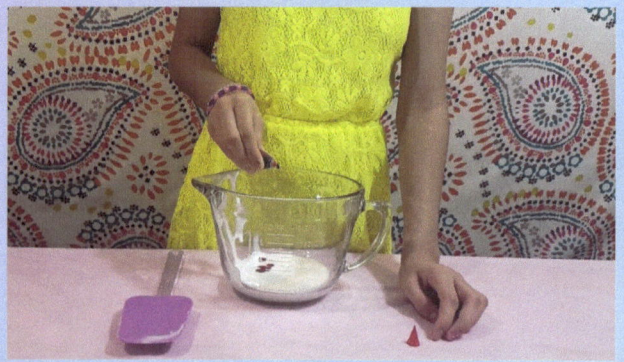

3) Add **Baking Soda** and mix well until dissolved

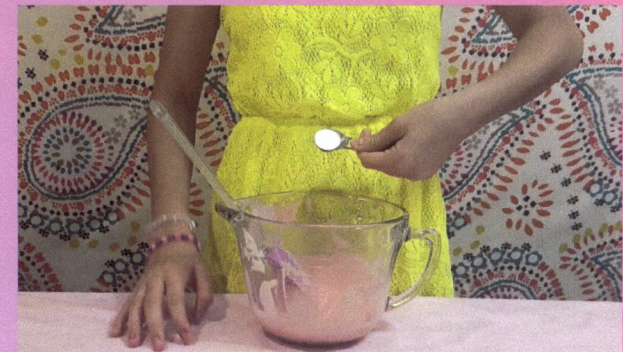

4) Add **Shaving Cream** with help of a spatula. Slowly add one cup at a time to make sure it mixes well.

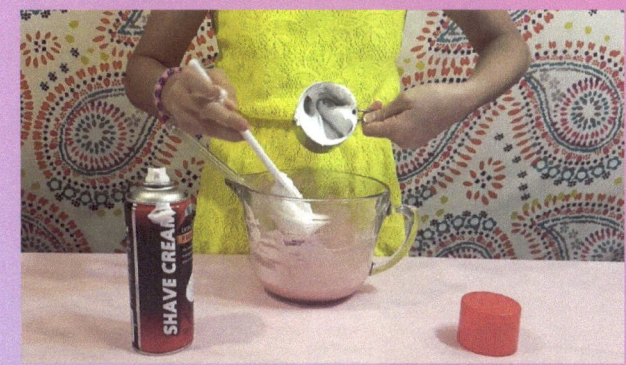

5) Add **Cherry Scent** and mix well.

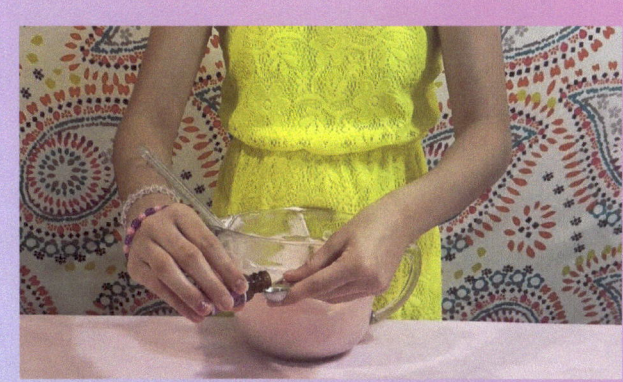

6) Add **Contact Lens Solution** slowly. Squirt directly from the bottle to mixing bowl. Don't over use contact lens solution or slime comes out hard like rubber. You need about 4 Tablespoons. No measuring spoons are being used, therefore, use your best judgement.

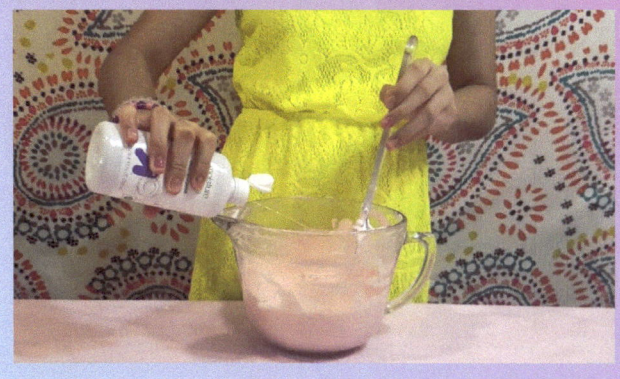

HOW TO MAKE SLIME

7) Use a **Spatula** to mix as you keep adding contact lens solution. Keep stirring until the slime doesn't stick to the bowl or your hands.

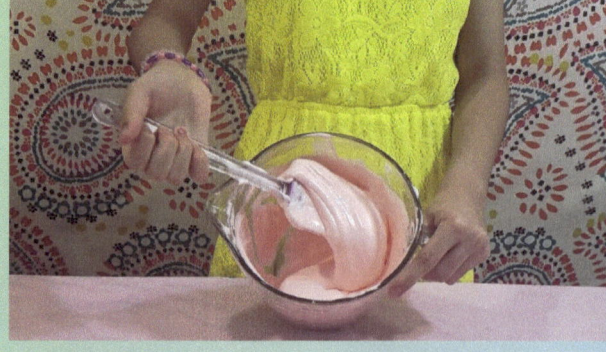

8) Once the glue starts to look like slime, **Knead** the mixture with your hands until you get the right slime consistency; smooth and soft enough to stretch with hands.

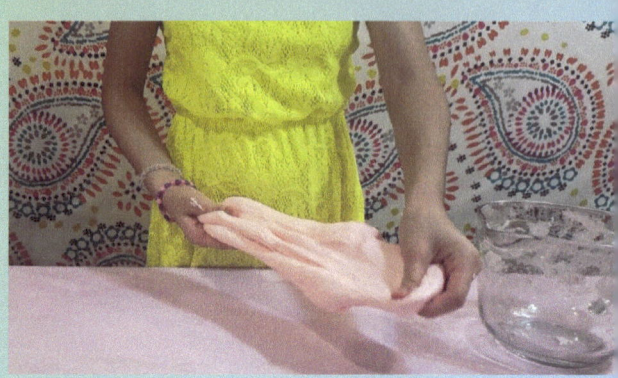

WHAT THE SLIME SHOULD LOOK LIKE

Stretched Cherry Gum Slime

Cherry Gum Slime in a **Storage Container**

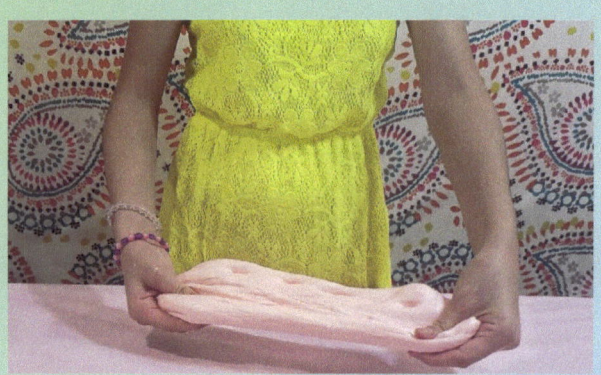
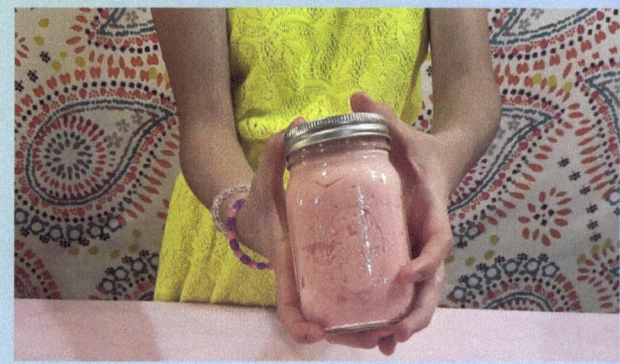

Now you have a super cool, cherry gum slime.

RECIPE 2. TWINKLE GALAXY SLIME

This slime is so fun to play with. It does take a little more work than the other slime recipes, but it is well worth it. The reason it's called twinkle galaxy slime is because it looks almost like a twinkling galaxy.

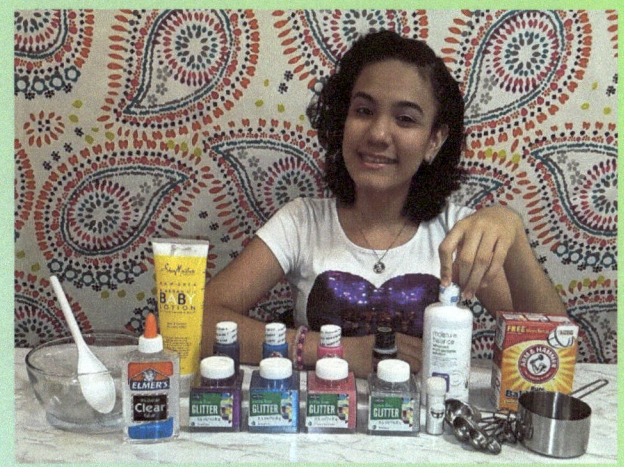

This slime is full of wonder and eye-catching colors. I really love the look the hologram powder gives it. This is so unique looking that it is worth every penny you spend.

You will be making four different color batches, so I recommend doing all four at the same time as it is much easier. The ingredient list is for each of the color. So just multiple by four

Ingredients
- $1/2$ Cup Clear PVA Glue each Batch
- $1/2$ Teaspoon Purple Acrylic Paint
- $1/2$ Teaspoon Blue Acrylic Paint
- $1/2$ Teaspoon Bright Pink Acrylic Paint
- $1/2$ Cup Teaspoon Metallic Silver Acrylic Paint
- 1 Teaspoon Matching Color Glitter each Paint Color
- 1 Teaspoon Hand Lotion each Bowl
- $1/8$ Teaspoon Hologram Powder each slime color
- $1/2$ Teaspoon Baking Soda each Slime Color
- 2 Tablespoons Contact Lens Solution for each Slime Color

HOW TO MAKE SLIME

Directions

1) Pour **<u>Clear</u> <u>Glue</u>** into all 4 mixing bowls.

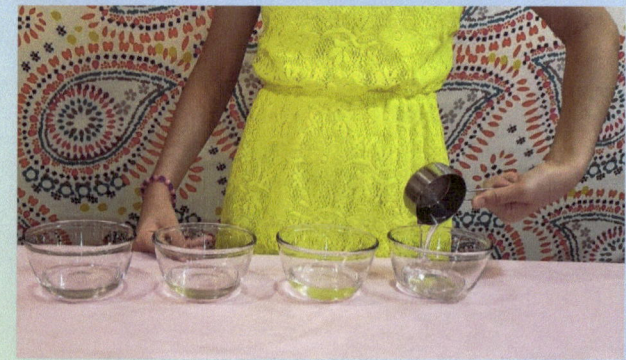

2) Add 2 Drops of **<u>Paint</u>** to each bowl (1 paint color per bowl) and mix well

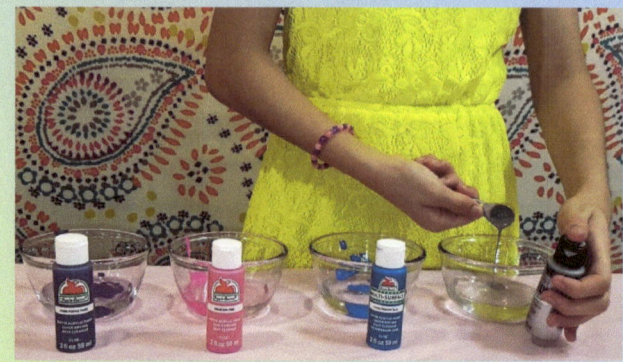

3) Add **<u>Glitter</u>** to each bowl to match the paint in it and mix well

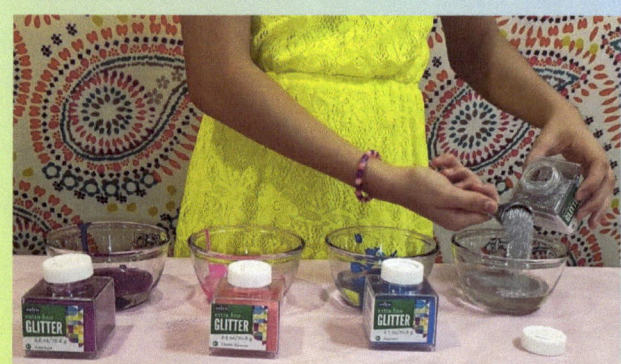

4) Add **<u>Hologram</u> <u>Powder</u>** to each bowl and mix well

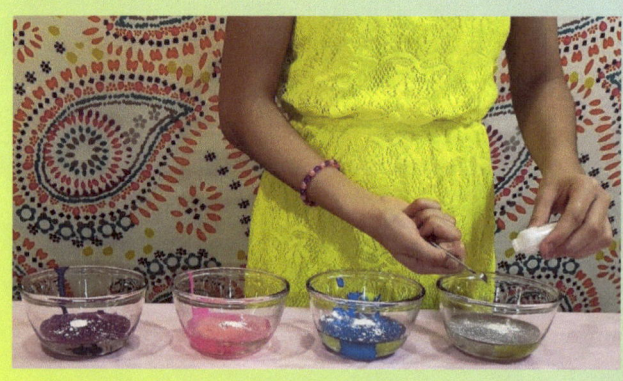

5) Add **Baking Soda** to each bowl and mix well until dissolved

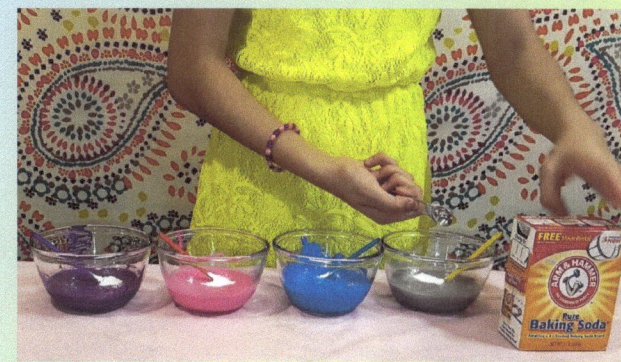

6) Add **Hand Lotion** to each bowl and mix well

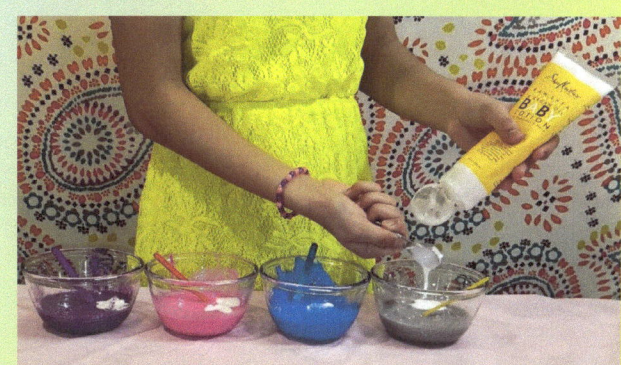

7) Add **Contact Lens Solution** slowly. Squirt directly from the bottle to mixing bowl. Don't over use contact lens solution or slime comes out hard like rubber. You need about 4 Tablespoons. No measuring spoons are being used, therefore, use your best judgement.

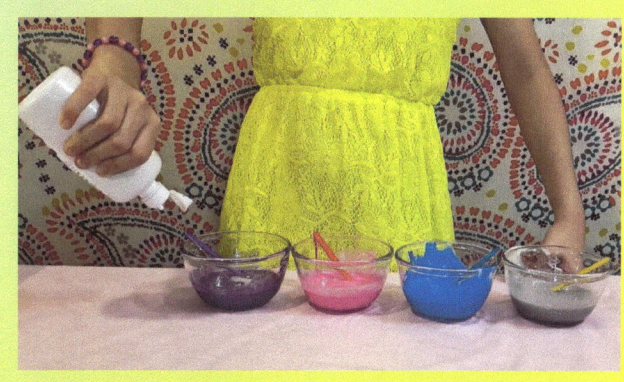

8) Use a **Spatula** to mix as you keep adding contact lens solution. Keep stirring until the slime doesn't stick to the bowl or your hands.

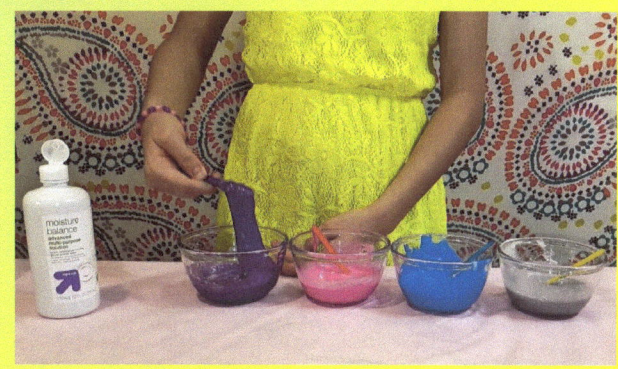

HOW TO MAKE SLIME

9) Once the glue starts to look like slime, **Knead** the mixture with your hands until you get the right slime consistency; smooth and soft enough to stretch with hands.

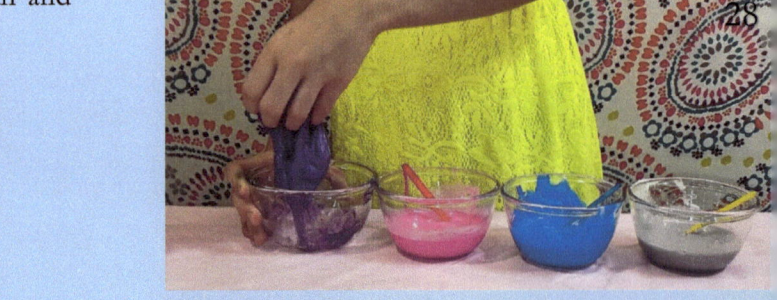

10) Get all four separate slimes out of their mixing bowls and place them on your table.

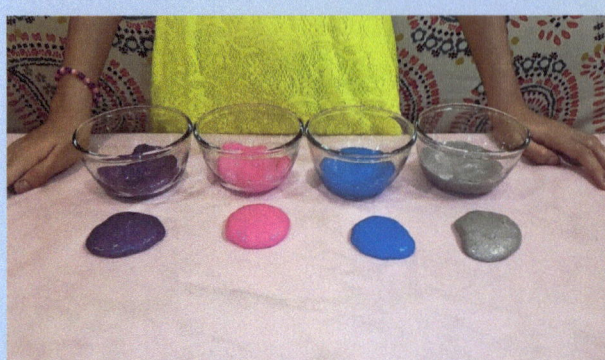

11) Stretch out on your table all four separate slimes **Side by Side**.

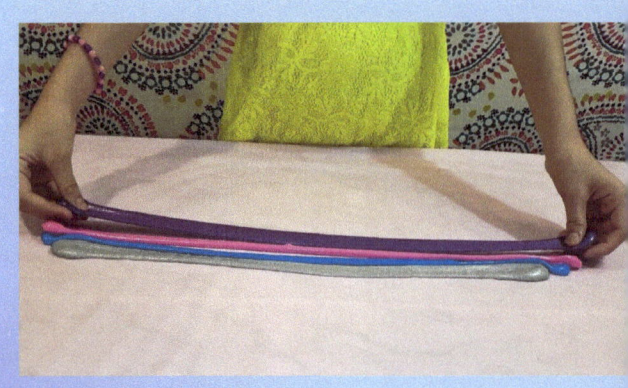

WHAT THE SLIME SHOULD LOOK LIKE

Stretched Twinkle Galaxy Slime

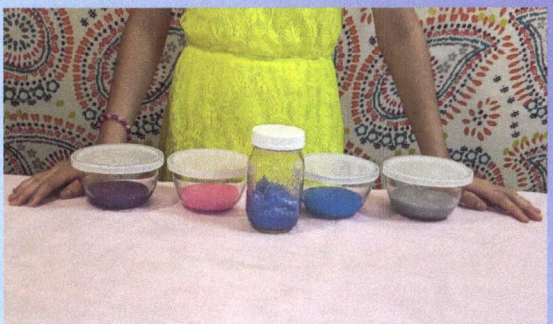

Twinkle Galaxy Slime in a **Storage Container**

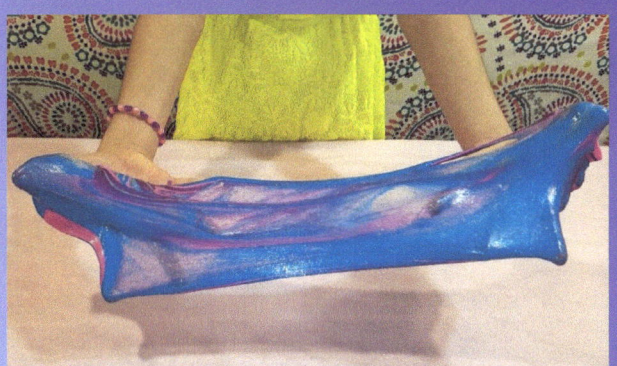

Now you have an eye catching, galaxy slime.

RECIPE 3. CRUNCHY BALL SLIME

The reason it's called crunchy slime is because it crunches and crackles. Kids just love the sound it makes and they can be there for many hours just poking it and smooching it.

One key ingredient is Kinetic foam or the generic name is Playfoam. This compound is made of styrofoam balls and gives slime a unique texture and sound. If you cannot find kinetic foam, just add plain styrofoam balls with same quantity as kinetic foam.

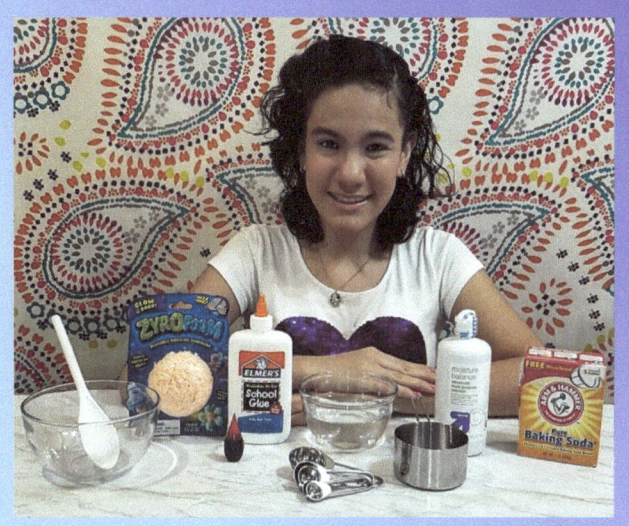

Ingredients
- 1 Cup White PVA Glue
- $\frac{1}{2}$ Cup Cold Water
- 8 Drops Orange Food Coloring
- $\frac{1}{2}$ Cup or 6-Ounces Kinetic Foam
- 1 Teaspoon Baking Soda
- 4 Tablespoons Contact Lens Solution

HOW TO MAKE SLIME

Directions

1) Pour **<u>White</u> <u>Glue</u>** into your mixing bowl.

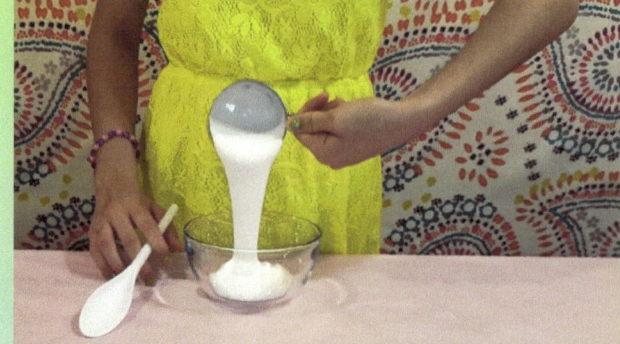

2) Add the **<u>Cold</u> <u>Water</u>** to bowl and mix well.

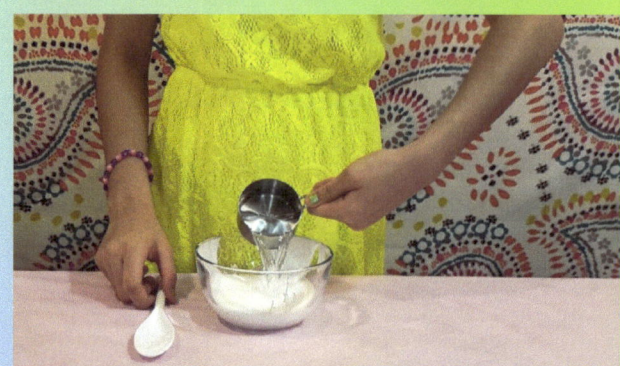

3) Add **<u>Orange</u> <u>Food</u> <u>Coloring</u>** (same color as kinetic foam) and mix well.

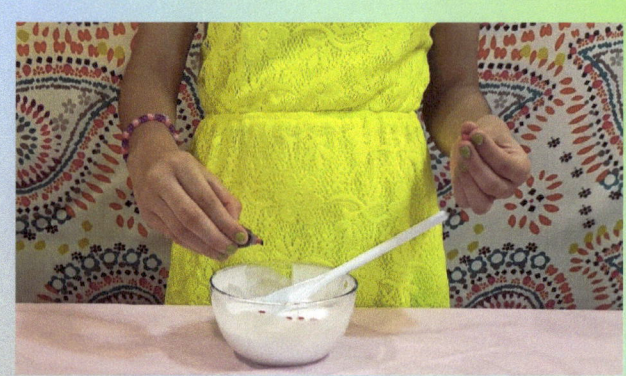

4) Add **<u>Baking</u> <u>Soda</u>** and mix well until dissolved

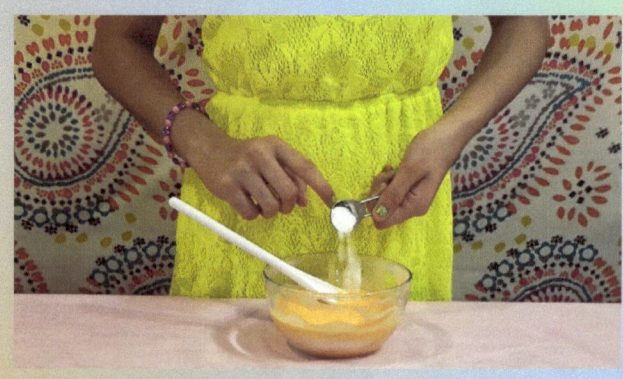

5) Add the **Kinetic Foam** and knead very well together.

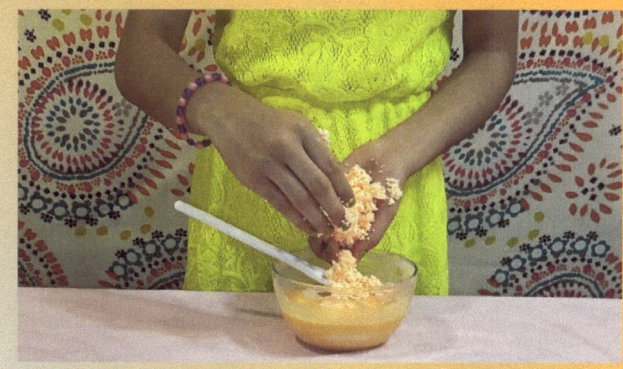

6) Add **Contact Lens Solution** slowly. Squirt directly from the bottle to mixing bowl. Don't over use contact lens solution or slime comes out hard like rubber. You need about 4 Tablespoons. No measuring spoons are being used, therefore, use your best judgement.

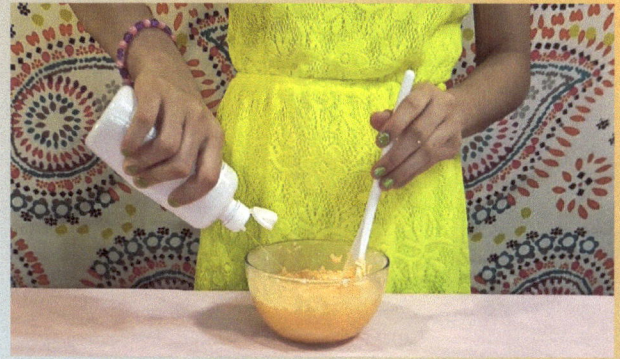

7) Use a **Spatula** to mix as you keep adding contact lens solution. Keep stirring until the slime doesn't stick to the bowl or your hands.

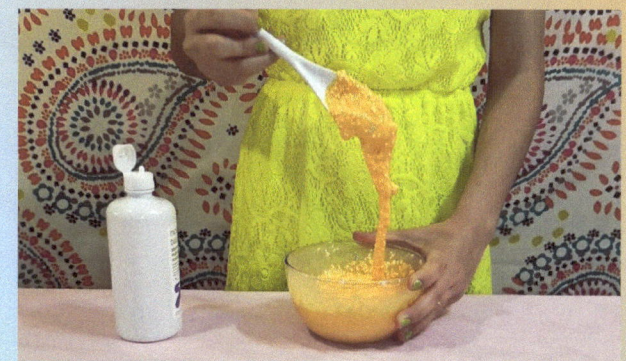

8) Once the glue starts to look like slime, **Knead** the mixture with your hands until you get the right slime consistency; smooth and soft enough to stretch with hands.

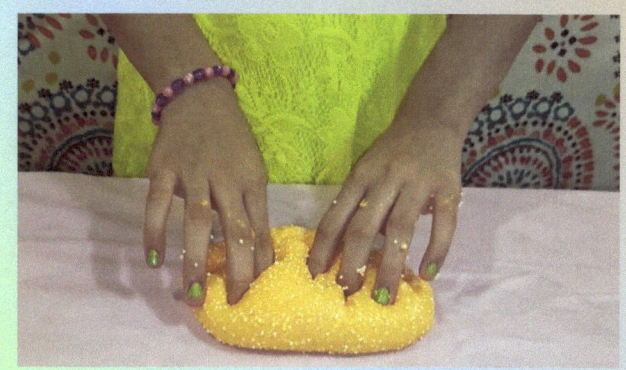

WHAT THE SLIME SHOULD LOOK LIKE

Stretched Crunchy Ball Slime

Crunchy Ball Slime in a **Storage Container**

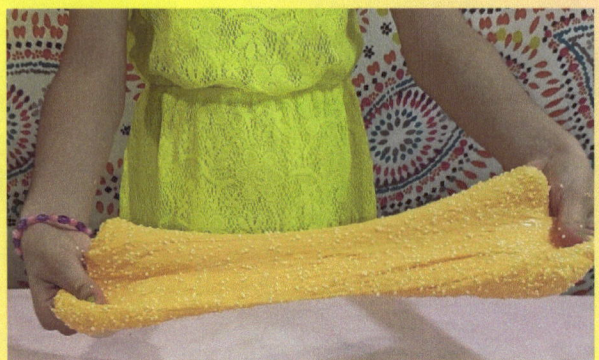
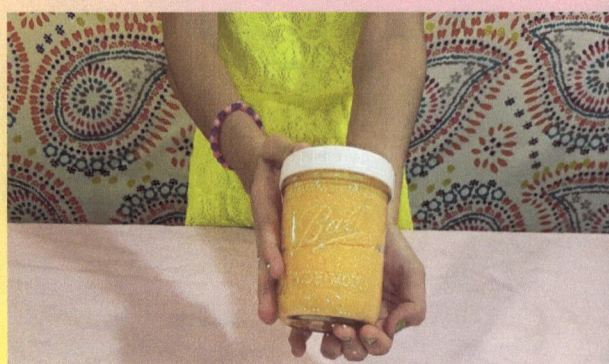

Now you have a super crunchy slime.

RECIPE 4. ALICORN SLIME

I love Unicorns. They are so beautiful. Unicorns were magical because of their horn. A Unicorn's horn, also known as Alicorn, was said to have magical powers and used as medicine for kings and queens. The reason this recipe is called Alicorn slime is because the unique colors used to make it represents that of a unicorn horn.

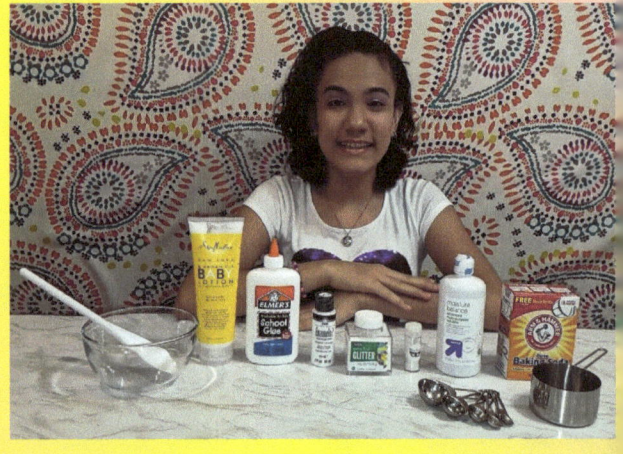

Ingredients

- 1Cup White PVA Glue
- 1 Tablespoon White Acrylic Paint
- 2 Teaspoons Extra Fine White Glitter
- 1 Tablespoon Hand Lotion
- 1 Teaspoon Hologram Powder
- 1 Teaspoon Baking Soda
- 4 Tablespoons Contact Lens Solution

Directions

1) Pour **White Glue** into your mixing bowl.

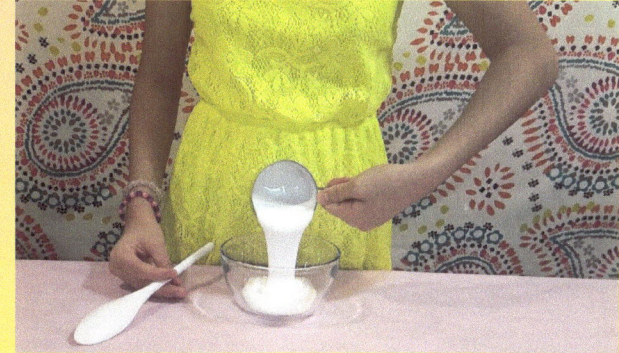

2) Add **White Paint** and mix well

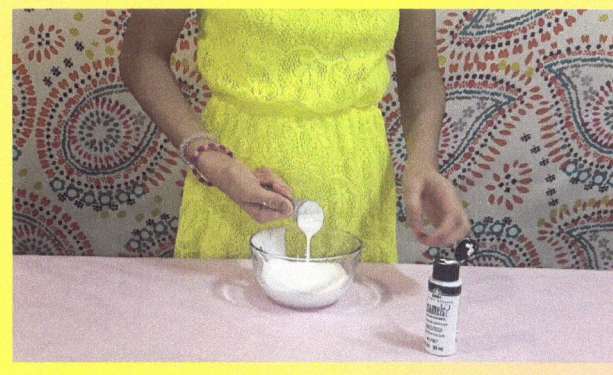

3) Add **Extra Fine White Glitter** and mix well

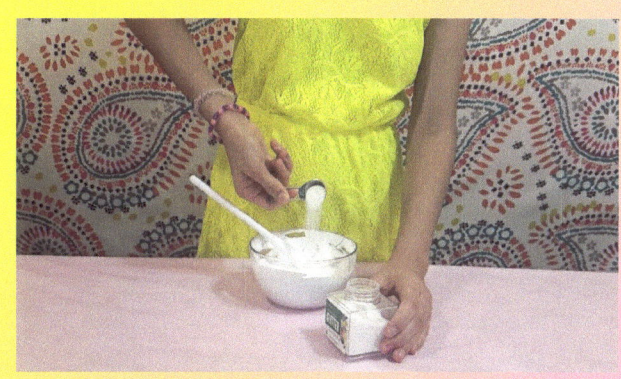

4) Add **Hologram Powder** and mix well

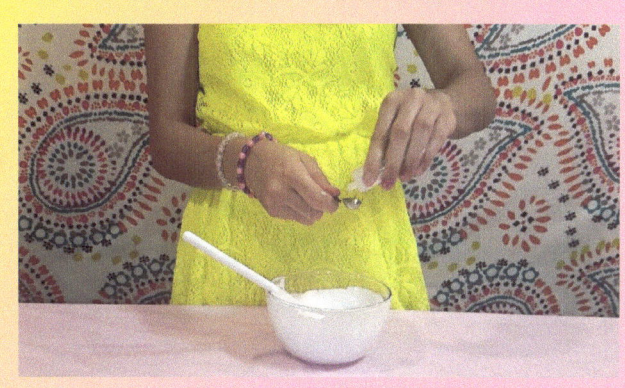

HOW TO MAKE SLIME

5) Add **Hand Lotion** and mix well

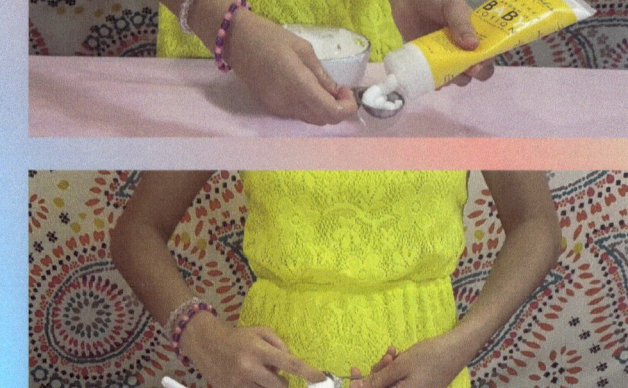

6) Add **Baking Soda** and mix well until dissolved

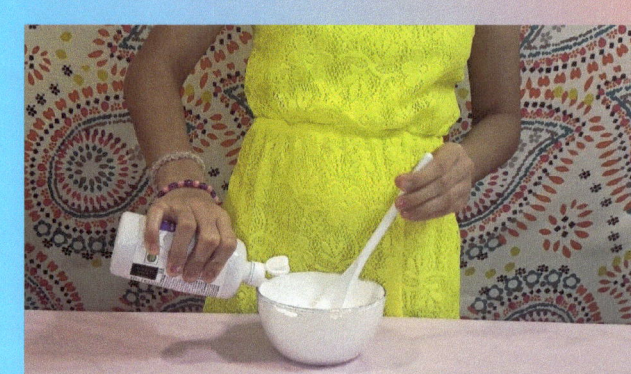

7) Add **Contact Lens Solution** slowly. Squirt directly from the bottle to mixing bowl. Don't over use contact lens solution or slime comes out hard like rubber. You need about 4 Tablespoons. No measuring spoons are being used, therefore, use your best judgement.

8) Use a **Spatula** to mix as you keep adding contact lens solution. Keep stirring until the slime doesn't stick to the bowl or your hands.

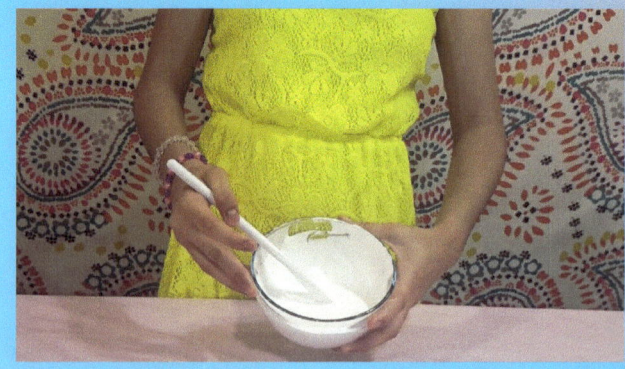

9) Once the glue starts to look like slime, **Knead** the mixture with your hands until you get the right slime consistency; smooth and soft enough to stretch with hands.

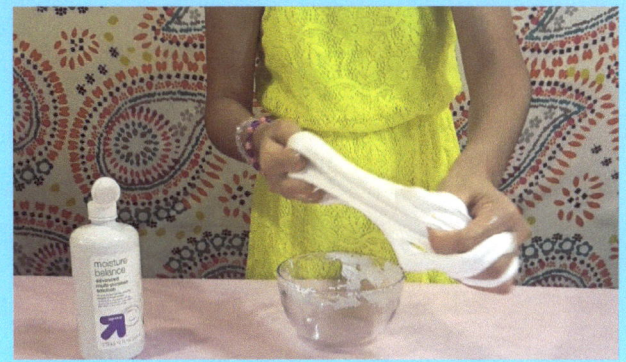

WHAT THE SLIME SHOULD LOOK LIKE

Stretched Alicorn Slime

Alicorn Slime in a **Storage Container**

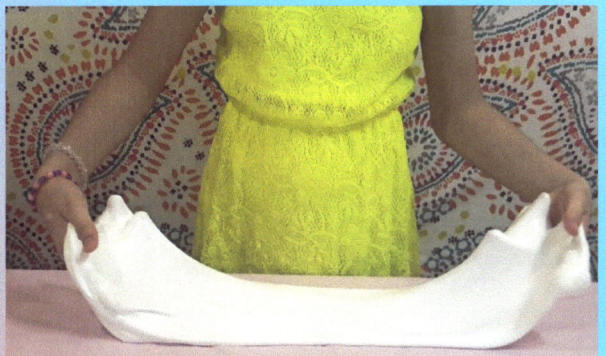
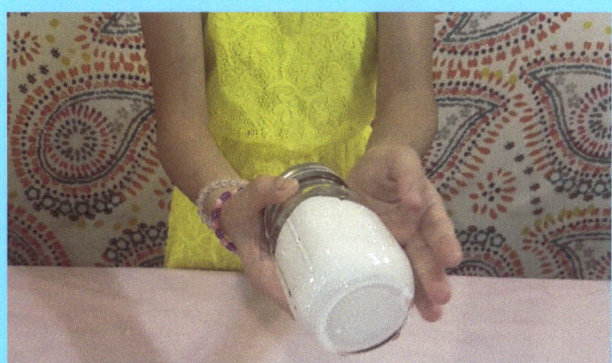

Now you have a super magical slime.

RECIPE 5. GOOGLY MONSTER SLIME

This is a creepy recipe. This slime is called Googly Monster because of the green color, googly eyes and glow in the dark paint we use. Just like a green creepy monster with lots of eyes, this slime is very unique and one of a kind.

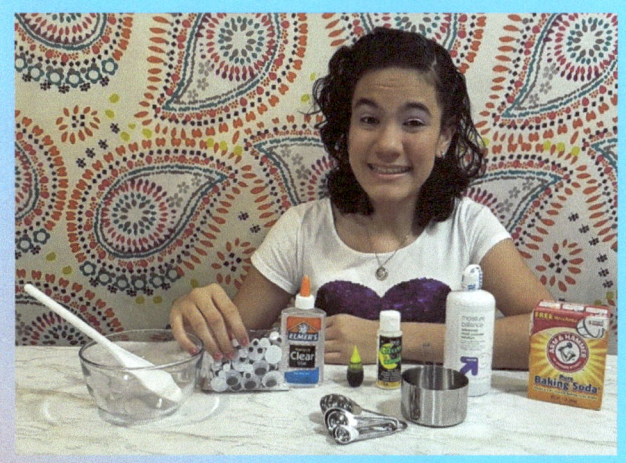

HOW TO MAKE SLIME

Ingredients

- 1 Cup Clear PVA Glue
- 1 Drop Neon Green Food Coloring
- 1 Tablespoon Glow in the Dark Gel or Paint
- 1 Bag with 60 count Googly Eyes
- 1 Teaspoon Baking Soda
- 4 Tablespoons Contact Lens Solution

Directions

1) Pour **Clear Glue** into your mixing bowl.

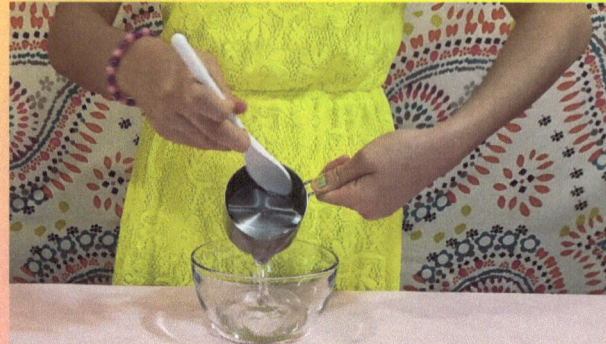

2) Add **Neon Green Food Coloring** and mix well.

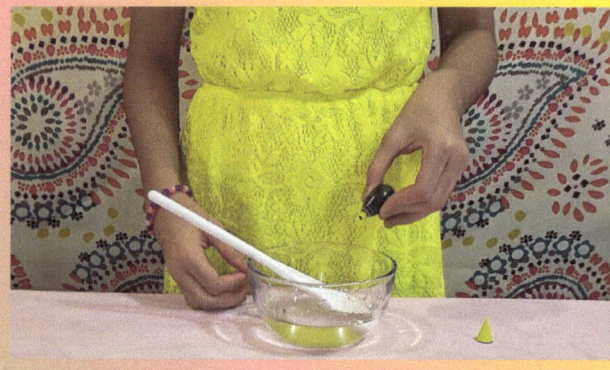

3) Add **Glow in the Dark Paint** and mix well

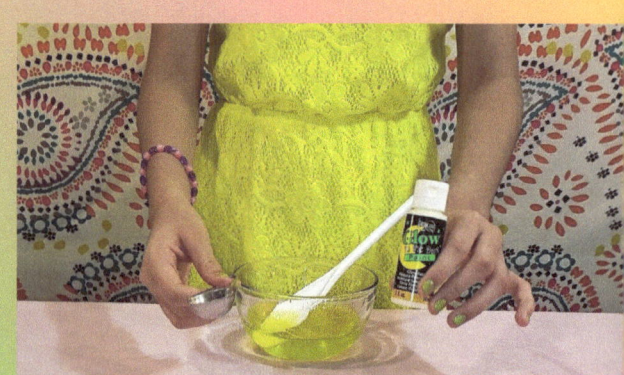

4) Add **Baking Soda** and mix well until dissolved

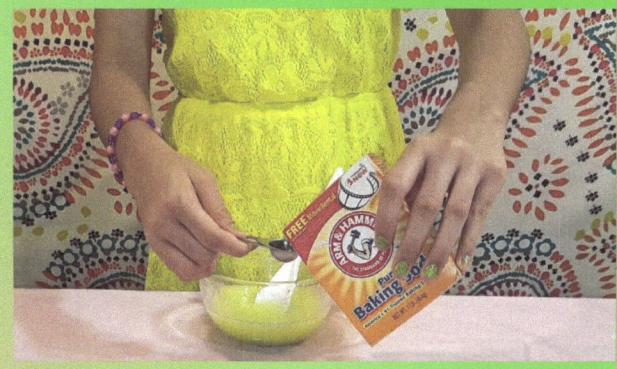

5) Add **Googly Eyes**.

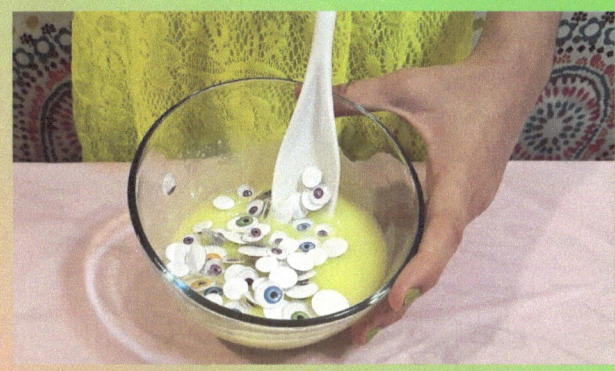

6) Add **Contact Lens Solution** slowly. Squirt directly from the bottle to mixing bowl. Don't over use contact lens solution or slime comes out hard like rubber. You need about 4 Tablespoons. No measuring spoons are being used, therefore, use your best judgement.

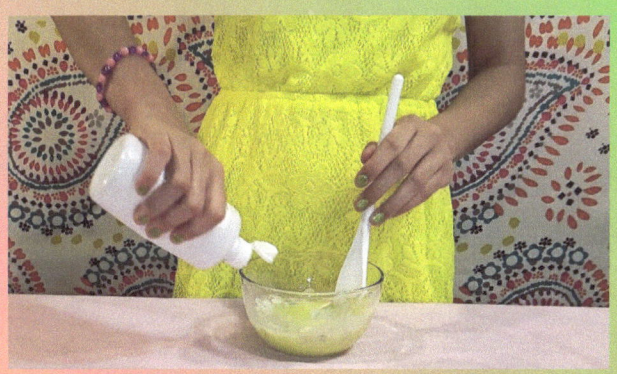

7) Use a **Spatula** to mix as you keep adding contact lens solution. Keep stirring until the slime doesn't stick to the bowl or your hands.

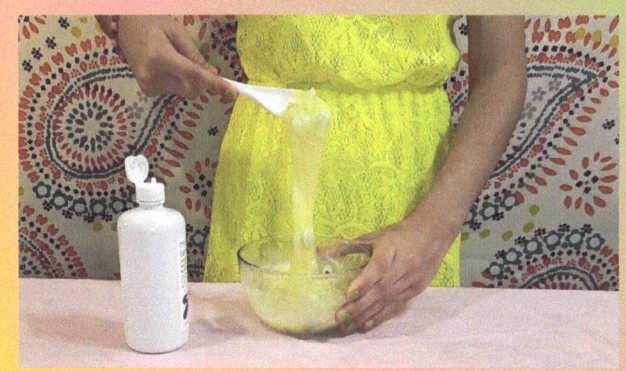

HOW TO MAKE SLIME

8) Once the glue starts to look like slime, **Knead** the mixture with your hands until you get the right slime consistency; smooth and soft enough to stretch with hands.

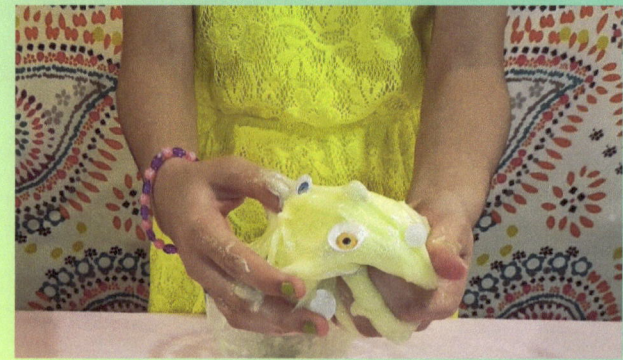

WHAT THE SLIME SHOULD LOOK LIKE

Stretched Googly Monster Slime

Googly Monster Slime in a **Storage Container**

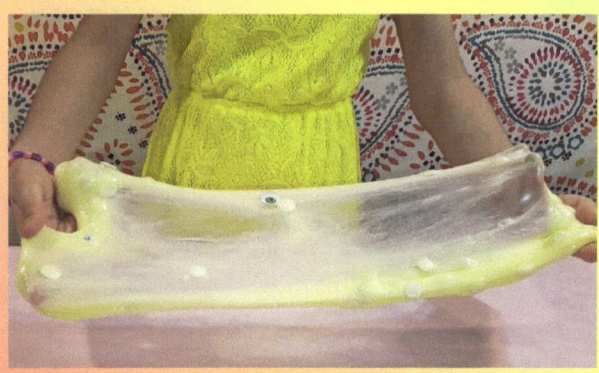

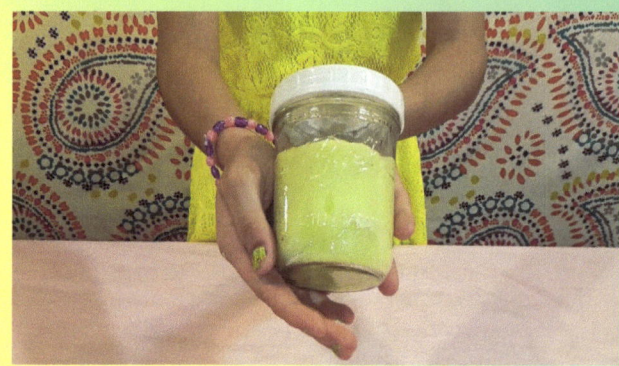

Now you have a creepy slime. You can play with the slime now, but if you want to activate the glow in the dark properties, you must let it sit under direct light for a few hours.

RECIPE 6. FISH BOWL SLIME

This slime is so adorable. It makes an incredible crunchy sound. Kids are all about senses, as we love to touch and look at things. This is called Fish Bowl slime because the little beads used in this slime look like the little pebbles in a fish bowl. This is one of my top 3 favorites.

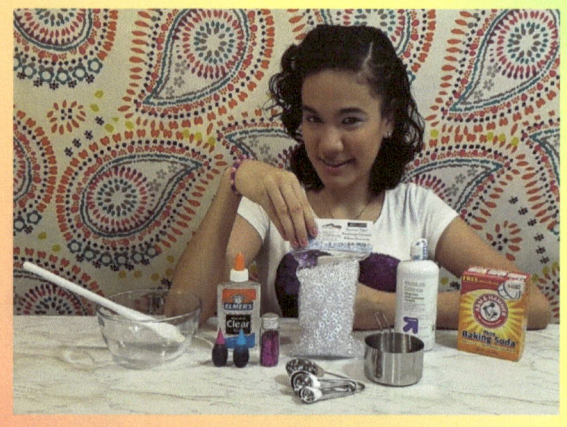

KUKI SHAMUS

Ingredients
- 1 Cup Clear PVA Glue
- 12 Drops Neon Pink Food Coloring
- 2 Drops Neon Blue Food Coloring
- 1 Teaspoon Purple Sequins
- $\frac{1}{2}$ Cup Decorative Beads
- 1 Teaspoon Baking Soda
- 4 Tablespoons Contact Lens Solution

Directions

1) Pour **Clear Glue** into your mixing bowl.

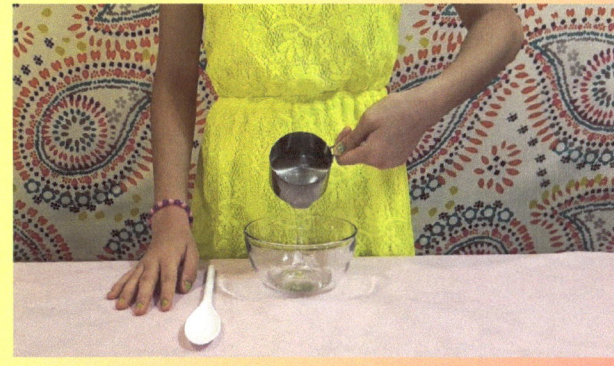

2) Add **Neon Purple Food Coloring** and mix well.

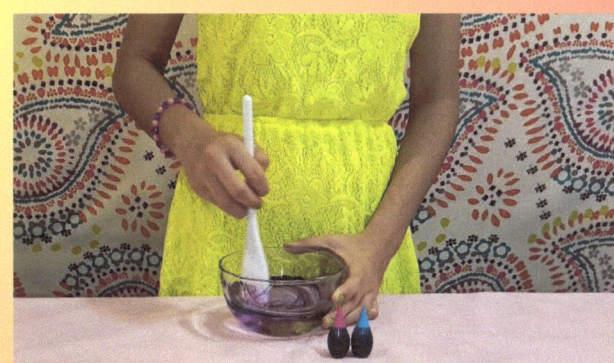

3) Add **Purple Sequins** to bowl and mix well

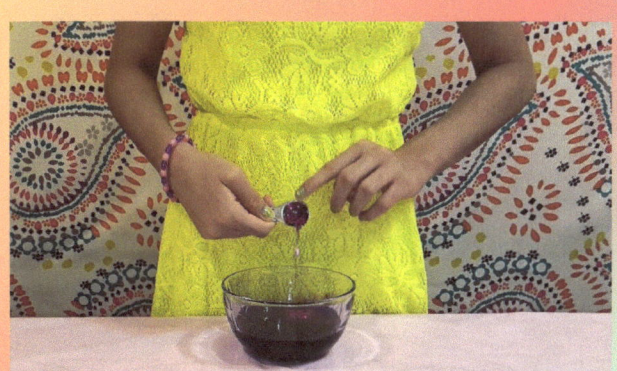

HOW TO MAKE SLIME

4) Add **Baking Soda** and mix well until dissolved

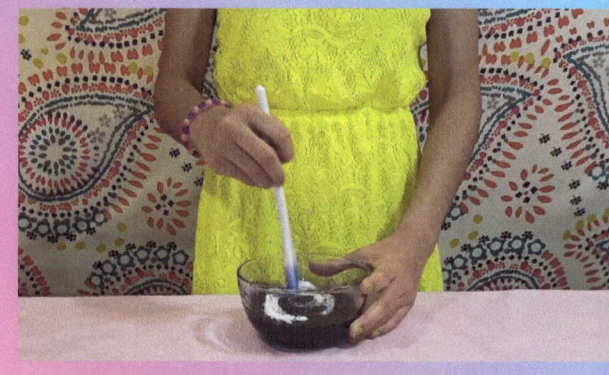

5) Add **Contact Lens Solution** slowly. Squirt directly from the bottle to mixing bowl. Don't over use contact lens solution or slime comes out hard like rubber. You need about 4 Tablespoons. No measuring spoons are being used, therefore, use your best judgement.

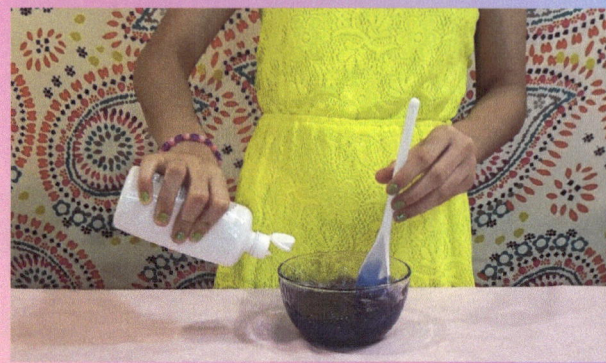

6) Use a **Spatula** to mix as you keep adding contact lens solution. Keep stirring until the slime doesn't stick to the bowl or your hands.

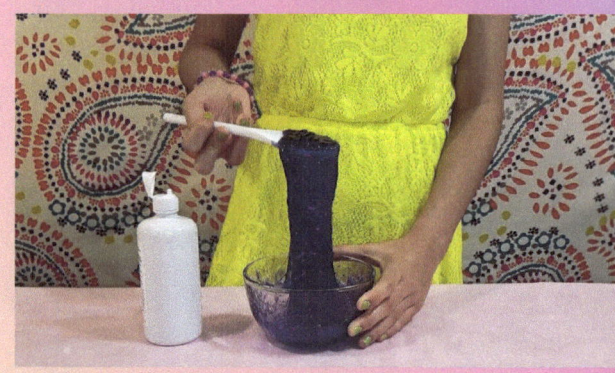

7) Once the glue starts to look like slime, **Knead** the mixture with your hands until you get the right slime consistency; smooth and soft enough to stretch with hands.

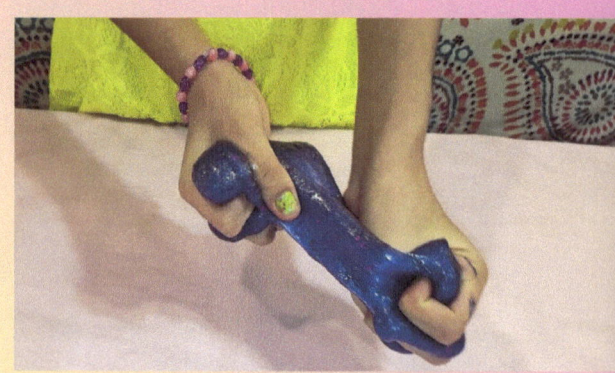

8) Add **Decorative Beads** and mix well

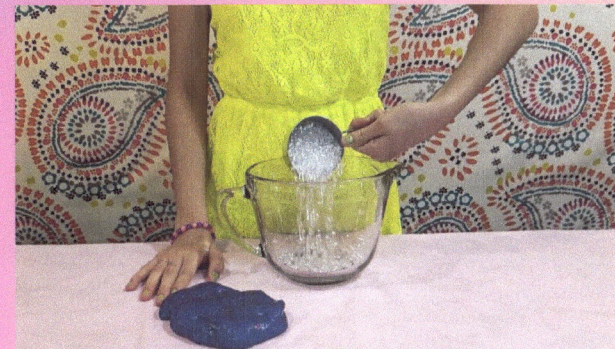

9) Knead the mixture with your hands. If slime is not sticking to the beads, add a little bit of water to get the slime sticky again.

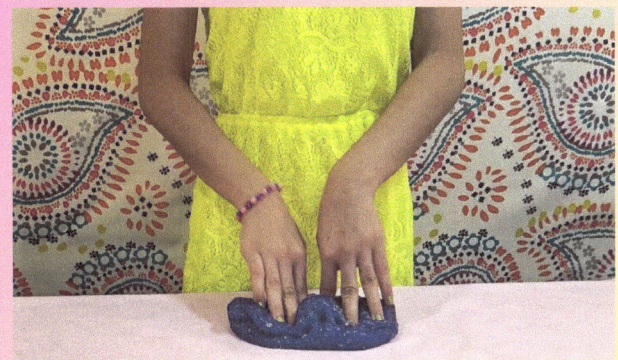

WHAT THE SLIME SHOULD LOOK LIKE

Stretched Fish Bowl Slime

Fish Bowl Slime in a **Storage Container**

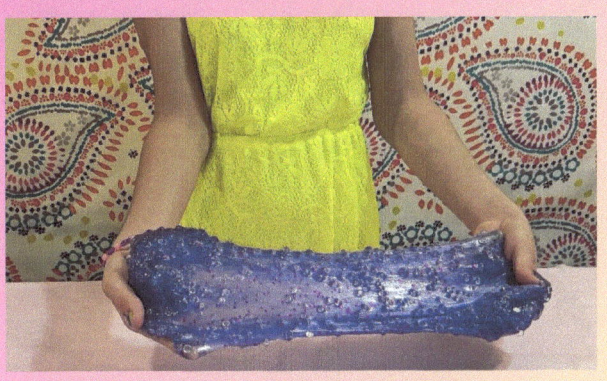
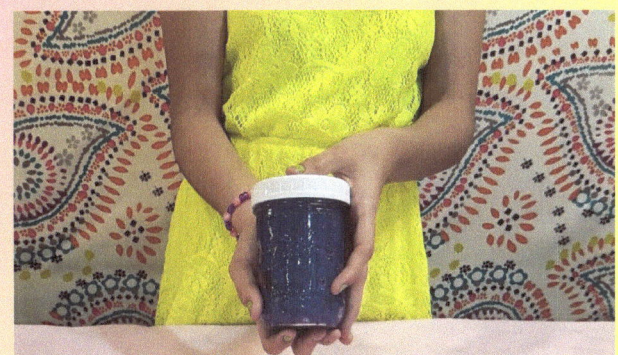

Now you have a clacky slime.

HOW TO MAKE SLIME

RECIPE 7. PEARLY WHITES SLIME

Nothing says elegance more than pearls. I just love that pearly, shiny finish. This slime is call Pearly Whites because we are making a white pearl finish to the slime.

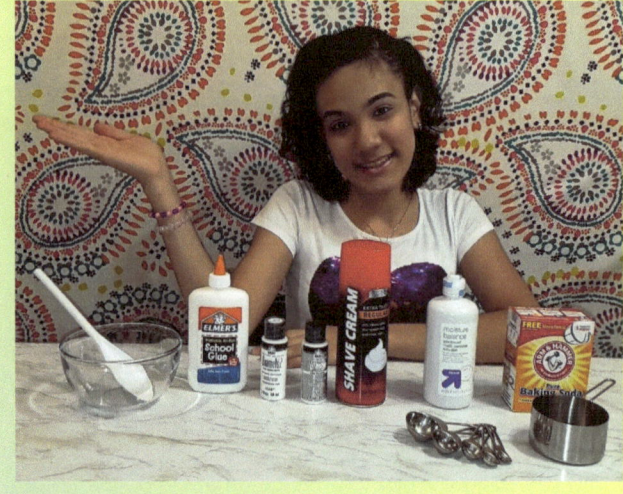

Ingredients

- 1 Cup White PVA Glue
- 2 Tablespoons White Acrylic Paint
- 2 Tablespoons Hologram Acrylic Paint
- 1 Cup Shaving Cream
- 1 Teaspoon Baking Soda
- 4 Tablespoons Contact Lens Solution

Directions

1) Pour **White Glue** into your mixing bowl.

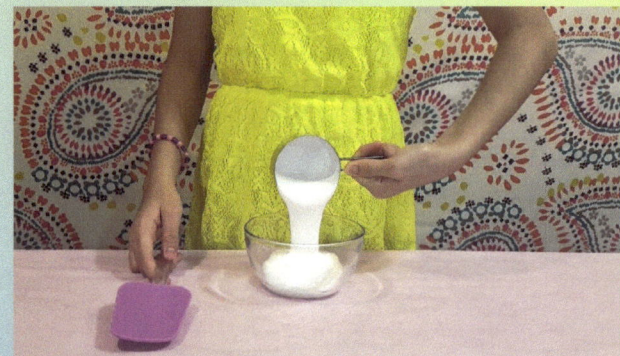

2) Add **White Paint** and mix well.

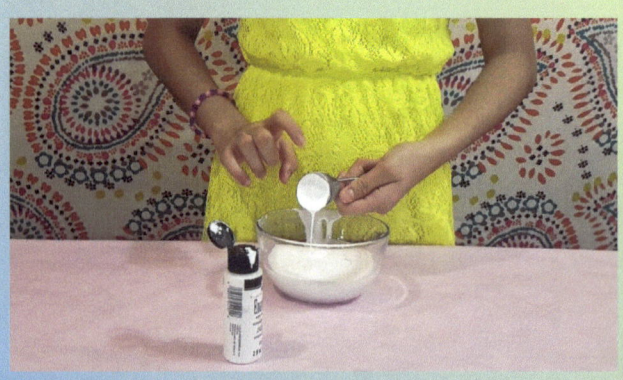

3) Add **Hologram** **Paint** and mix well.

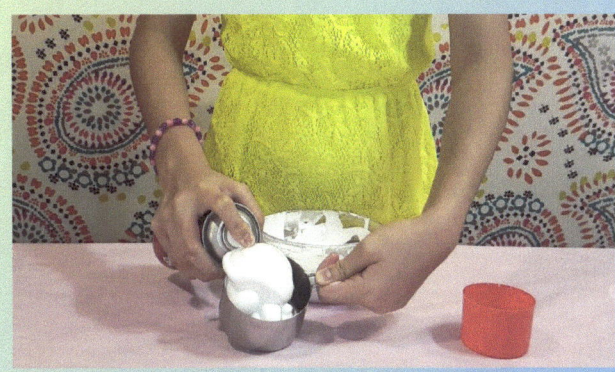

4) Add **Shaving** **Cream** and mix well.

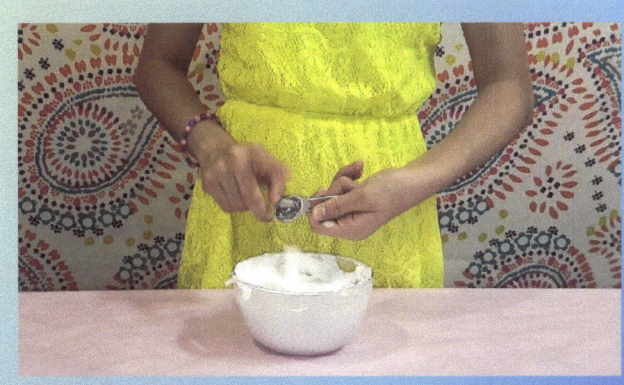

5) Add **Baking** **Soda** and mix well until dissolved.

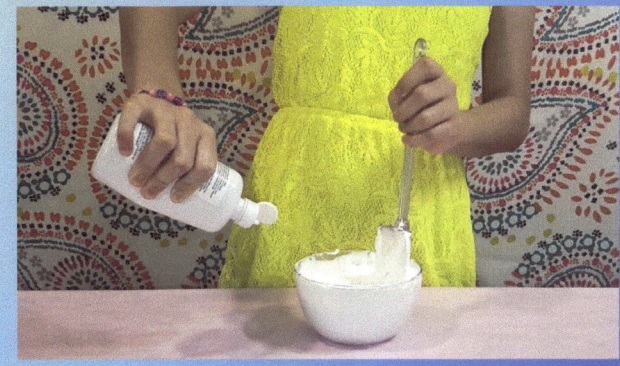

6) Add **Contact** **Lens** **Solution** slowly. Squirt directly from the bottle to mixing bowl. Don't over use contact lens solution or slime comes out hard like rubber. You need about 4 Tablespoons. No measuring spoons are being used, therefore, use your best judgement.

HOW TO MAKE SLIME

7) Use a **Spatula** to mix as you keep adding contact lens solution. Keep stirring until the slime doesn't stick to the bowl or your hands.

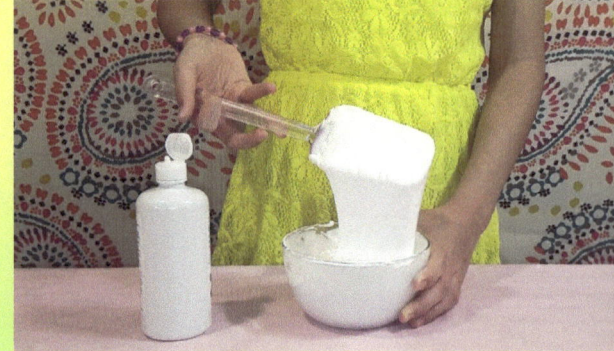

8) Once the glue starts to look like slime, **Knead** the mixture with your hands until you get the right slime consistency; smooth and soft enough to stretch with hands.

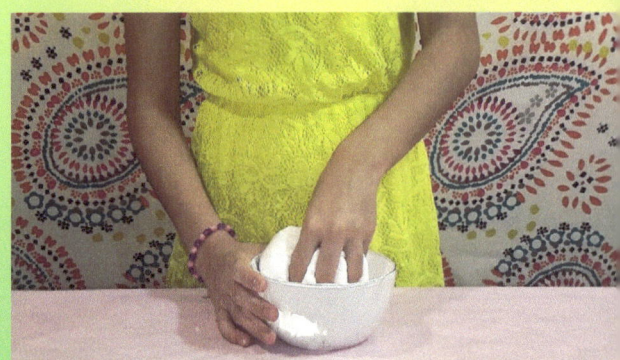

WHAT THE SLIME SHOULD LOOK LIKE

Stretched Pearly Whites Slime

Pearly Whites Slime in a **Storage Container**

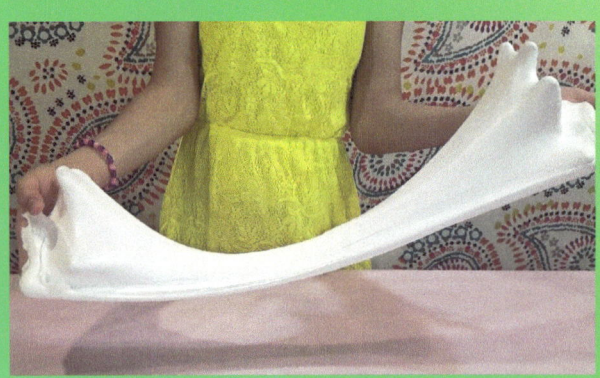
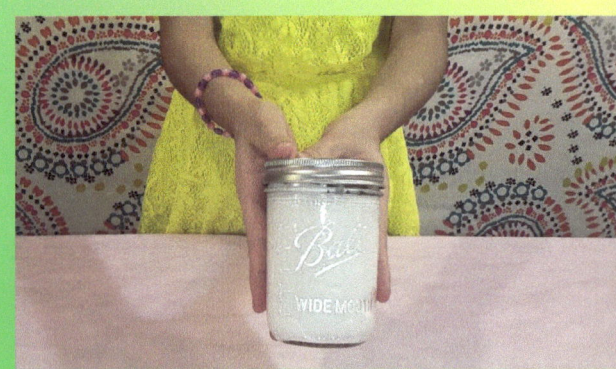

Now you have a super stretchy slime.

Recipe 8. Glow in the Dark Slime

This is another fun, unique slime recipe. Many kids love to make this and keep it in a clear container in their room to play with it at night. This is a glow in the dark slime because we use glow in the dark paint to actually make it glow at night. My youngest sister loves hiding in dark places while playing with it.

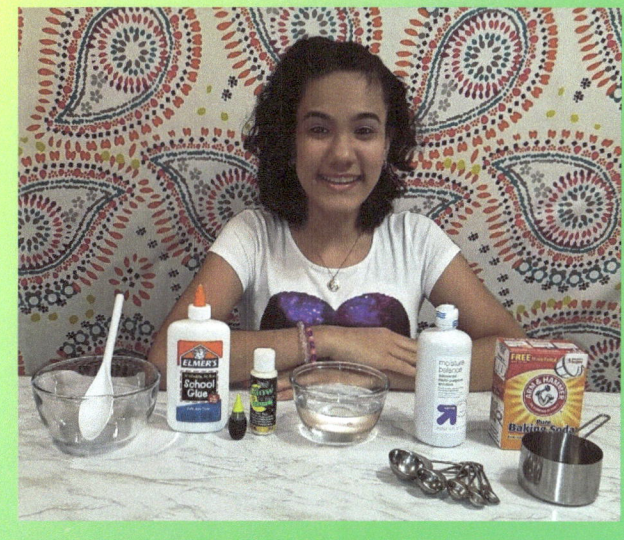

Ingredients

- 1/2 Cup White PVA Glue
- 1/2 Cup Cold Water
- 9 Drops Neon Green Food Coloring
- 3 Tablespoons Glow in the Dark Paint
- 1 Teaspoon Baking Soda
- 4 Tablespoons Contact Lens Solution

Directions

1) Pour **White Glue** into your mixing bowl.

2) Add the **Cold Water** to bowl and mix well.

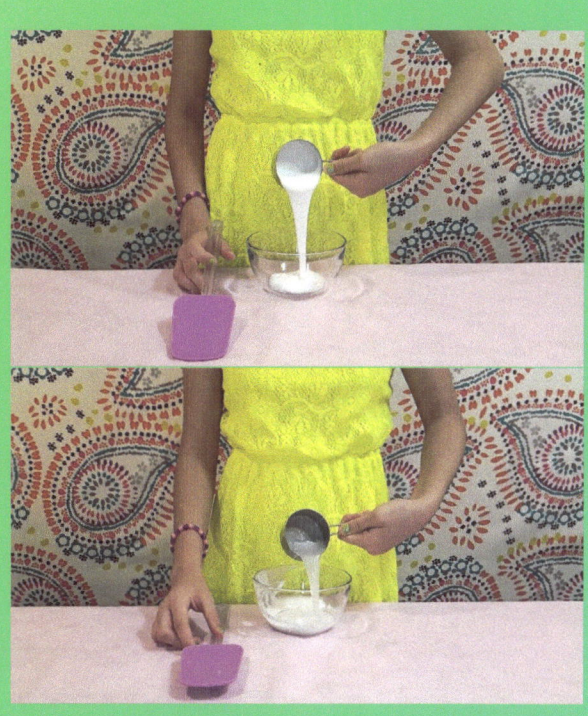

HOW TO MAKE SLIME

3) Add **Neon Green Food Coloring** and mix well.

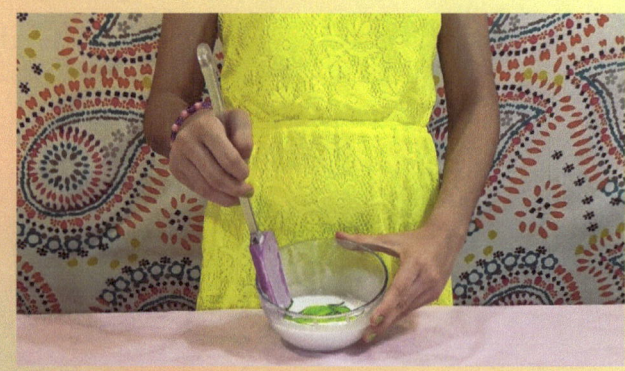

4) Add **Glow in the Dark Paint** mix well

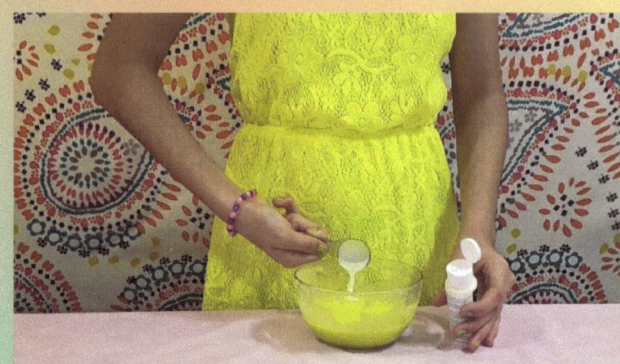

5) Add **Baking Soda** and mix well until dissolved

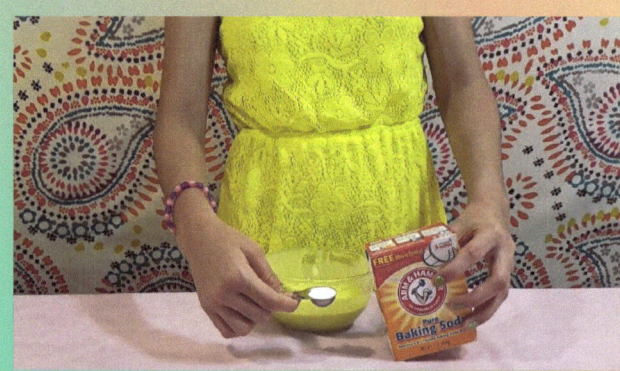

6) Add **Contact Lens Solution** slowly. Squirt directly from the bottle to mixing bowl. Don't over use contact lens solution or slime comes out hard like rubber. You need about 4 Tablespoons. No measuring spoons are being used, therefore, use your best judgement.

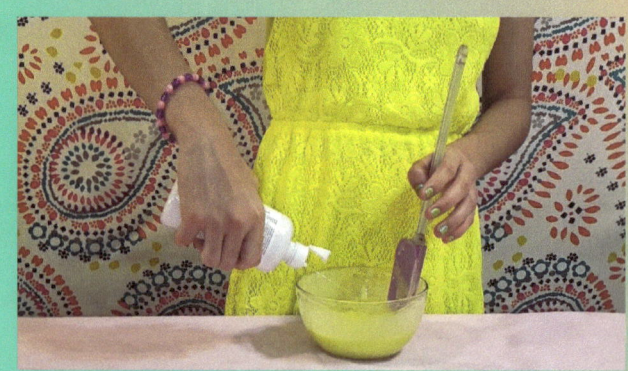

7) Use a **Spatula** to mix as you keep adding contact lens solution. Keep stirring until the slime doesn't stick to the bowl or your hands.

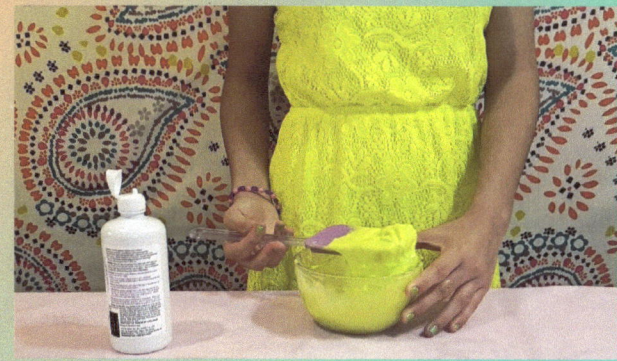

8) Once the glue starts to look like slime, **Knead** the mixture with your hands until you get the right slime consistency; smooth and soft enough to stretch with hands.

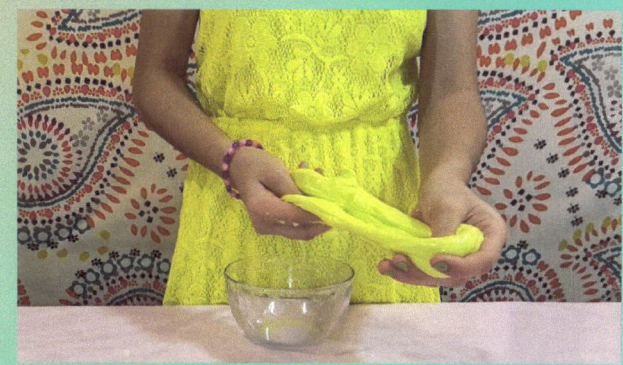

You can play with the slime now, but if you want to activate the glow in the dark properties you must let it sit under direct light for a few hours.

WHAT THE SLIME SHOULD LOOK LIKE

Stretched Glow in the Dark Slime

Glow in the Dark Slime in a **Storage Container**

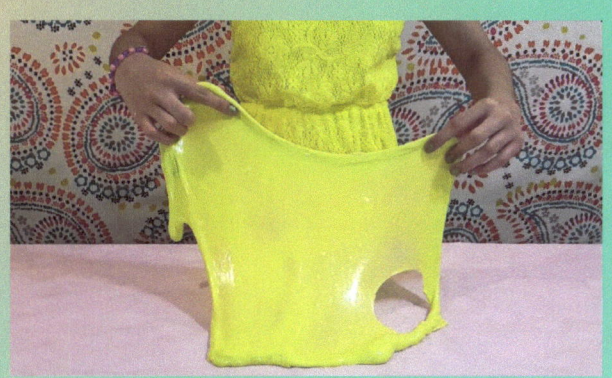
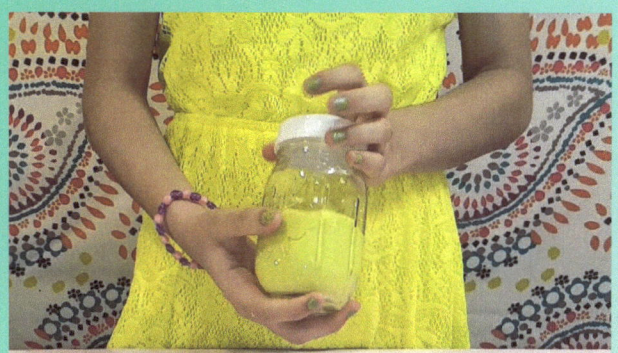

Now you have an awesome glow in the dark slime. You can play with the slime now, but if you want to activate the glow in the dark properties, you must let it sit under direct light for a few hours.

HOW TO MAKE SLIME

RECIPE 9. SUNNY FOAM SLIME

Foam slime has a very unique texture. Slime is all about the texture and the feel when it is in your hands. This is called Sunny Foam slime because we use styrofoam beads and make it extremely glittery to give it its unique texture and sound.

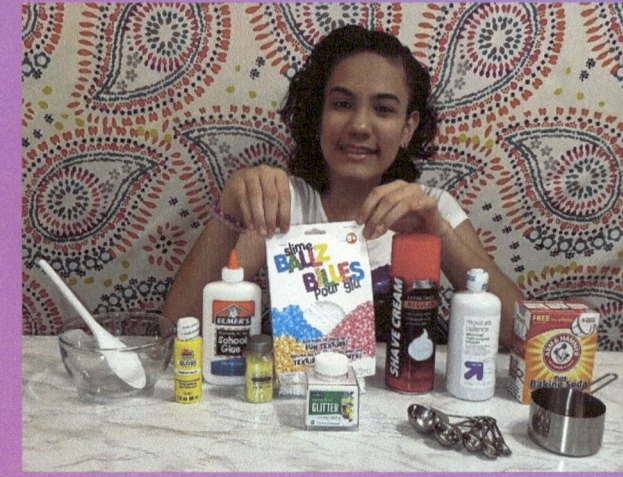

Ingredients

- 1 Cup White PVA Glue
- 2 Tablespoons Yellow Acrylic Paint
- 2 Tablespoons Crystal Glitter
- 1 Tablespoon Yellow Sequins
- 3 Cups Shaving Cream
- 2 Cups Styrofoam beads
- 1 Teaspoon Baking Soda
- 4 Tablespoons Contact Lens Solution

Directions

1) Pour **White Glue** into your mixing bowl.

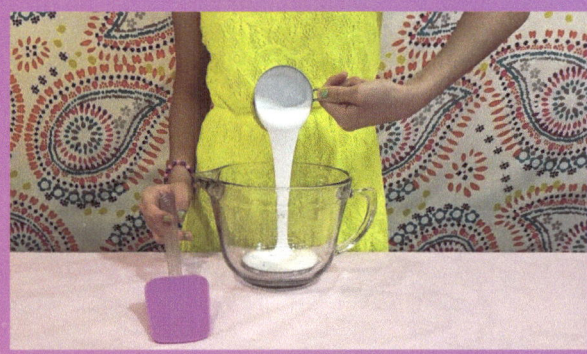

2) Add **Yellow Paint** and mix well

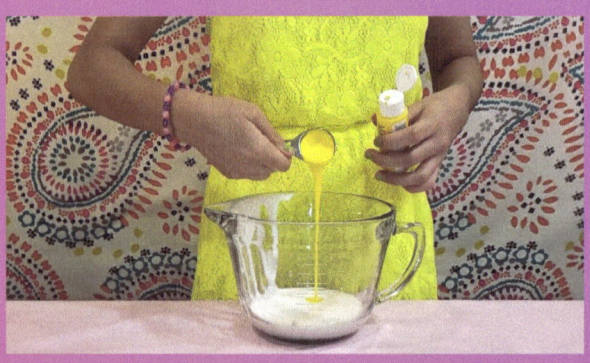

KUKI SHAMUS

3) Add **Crystal Glitter** and mix well

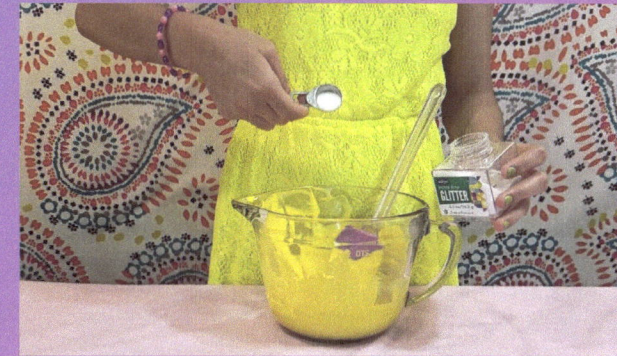

4) Add **Yellow Sequins** to bowl and mix well

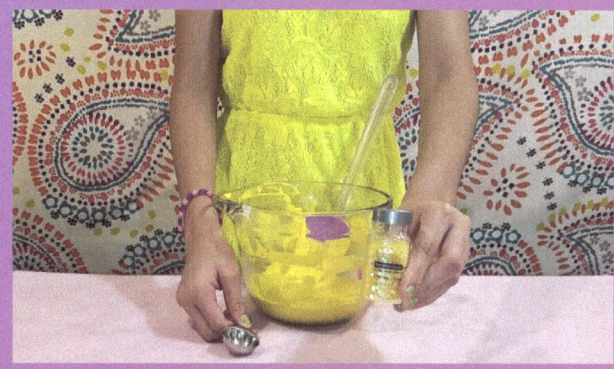

5) Add **Baking Soda** and mix well until dissolved

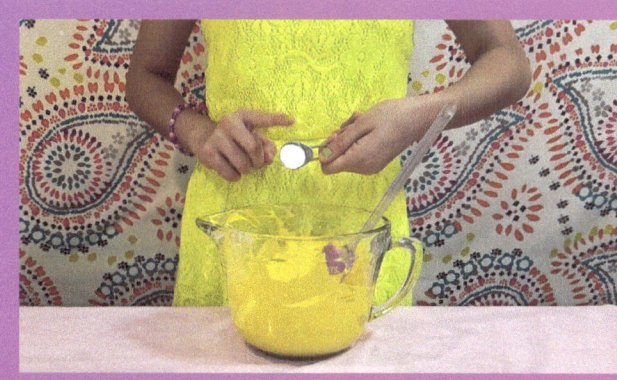

6) Add **Shaving Cream** with help of a spatula. Slowly add one cup at a time to make sure it mixes well.

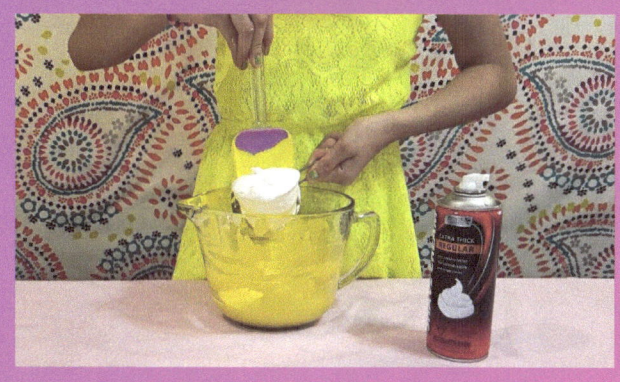

HOW TO MAKE SLIME

7) Add <u>**Styrofoam Beads**</u> over slime. Mix and knead well until they are fully combined together.

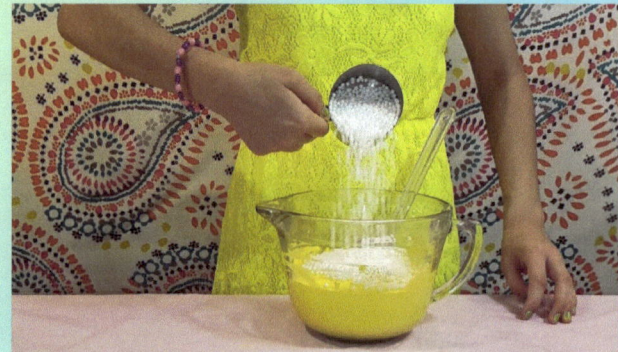

8) Add <u>**Contact Lens Solution**</u> slowly. Squirt directly from the bottle to mixing bowl. Don't over use contact lens solution or slime comes out hard like rubber. You need about 4 Tablespoons. No measuring spoons are being used, therefore, use your best judgement.

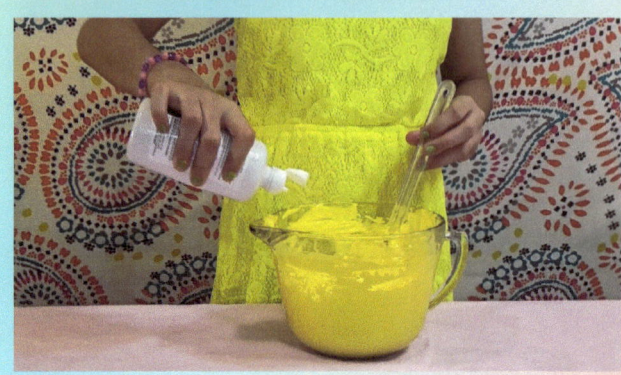

9) Use a <u>**Spatula**</u> to mix as you keep adding contact lens solution. Keep stirring until the slime doesn't stick to the bowl or your hands.

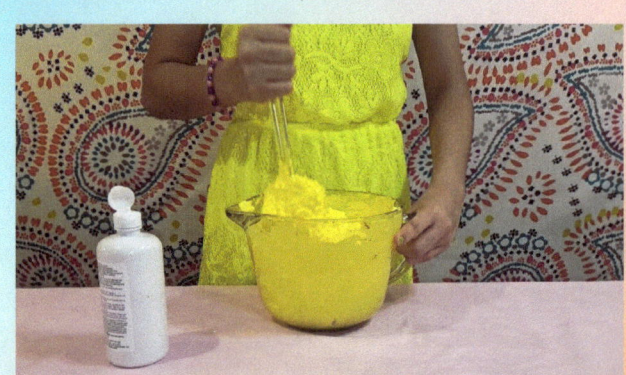

10) Once the glue starts to look like slime, <u>**Knead**</u> the mixture with your hands until you get the right slime consistency; smooth and soft enough to stretch with hands.

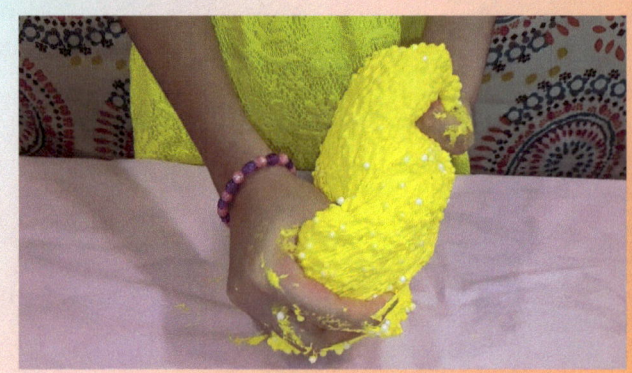

WHAT THE SLIME SHOULD LOOK LIKE

Stretched Sunny Foam Slime

Sunny Foam Slime in a **Storage Container**

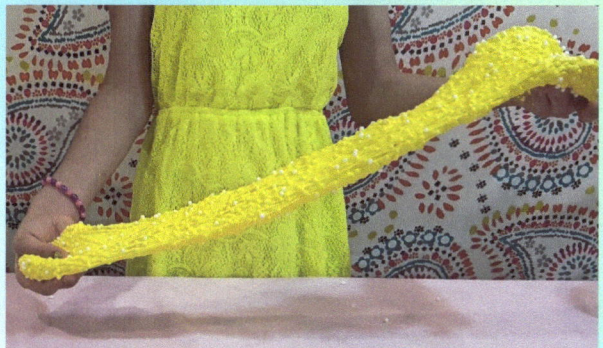
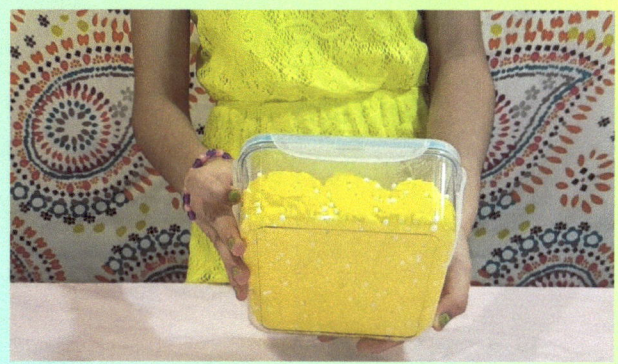

Now you have a unique texture slime

RECIPE 10. 1-2 SIMPLE SLIME

This recipe is called 1-2 Simple Slime because you only need 2 ingredients. For some reason, only 2 types of glue work for this recipe: Elmer's wood glue and HDX Home Depot brand. ONLY use shaving gel as this is the only thing that activates wood glue.

Note 1: Do not add anything else or the consistency of your slime will be lost.

Note 2: Wood glue sticks to wood, so make sure you use a plastic spatula for mixing and not a wood stick.

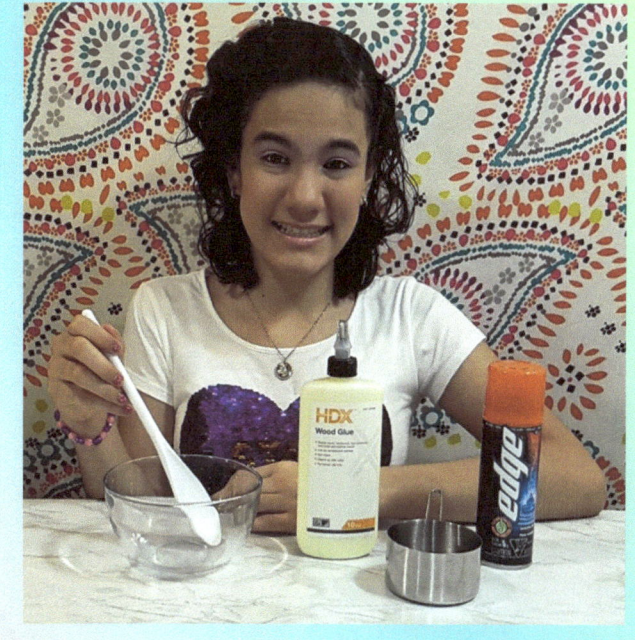

Ingredients

- $\frac{1}{2}$ Cup Wood Glue
- $\frac{1}{4}$ Cup Shaving Gel

HOW TO MAKE SLIME

Directions

1) Pour **Wood Glue** into your mixing bowl.

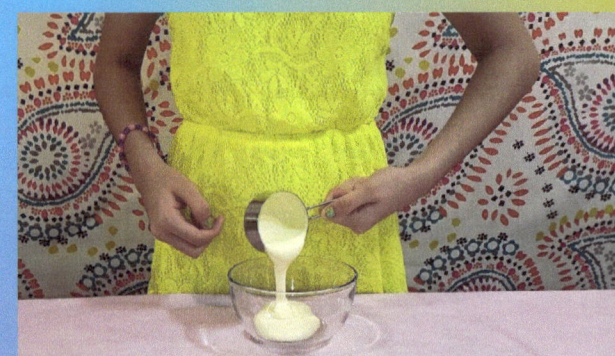

2) Add **Shaving Gel** slowly with small squirts at a time You will need about 4 Tablespoons but it is difficult to measure because we will squirt it directly from the bottle to the mixing bowl.

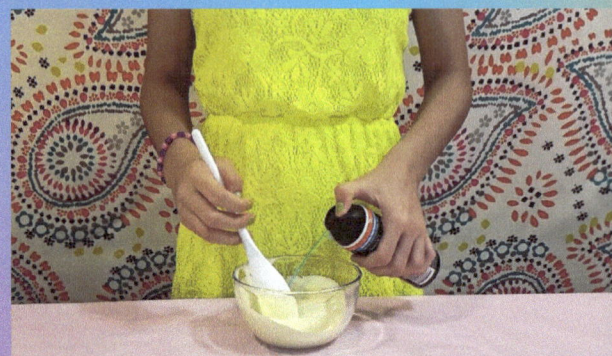

3) Once the glue starts to look like slime, **Knead** the mixture with your hands until you get the right slime consistency; smooth and soft enough to stretch with hands.

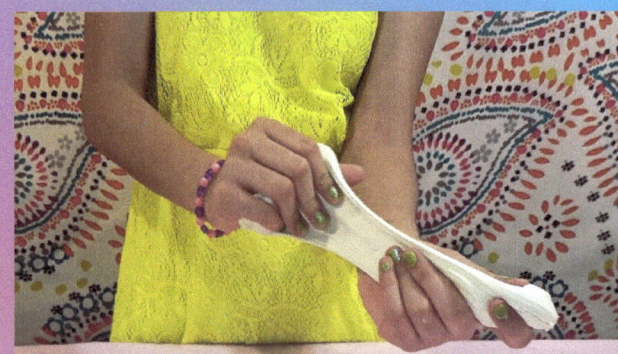

WHAT THE SLIME SHOULD LOOK LIKE

Stretched 1-2 Simple Slime

1-2 Simple Slime in a **Storage Container**

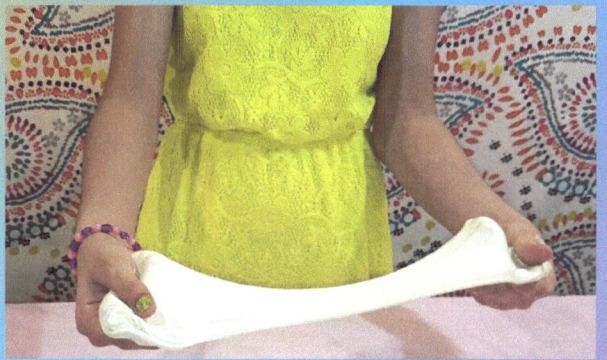
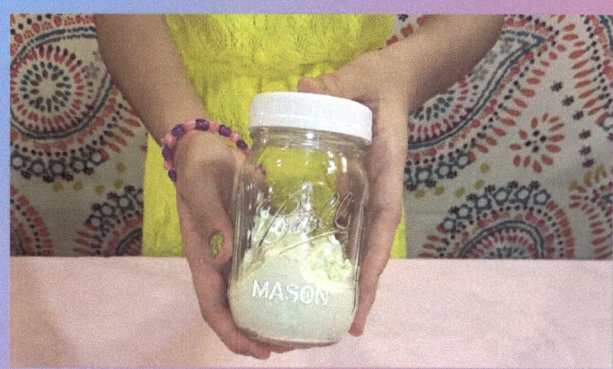

Now you have a 1-2 buckle my shoe, soft slime.

RECIPE 11. FRUITY EDIBLE SLIME

YES!!! Finally, something we can play with and eat. This slime is edible, so we can eat it once we are done. This recipe calls for gummy bears or gummy worms. You can replace corn starch and powder sugar for flour instead if you prefer to have it less sweet. Just make sure to use the same quantities if you do such replacements.

Note 1: The bowl will get very hot so have a parent supervising when making this.

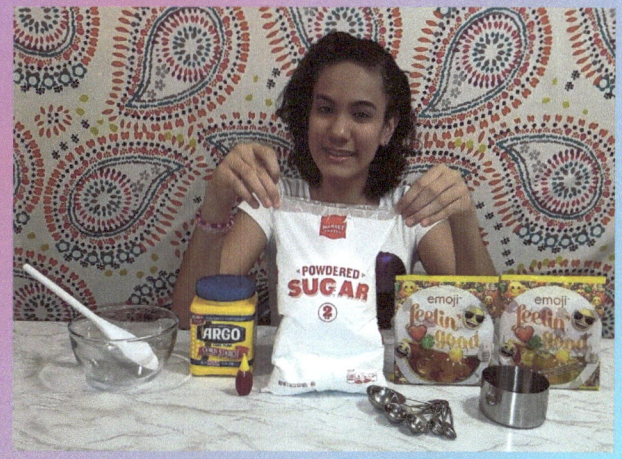

Note 2: No Gummy Bears were hurt in the process of making this book lol. Let's get started.

Ingredients

- 1 Cup Gummy Bears or other Gummies
- 1 Drop Yellow Food Coloring (optional)
- 6 Tablespoons Powdered Sugar
- 6 Tablespoons Corn Starch

HOW TO MAKE SLIME

Directions

1) Pour **<u>Gummy Bears</u>** into your mixing bowl.

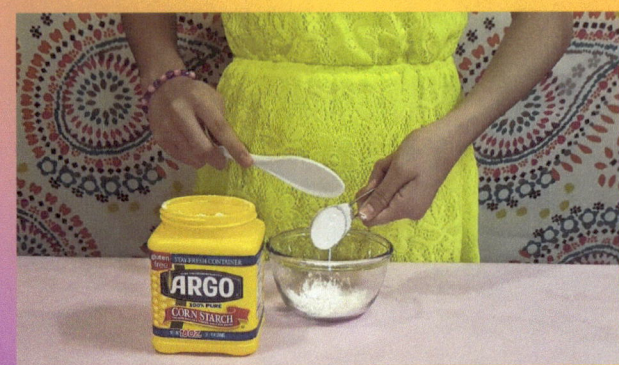

2) Pour **<u>Corn Starch</u>** into a separate bowl.

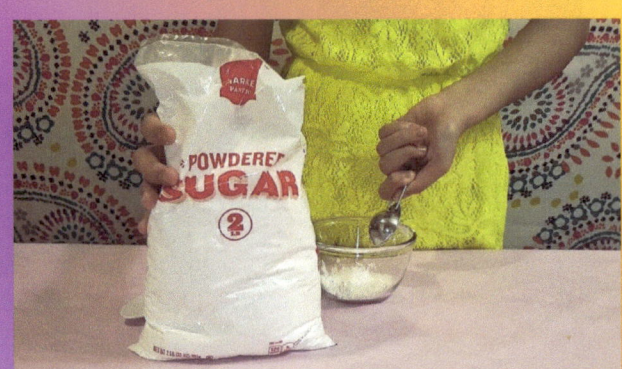

3) Add **<u>Powdered Sugar</u>** to Corn Starch and mix well.

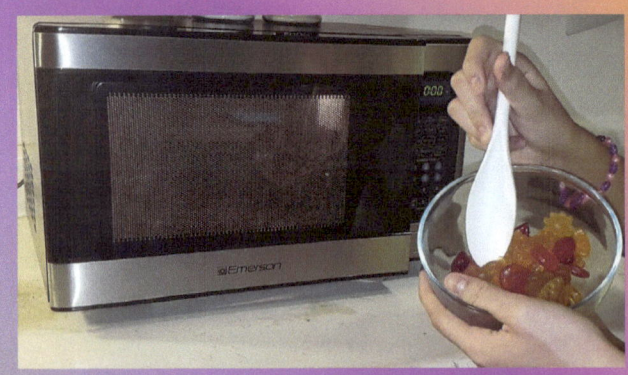

4) **<u>Microwave</u>** the Gummy Bears to melt them using five second increments. Do this about six to eight times depending on how powerful your microwave is.

5) Take bowl out of microwave and use a spatula to see how melted the Gummy Bears are. Do this until they are very soft and **Completely Melted**. Be careful because gummy bears burn quickly. If you want to add food coloring this is when you do it.

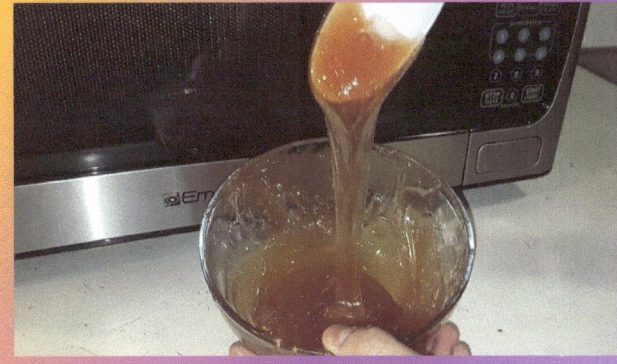

6) Once gummy mixture is not hot but warm **Combine** powder mixture one tablespoon at a time. Mix all together well until the mixture starts taking form like slime. You may or may not need all powder mixture based upon the brand of gummies you have. Some may require a little more.

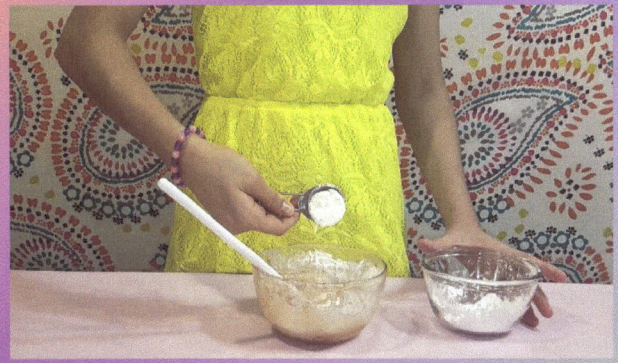

7) With your hand knead the mixture until is smooth and soft enough to stretch with hands.

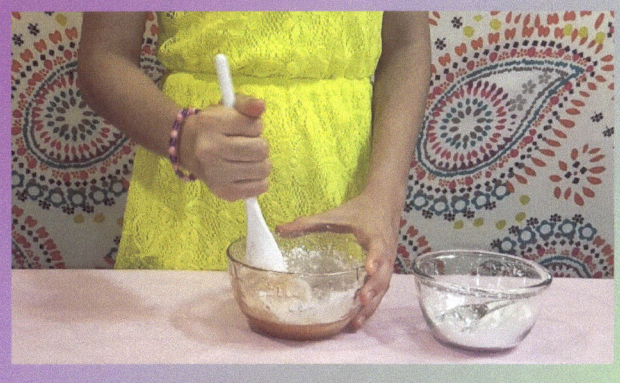

8) Once the gummy mixture starts to look like slime, **Knead** the mixture with your hands until you get the right slime consistency; smooth and soft enough to stretch with hands.

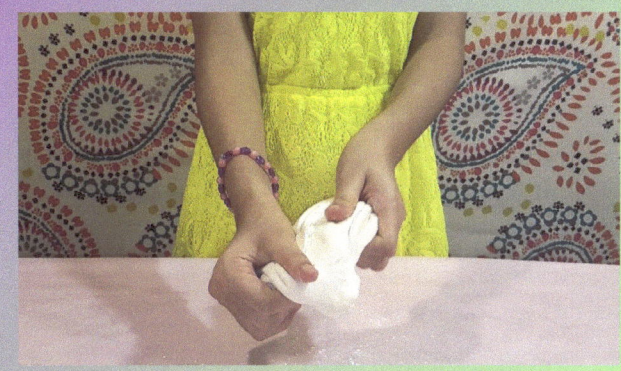

HOW TO MAKE SLIME

WHAT THE SLIME SHOULD LOOK LIKE

<u>Stretched</u> Fruity Edible Slime

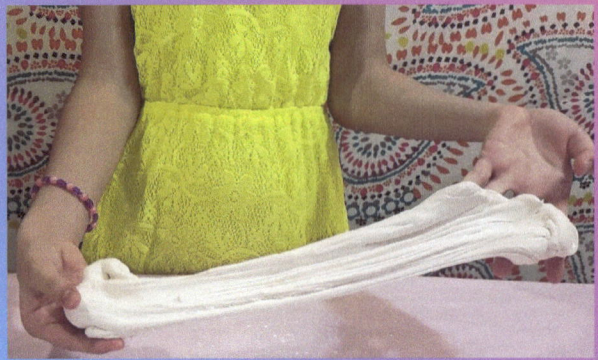

Fruity Edible Slime in a <u>Storage</u> <u>Container</u>

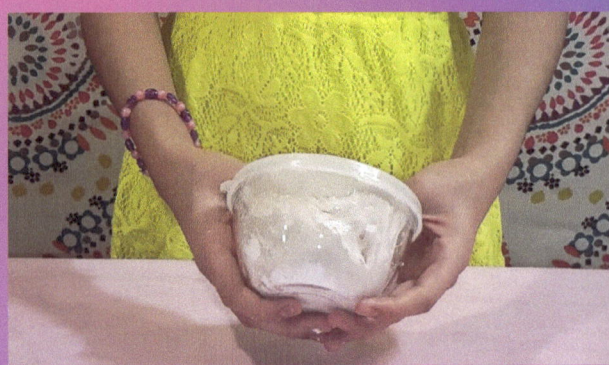

Now you have a tasty treat edible slime!

RECIPE 12. NACHO CHEESY SLIME

Nacho Cheesy slime is called that because the slime is yellow like nacho cheese. This slime is very stretchy and clucky. The key to making this slime look real is in the paint. Look for a color close to real cheddar cheese, thus more orange than yellow. Be careful, as you might get hungry when you make this slime *wink*.

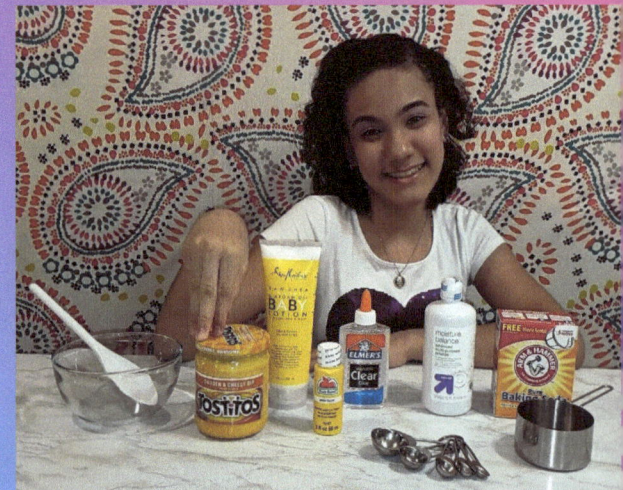

<u>Ingredients</u>

- 1 Cup Clear PVA Glue
- 3 Tablespoons Yellowy/Orange Acrylic Paint
- 3 Tablespoons Hand Lotion
- 1 Teaspoon Baking Soda
- 4 Tablespoons Contact Lens Solution
- 1 Nacho Cheese Container (optional)

KUKI SHAMUS

Directions

1) Pour **Clear** **Glue** into your mixing bowl.

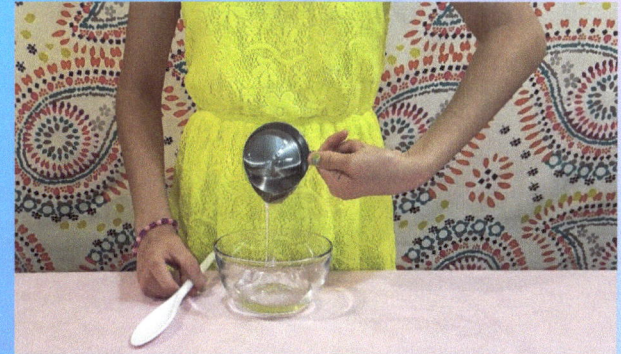

2) Add **Yellow**/**Orange** **Paint** and mix well

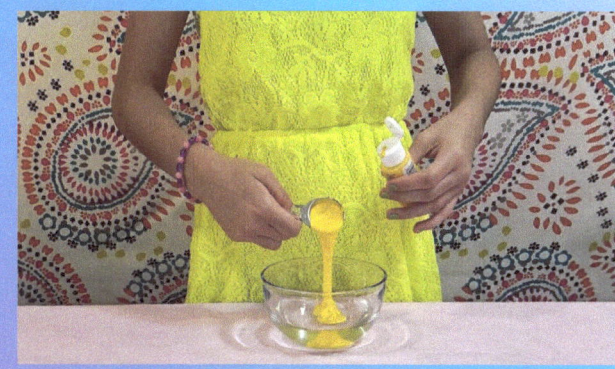

3) Add **Hand** **Lotion** and mix well

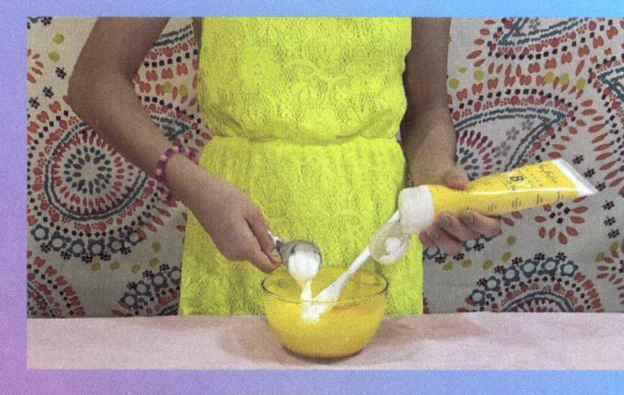

4) Add **Baking** **Soda** and mix well until dissolved

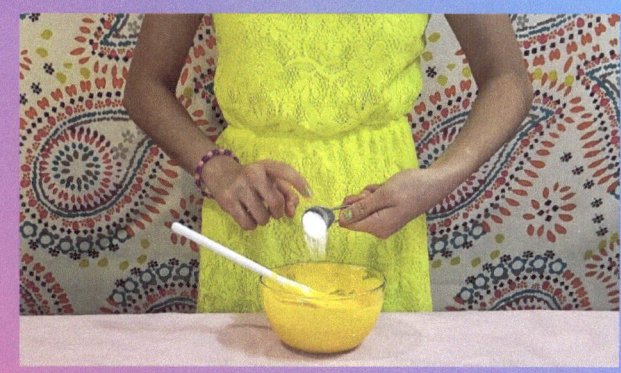

HOW TO MAKE SLIME

5) Add **Contact Lens Solution** slowly. Squirt directly from the bottle to mixing bowl. Don't over use contact lens solution or slime comes out hard like rubber. You need about 4 Tablespoons. No measuring spoons are being used, therefore, use your best judgement.

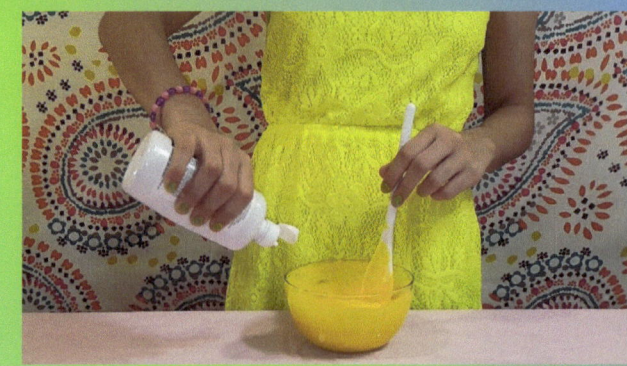

6) Use a **Spatula** to mix as you keep adding contact lens solution. Keep stirring until the slime doesn't stick to the bowl or your hands.

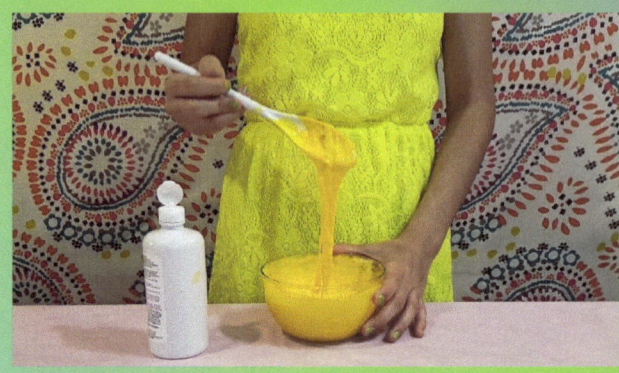

7) Once the glue starts to look like slime, **Knead** the mixture with your hands until you get the right slime consistency; smooth and soft enough to stretch with hands.

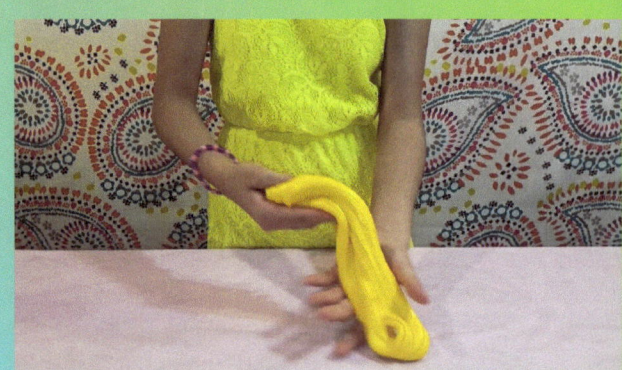

WHAT THE SLIME SHOULD LOOK LIKE

<u>Stretched</u> Nacho Cheesy Slime

Nacho Cheesy Slime in a <u>Storage Container</u>

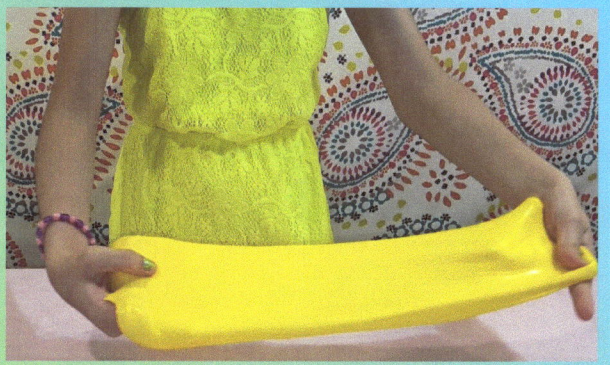
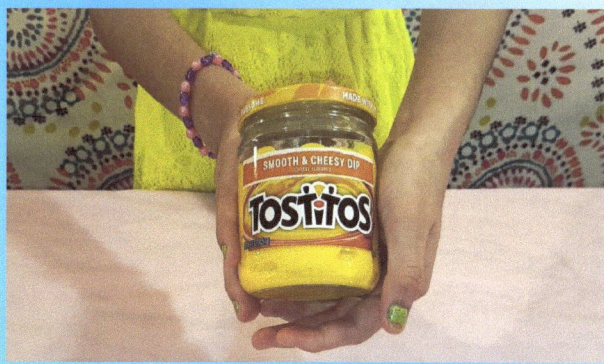

Now you have a stretchy soft slime!

RECIPE 13. HYDRA SLIME

I love mythological creatures like unicorns and mermaids, but there is one Greek creature that I find very interesting: a Hydra. A Hydra is an ancient serpent-like water monster with reptilian traits and many heads that multiplied if they were cut off.

I'm going to make this slime very green and metallic so that it resembles the skin of a Hydra. This slime is very stretchy and light. You can poke it all day long.

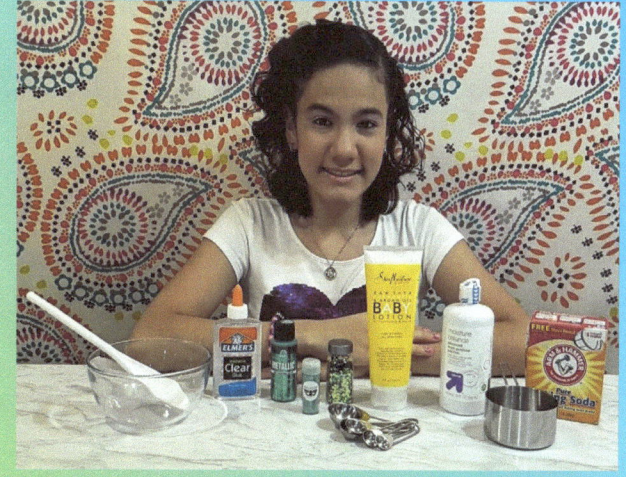

<u>Ingredients</u>

- 1 Cup of Clear PVA Glue
- 2 Tablespoons Metallic Green Acrylic Paint
- 1 Tablespoon Green Sequins
- 1 Tablespoon Hand Lotion per bowl
- $\frac{1}{2}$ Teaspoon Green Hologram Powder
- 1 Teaspoon Baking Soda
- 4 Tablespoons Contact Lens Solution

HOW TO MAKE SLIME

Directions

1) Pour **Clear Glue** into your mixing bowl.

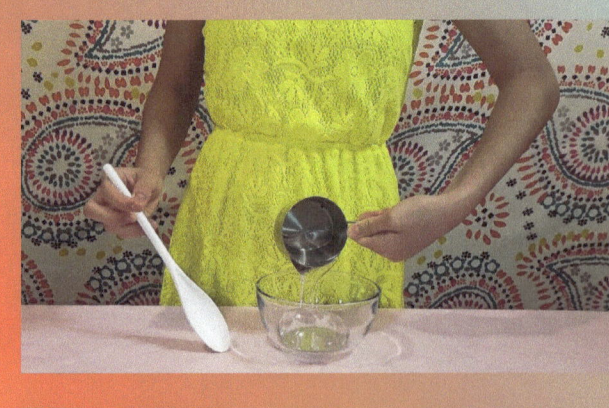

2) Add **Green Paint** to bowl and mix well

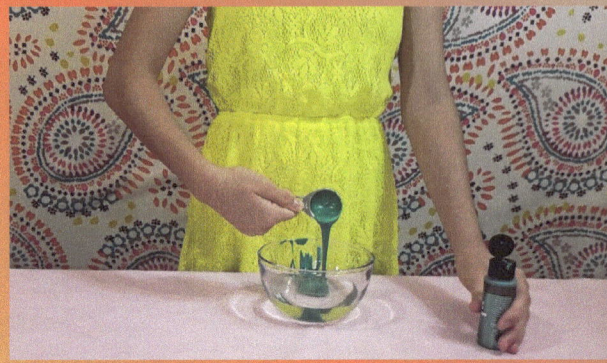

3) Add **Green Sequins** to bowl and mix well

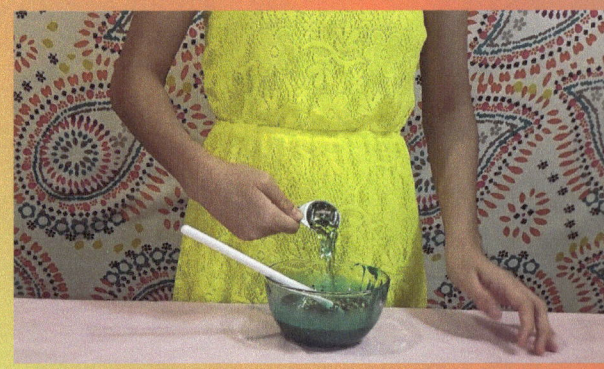

4) Add **Green Hologram Powder** and mix well

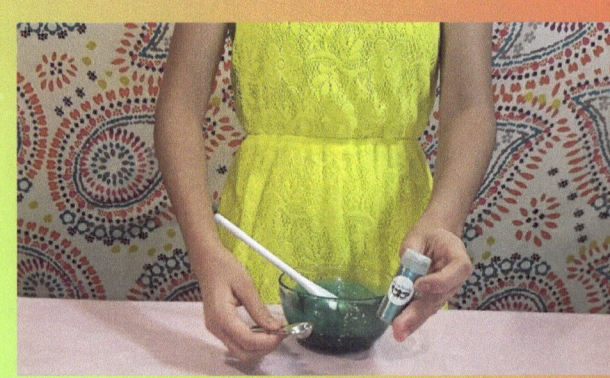

5) Add **Hand Lotion** and mix well

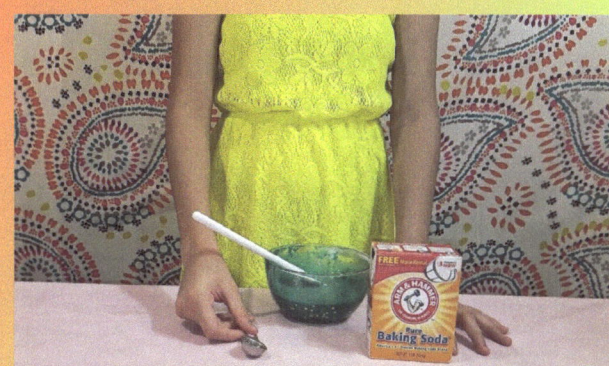

6) Add **Baking Soda** and mix well until dissolved

7) Add **Contact Lens Solution** slowly. Squirt directly from the bottle to mixing bowl. Don't over use contact lens solution or slime comes out hard like rubber. You need about 4 Tablespoons. No measuring spoons are being used, therefore, use your best judgement.

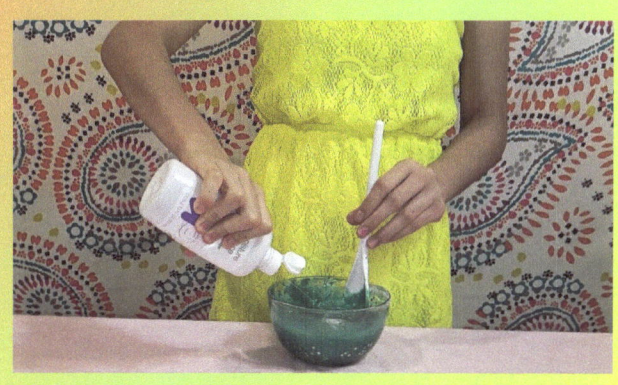

8) Use a **Spatula** to mix as you keep adding contact lens solution. Keep stirring until the slime doesn't stick to the bowl or your hands.

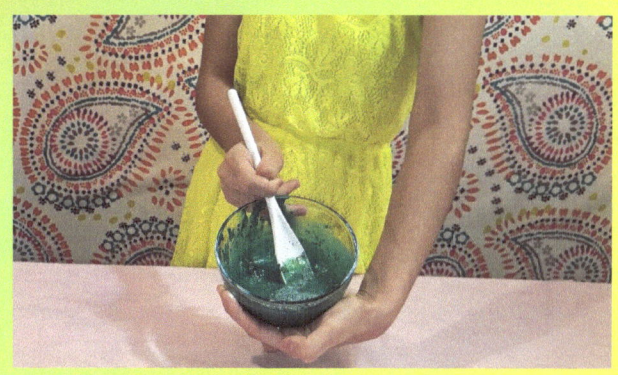

HOW TO MAKE SLIME

9) Once the glue starts to look like slime, **Knead** the mixture with your hands until you get the right slime consistency; smooth and soft enough to stretch with hands.

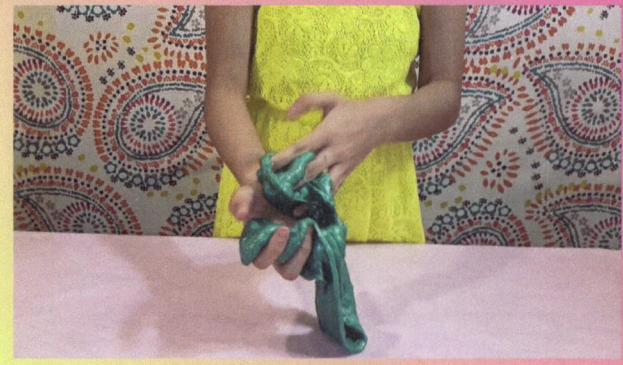

WHAT THE SLIME SHOULD LOOK LIKE

Stretched Hydra Slime

Hydra Slime in a **Storage Container**

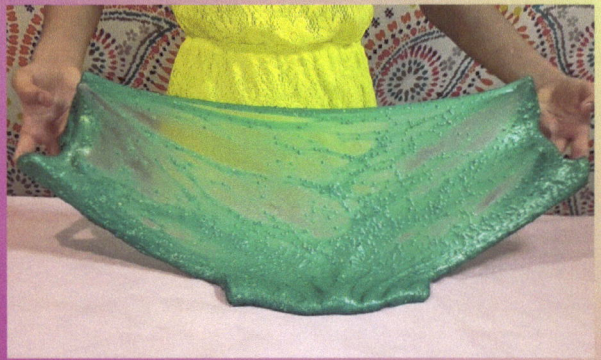
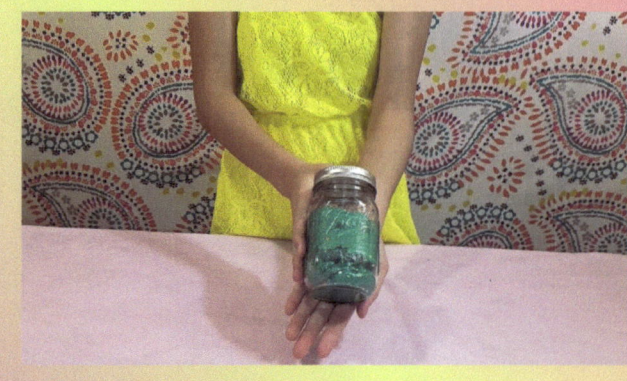

Now you have a fantastic, cool looking slime!

RECIPE 14. GOLD RUSH SLIME

This satisfying giggly slime is amazing. I love how the consistency looks like liquid gold. You need the pearl gold powder. Otherwise, it won't have the realistic look of gold. You can use metallic gold acrylic paint, although it just won't look as shimmery and liquid like.

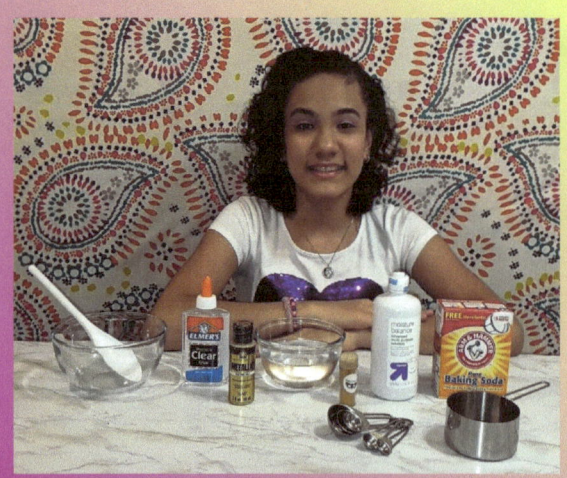

KUKI SHAMUS

Ingredients

- 2 Tablespoons Gold Metallic Acrylic Paint
- 1 Teaspoon Gold Pearl pigment powder
- 4 Tablespoons Contact Lens Solution
- 1 Teaspoon Baking Soda
- 1 Cup Clear PVA Glue
- $\frac{1}{4}$ Cup Cold Water

Directions

1) Pour **Clear Glue** into your mixing bowl.

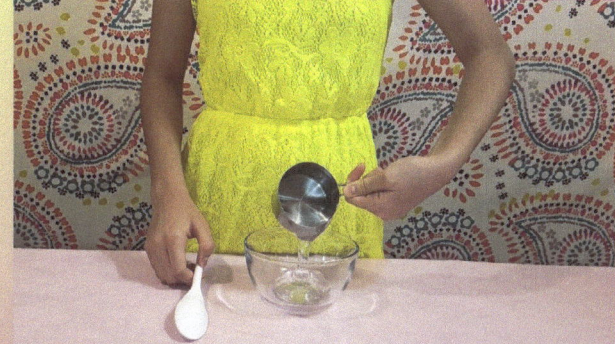

2) Add **Cold Water** to bowl and mix well

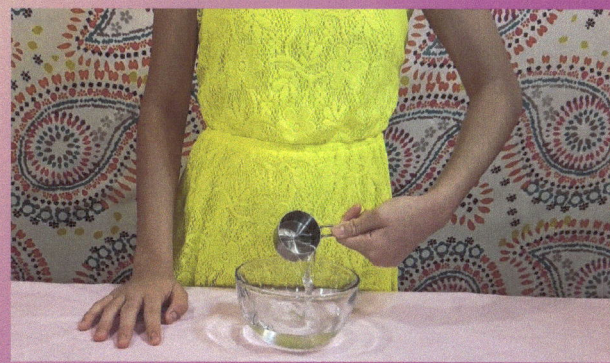

3) Add **Gold Metallic Paint** and mix well

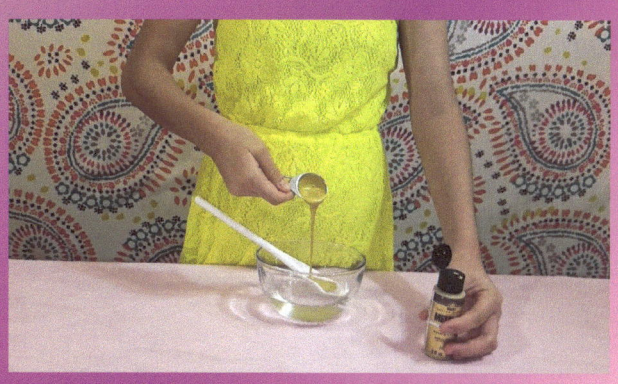

HOW TO MAKE SLIME

4) Add **Gold** **Pearl** **Pigment** **Powder** and mix

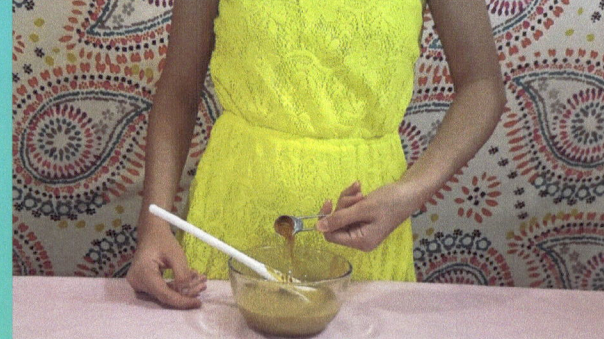

5) Add **Baking** **Soda** and mix well until dissolved

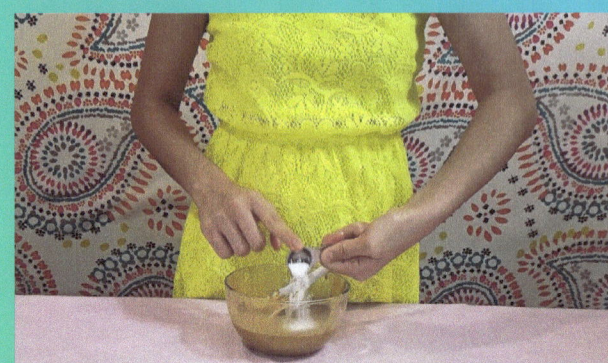

6) Add **Contact** **Lens** **Solution** slowly. Squirt directly from the bottle to mixing bowl. Don't over use contact lens solution or slime comes out hard like rubber. You need about 4 Tablespoons. No measuring spoons are being used, therefore, use your best judgement.

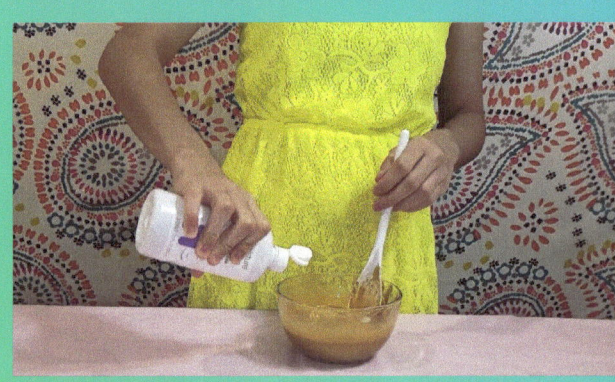

7) Use a **Spatula** to mix as you keep adding contact lens solution. Keep stirring until the slime doesn't stick to the bowl or your hands.

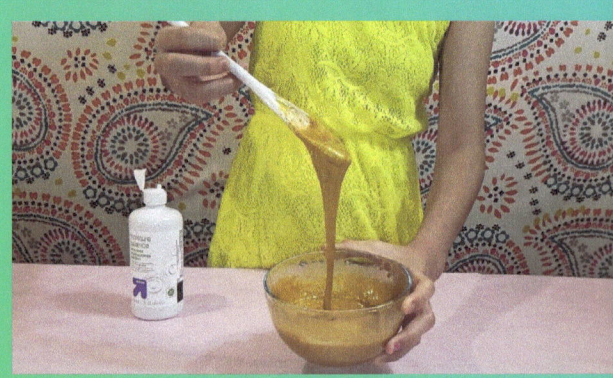

8) Once the glue starts to look like slime, **Knead** the mixture with your hands until you get the right slime consistency; smooth and soft enough to stretch with hands.

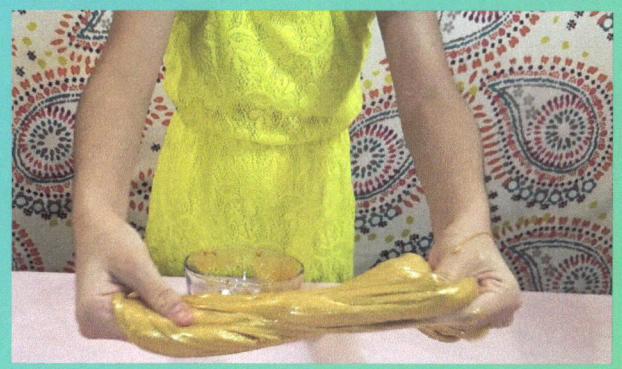

WHAT THE SLIME SHOULD LOOK LIKE

Stretched Gold Rush Slime

Gold Rush Slime in a **Storage Container**

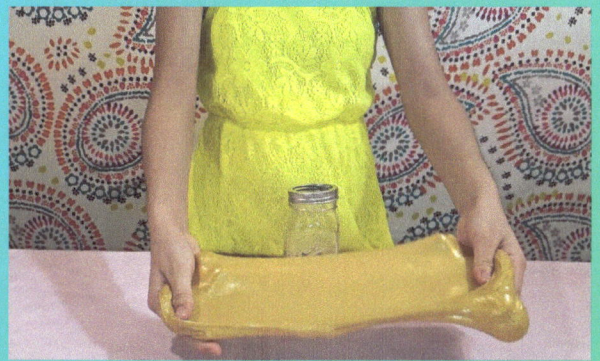

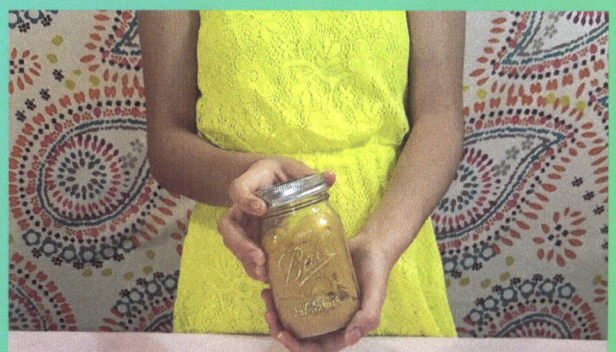

Now you have a beautiful soft slime!

RECIPE 15. ABRACADABRA SLIME

Slime science is so amazing. This recipe is called Abracadabra because the slime changes color. That's right! This slime will transform color right before your eyes when cold temperature is applied to it. Then it will go back to its normal color after it warms up.

We will be needing Thermochromic Pigment. This ingredient is usually only found online and can be ordered in different colors. I really love pink, so I decided to use the black to pink pigment. As the temperature changes, it is so beautiful to view in real time.

HOW TO MAKE SLIME

Ingredients

- 1 Cup White PVA Glue
- 1 Tablespoon Thermochromic Pigment
- 1 Cup Shaving Cream
- 1 Teaspoon Baking Soda
- 4 Tablespoons Contact Lens Solution

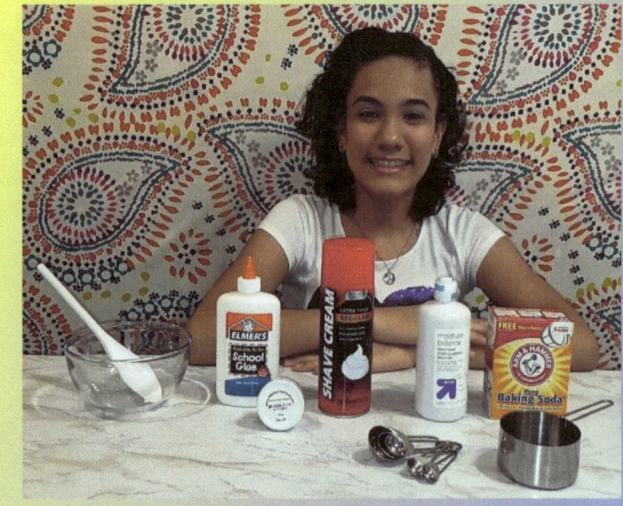

Directions

1) Pour **White Glue** into your mixing bowl.

2) Add **Shaving Cream** with help of a spatula. Slowly add one cup at a time to make sure it mixes well.

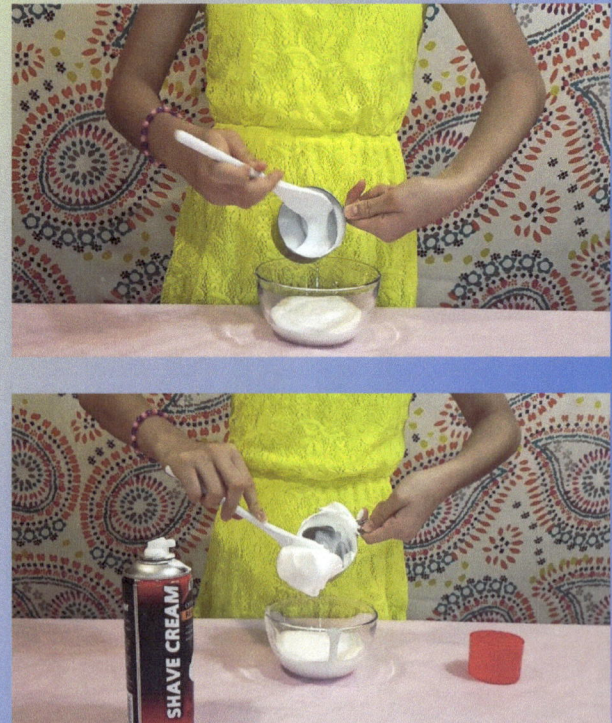

3) Add **Color Changing Pigment** and mix well

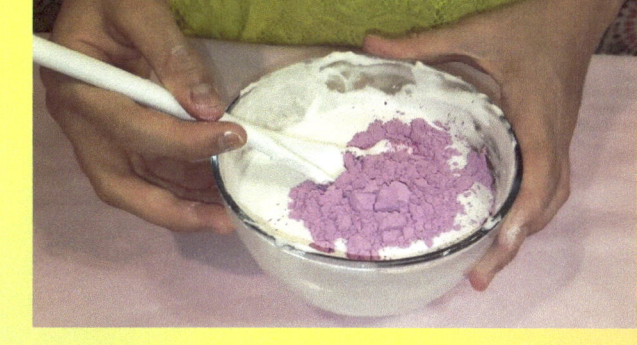

4) Add **Baking Soda** and mix well until dissolved

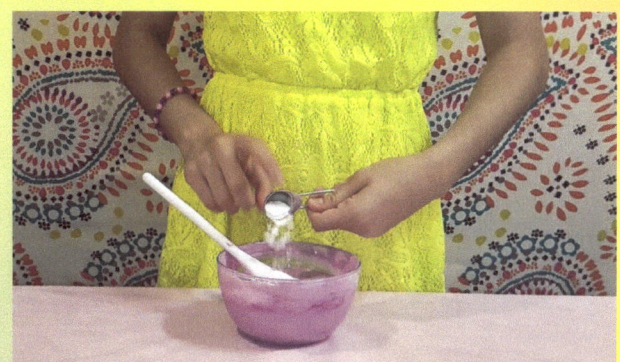

5) Add **Contact Lens Solution** slowly. Squirt directly from the bottle to mixing bowl. Don't over use contact lens solution or slime comes out hard like rubber. You need about 4 Tablespoons. No measuring spoons are being used, therefore, use your best judgement.

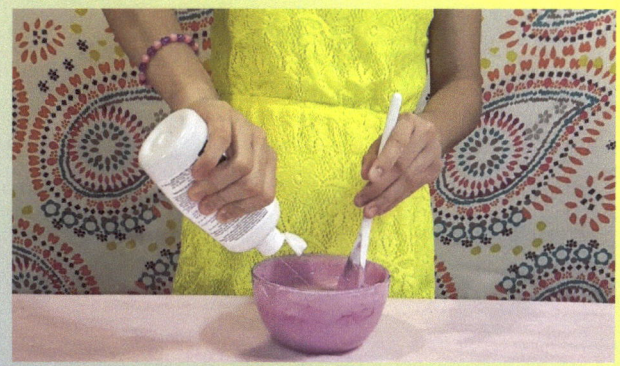

6) Use a **Spatula** to mix as you keep adding contact lens solution. Keep stirring until the slime doesn't stick to the bowl or your hands.

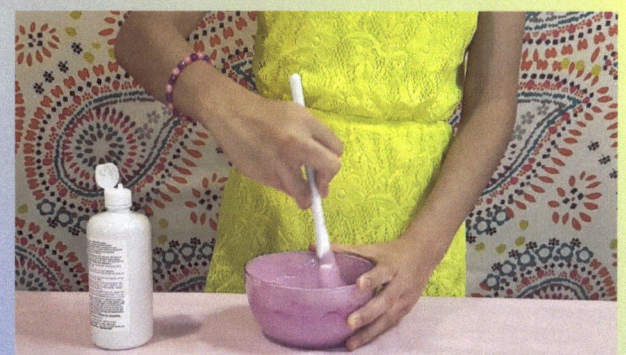

HOW TO MAKE SLIME

7) Once the glue starts to look like slime, **Knead** the mixture with your hands until you get the right slime consistency; smooth and soft enough to stretch with hands.

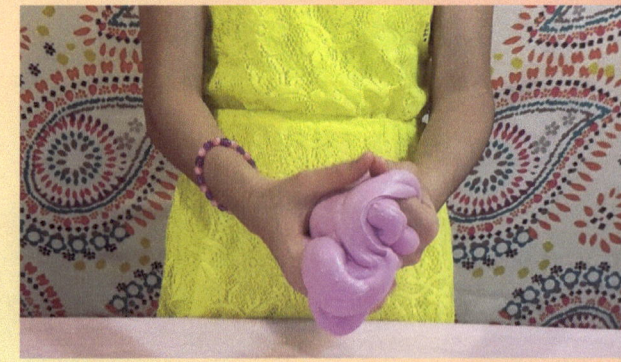

WHAT THE SLIME SHOULD LOOK LIKE

Stretched Abracadabra Slime

Abracadabra Slime in a **Storage Container**

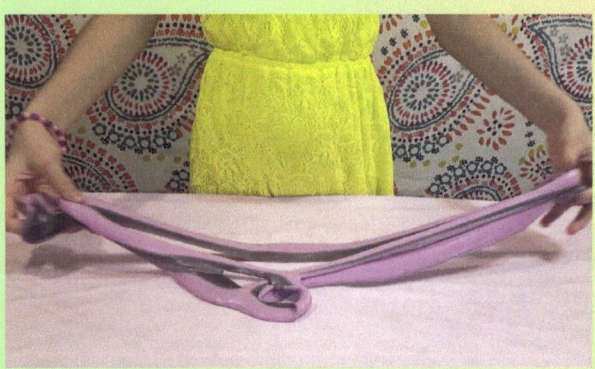
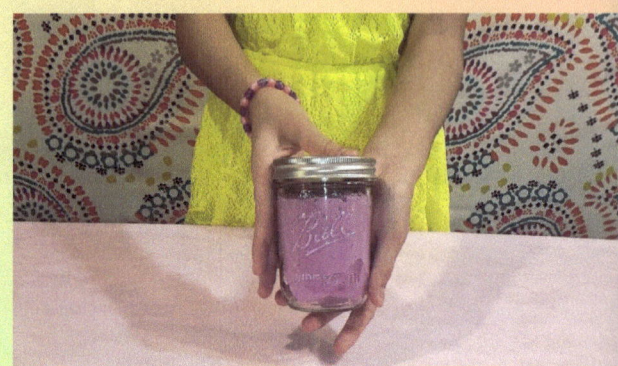

Abracadabra Slime **Color Transformation**

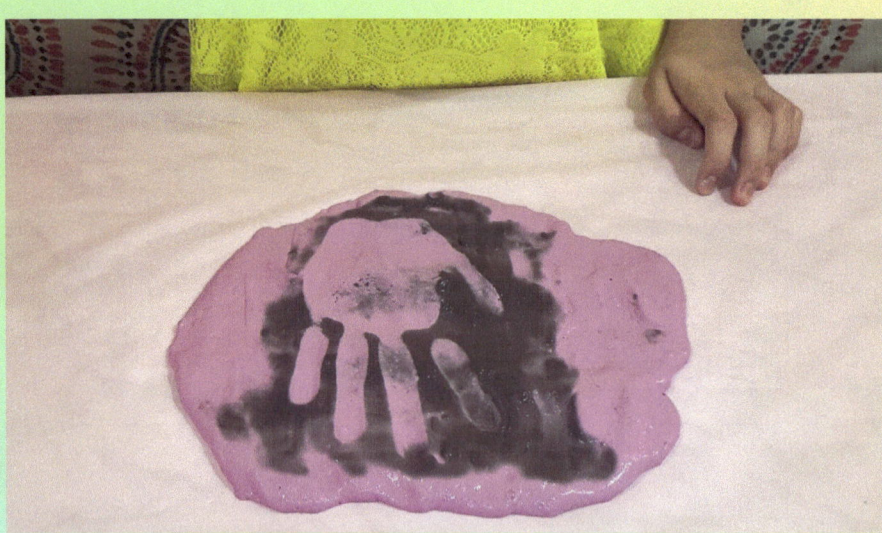

Now you have a magic color changing slime!

Recipe 16. Bubbly Slime

This recipe is called Bubbly Slime because it is so thin and stretchy that you can actually blow slime bubbles with it. Is very fun to play with.

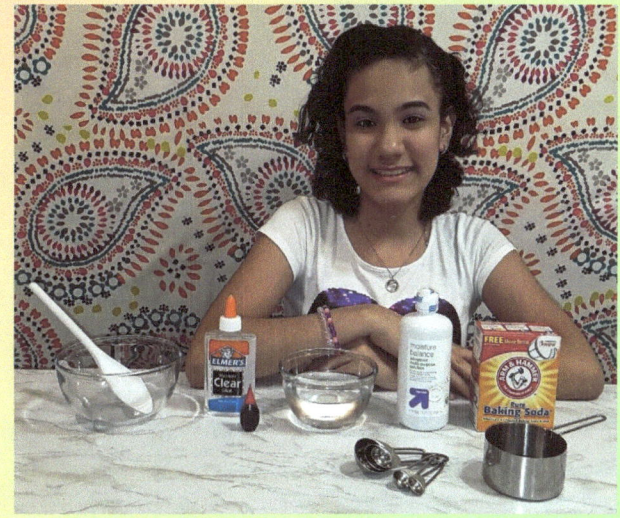

Ingredients

- 1 Cup Clear PVA Glue
- $1/4$ Cup Cold Water
- 8 Drops Red Food Coloring
- 2 Teaspoons Baking Soda
- 4 Tablespoons Contact Lens Solution

Directions

1) Pour **Clear Glue** into your mixing bowl.

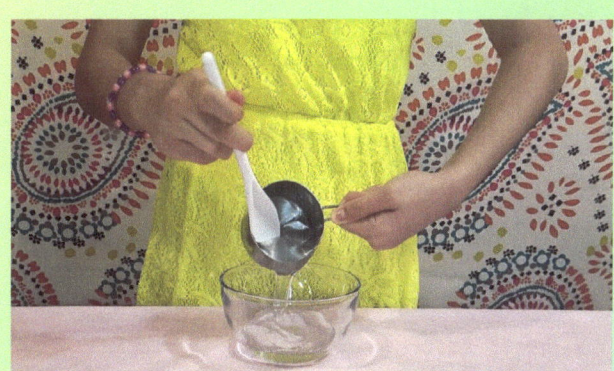

2) Add **Red Food Coloring** and mix well.

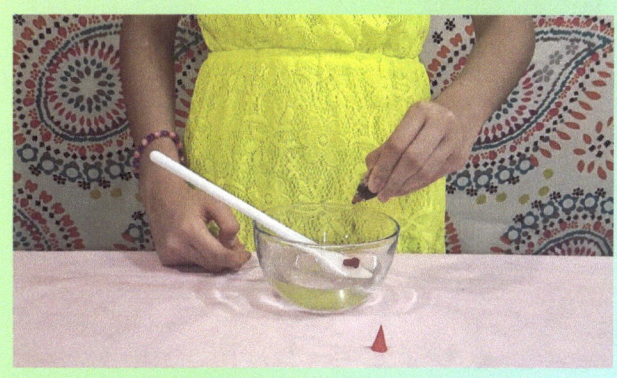

HOW TO MAKE SLIME

3) Add **Cold Water** into a second mixing bowl.

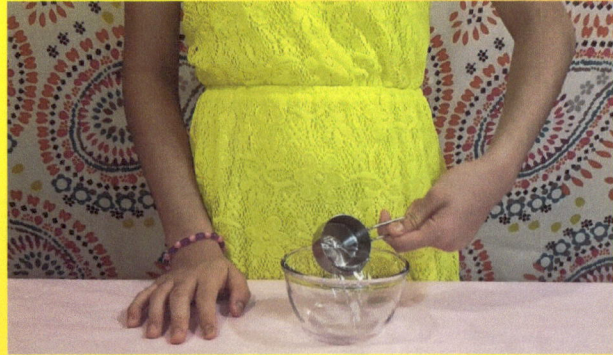

4) Add **Baking Soda** to that second bowl with Cold Water and mix well until dissolved.

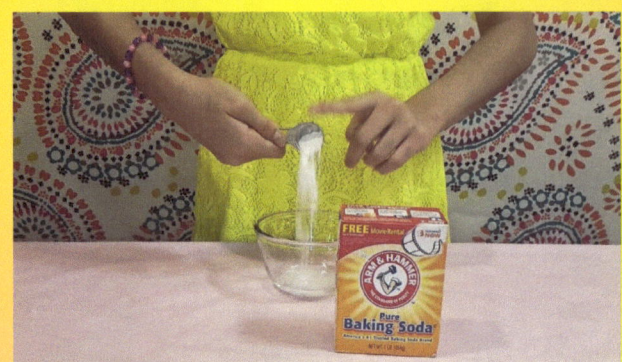

5) **Combine** the Baking Soda Water and Glue together. Add it a little at a time until the slime forms together.

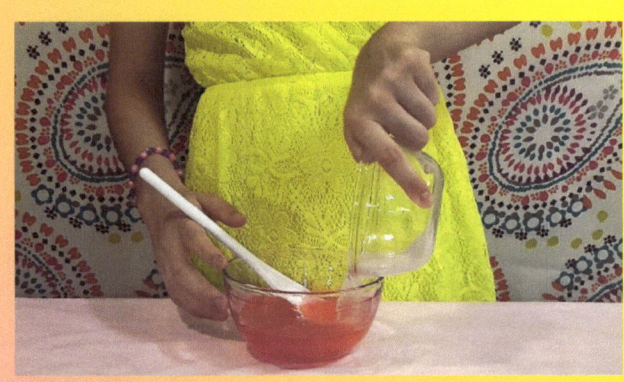

6) Add **Contact Lens Solution** slowly. Squirt directly from the bottle to mixing bowl. Don't over use contact lens solution or slime comes out hard like rubber. You need about 4 Tablespoons. No measuring spoons are being used, therefore, use your best judgement.

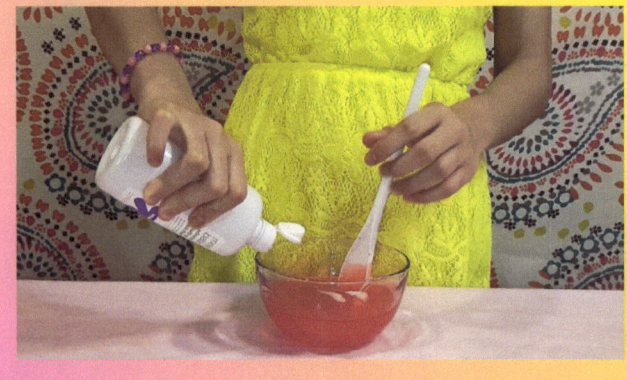

7) Use a **Spatula** to mix as you keep adding contact lens solution. Keep stirring until the slime doesn't stick to the bowl or your hand.

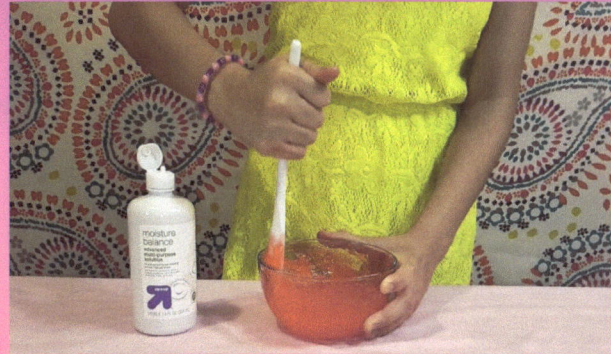

8) Once the glue starts to look like slime, **Knead** the mixture with your hands until you get the right slime consistency; smooth and soft enough to stretch with hands.

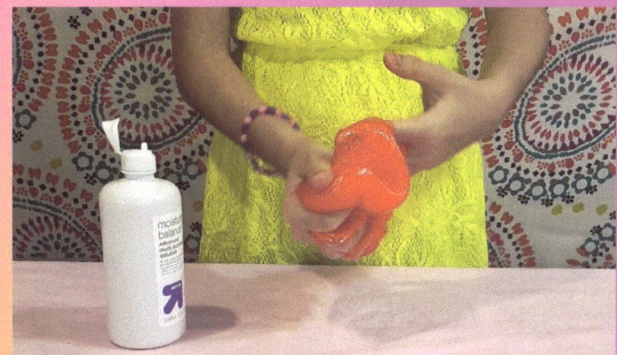

WHAT THE SLIME SHOULD LOOK LIKE
Stretched Bubbly Slime

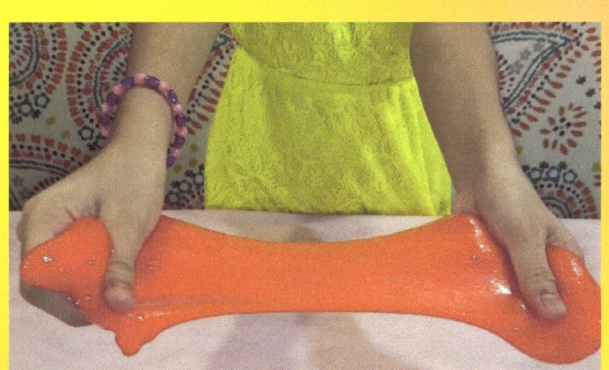

Bubbly Slime in a **Storage Container**

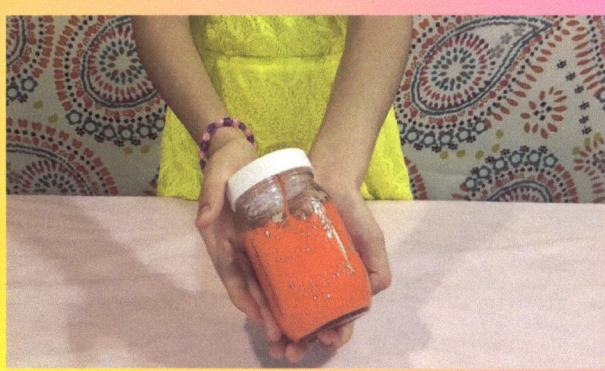

Blowing Big Bubbles using Bubbly Slime

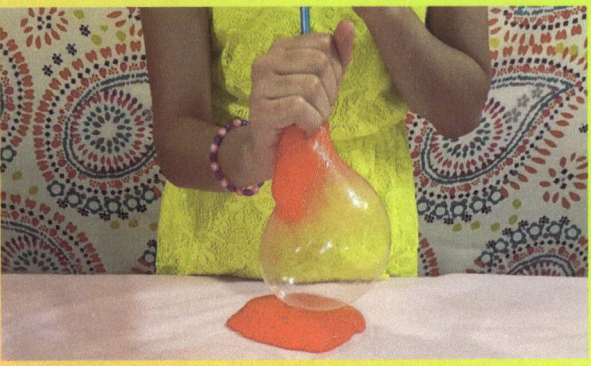

Now you have a bubble making slime!

RECIPE 17. KUKI COOKIE SLIME

The name of this slime comes from people always mistaking my name. My little sister started calling me Kuki Cookie because the sound is the same, however the spelling of my name is different. This slime is glossy and stretchy and just amazingly scented. It reminds me of holding cookies in my hands when I play with this slime.

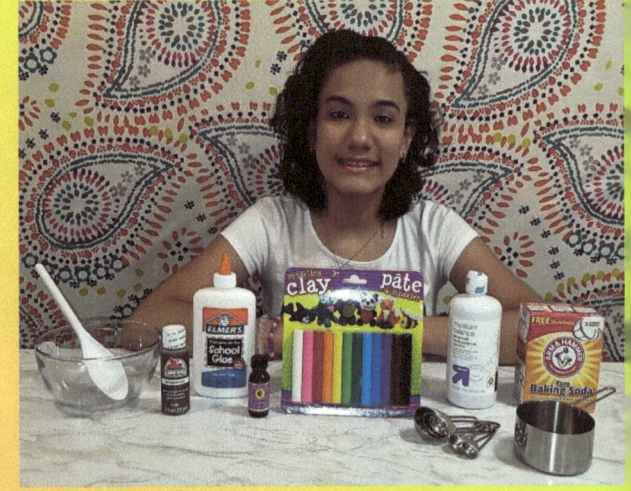

Ingredients

- 1 Cup White PVA Glue
- 2 Tablespoons Brown Acrylic Paint
- $\frac{1}{2}$ Teaspoon or 20 drops Grandma's Cookies Scent or Chocolate Scent
- 1 Stick Brown Molding Clay (optional)
- 1 Teaspoon Baking Soda
- 4 Tablespoons Contact Lens Solution

Directions

1) Pour **White Glue** into your mixing bowl.

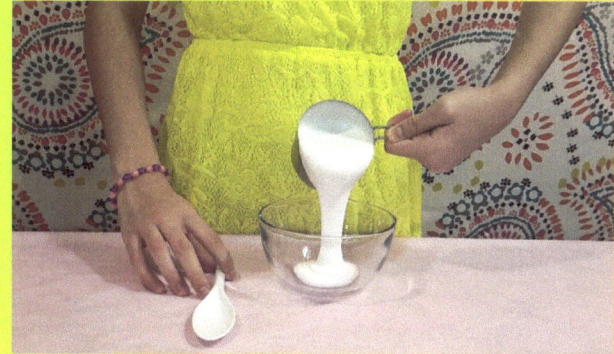

2) Add **Brown Paint** and mix well.

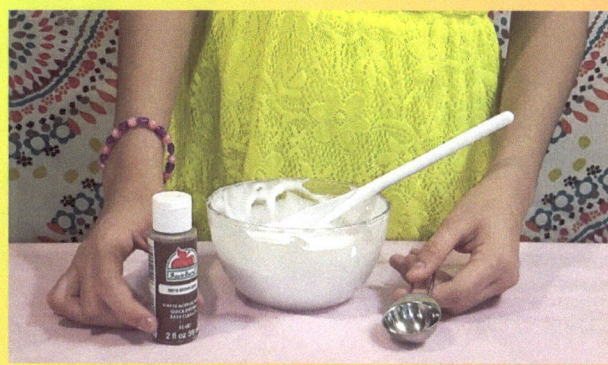

3) Add **Grandma's Cookies Scent** and mix well.

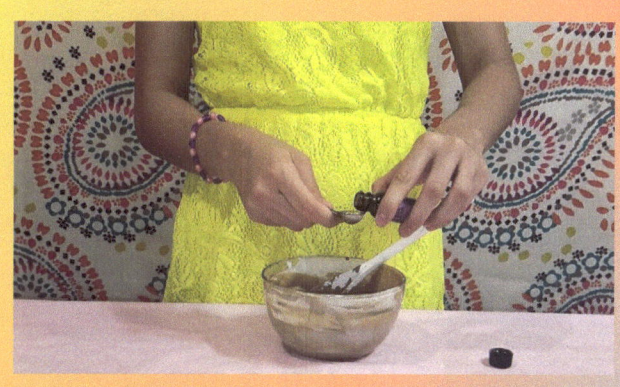

4) Add **Baking Soda** and mix well until dissolved.

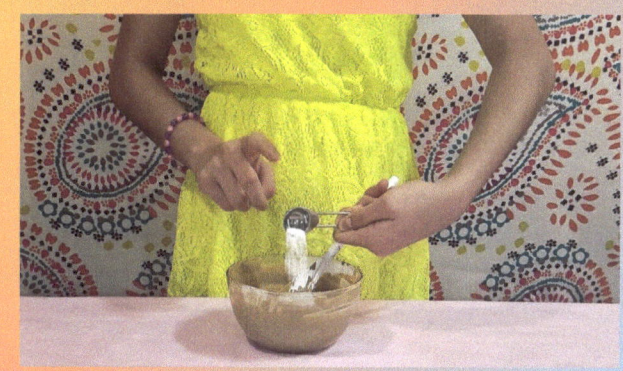

HOW TO MAKE SLIME

5) Add <u>**Contact Lens Solution**</u> slowly. Squirt directly from the bottle to mixing bowl. Don't over use contact lens solution or slime comes out hard like rubber. You need about 4 Tablespoons. No measuring spoons are being used, therefore, use your best judgement.

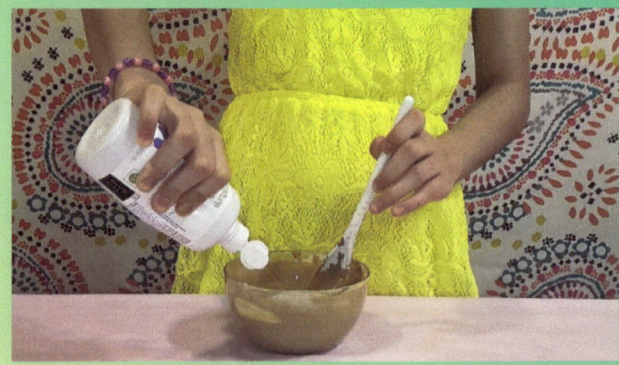

6) Use a <u>**Spatula**</u> to mix as you keep adding contact lens solution. Keep stirring until the slime doesn't stick to the bowl or your hands.

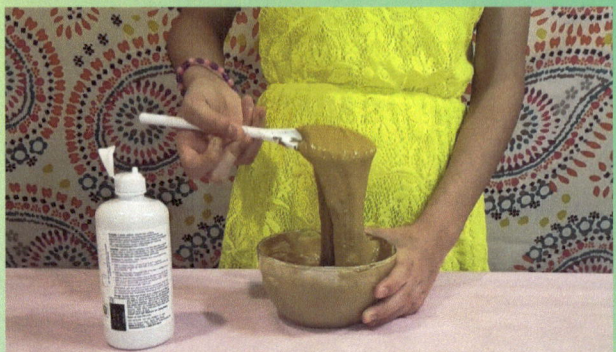

7) Once the glue starts to look like slime, <u>**Knead**</u> the mixture with your hands until you get the right slime consistency; smooth and soft enough to stretch with hands.

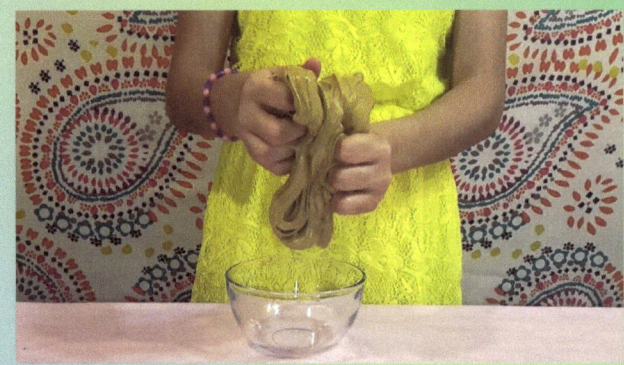

8) <u>**Shape the Slime**</u> to look like cookies. Take the brown modeling clay and make tiny pieces that look like chocolate chips.

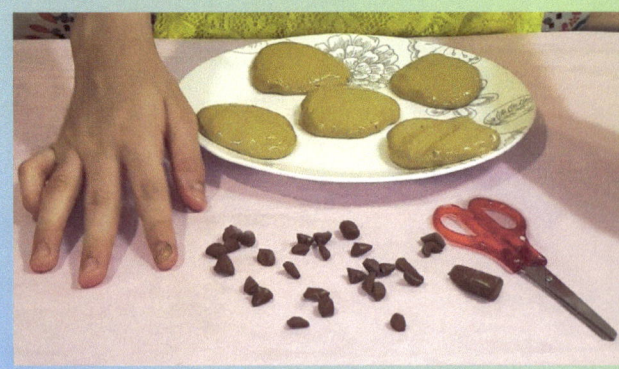

KUKI SHAMUS

9) Place these **Clay Pieces On Top** of the slime so the slime looks like chocolate chip cookies.

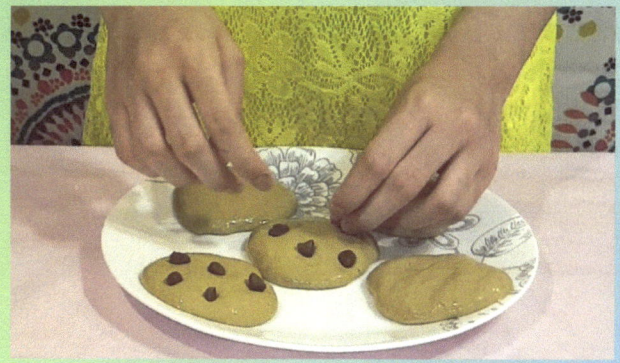

WHAT THE SLIME SHOULD LOOK LIKE

Stretched Kuki Cookie Slime

Kuki Cookie Slime in a **Storage Container**

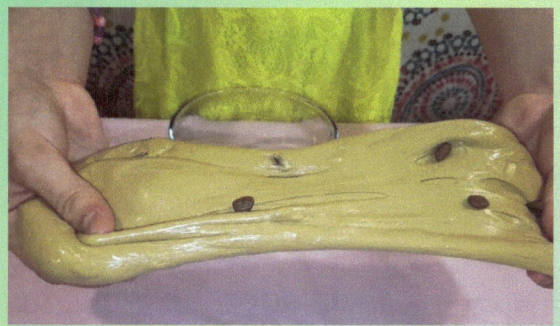

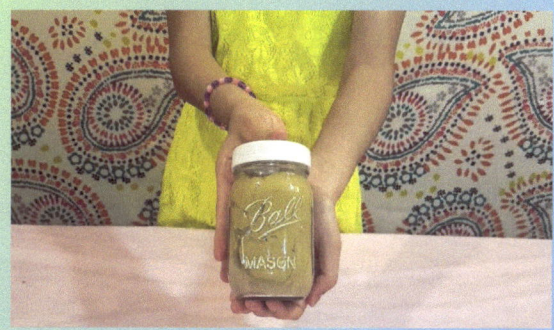

Show Me the Cookie in Kuki Cookie Slime

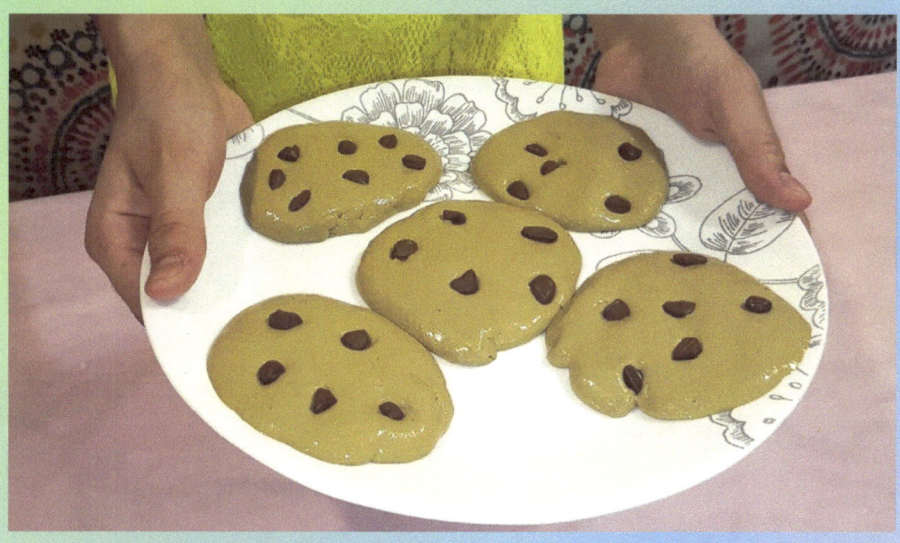

Now you have a delicious scented slime!

HOW TO MAKE SLIME

Recipe 18. Cotton Candy Slime

It is so pretty in pink. This is called Cotton candy slime because its pink and fluffy, just like that favorite treat people enjoy at carnivals. I just love how fluffy and light this slime is.

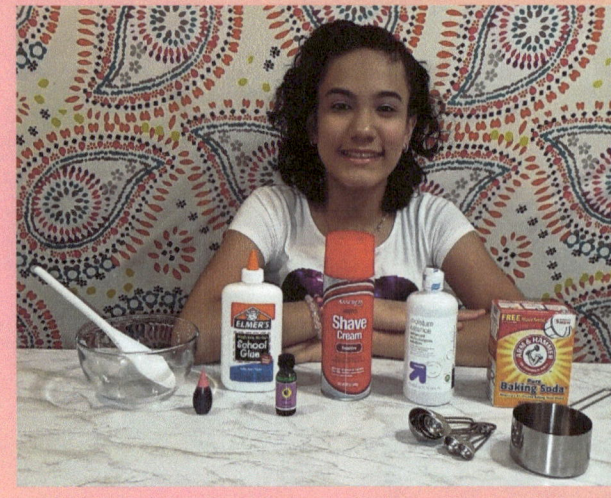

Ingredients

- 1 Cup White PVA Glue
- 10 Drops Pink Food Coloring
- 5 Cups Unscented Shaving Cream
- $\frac{1}{2}$ Teaspoon or 20 Drops Cotton Candy Scent
- 1 Teaspoon Baking Soda
- 4 Tablespoons Contact Lens Solution

Directions

1) Pour **White Glue** into your mixing bowl.

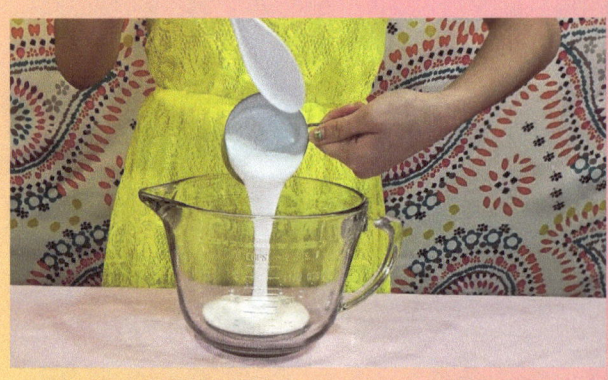

2) Add **Pink Food Coloring** and mix well.

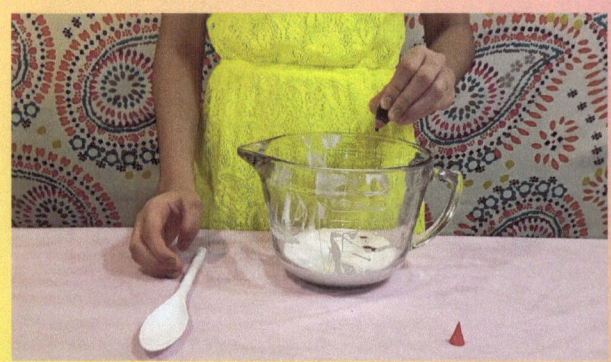

3) Add **Cotton Candy Scent** and mix well.

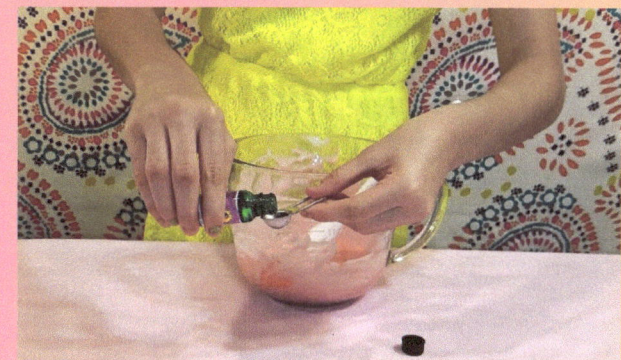

4) Add **Baking Soda** and mix well until dissolved.

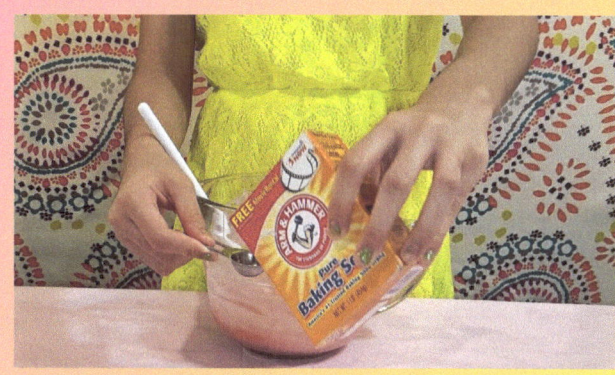

5) Add **Shaving Cream** with help of a spatula. Slowly add one cup at a time to make sure it mixes well.

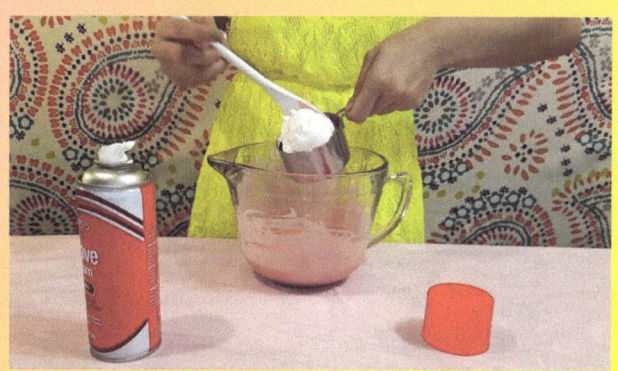

6) Add **Contact Lens Solution** slowly. Squirt directly from the bottle to mixing bowl. Don't over use contact lens solution or slime comes out hard like rubber. You need about 4 Tablespoons. No measuring spoons are being used, therefore, use your best judgement.

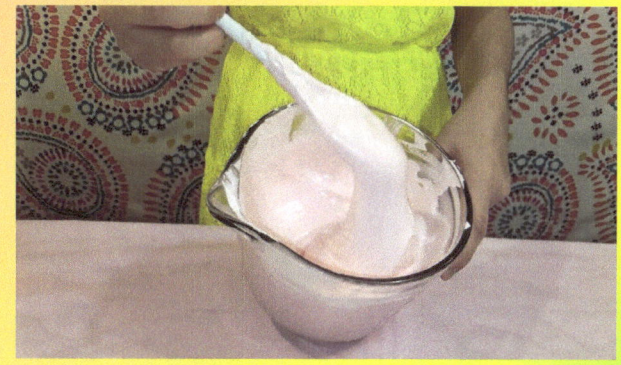

HOW TO MAKE SLIME

7) Use a **Spatula** to mix as you keep adding contact lens solution. Keep stirring until the slime doesn't stick to the bowl or your hands.

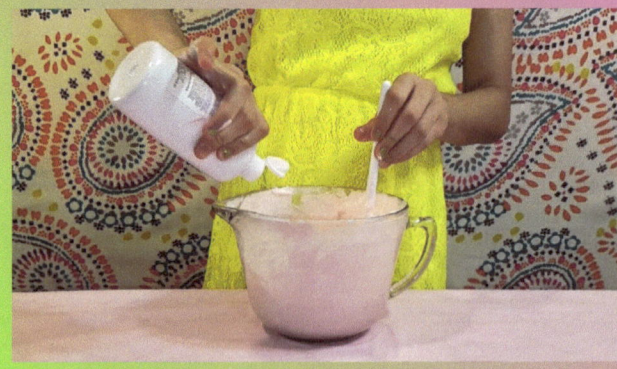

8) Once the glue starts to look like slime, **Knead** the mixture with your hands until you get the right slime consistency; smooth and soft enough to stretch with hands.

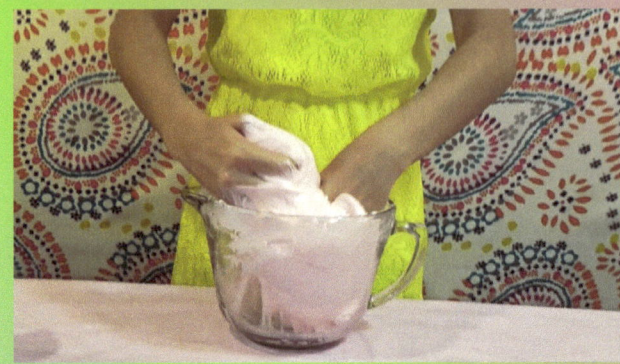

WHAT THE SLIME SHOULD LOOK LIKE

Stretched Cotton Candy Slime   Cotton Candy Slime in a **Storage Container**

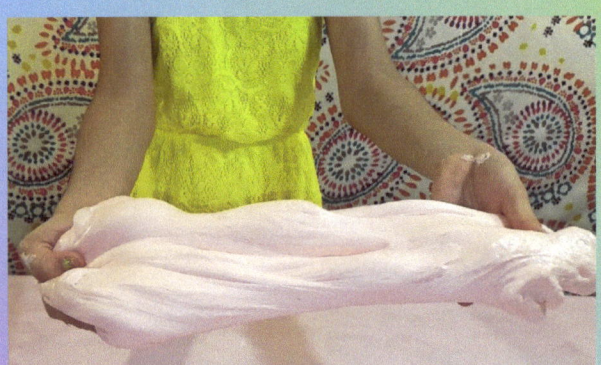
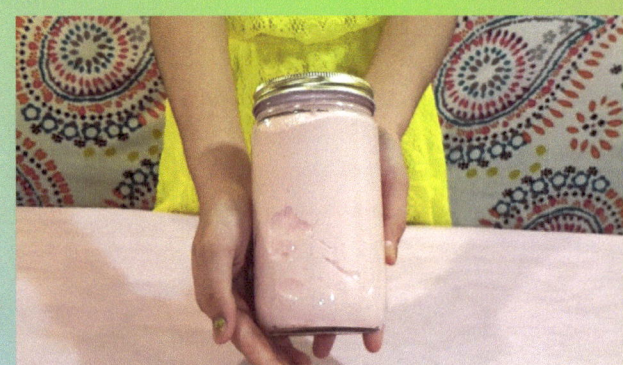

Now you have a fluffy scented slime!

Recipe 19. Jack O' Slime

Two of the most loved holidays by kids are Halloween and Christmas. I wanted to add a Halloween recipe to have an activity you can do at home besides carving a pumpkin on Halloween.

You can also make this as a gift to give all your classmates, friends or neighbors for Halloween. It's very inexpensive and SO cute because we add glow in the dark paint to make it glow for Halloween Night.

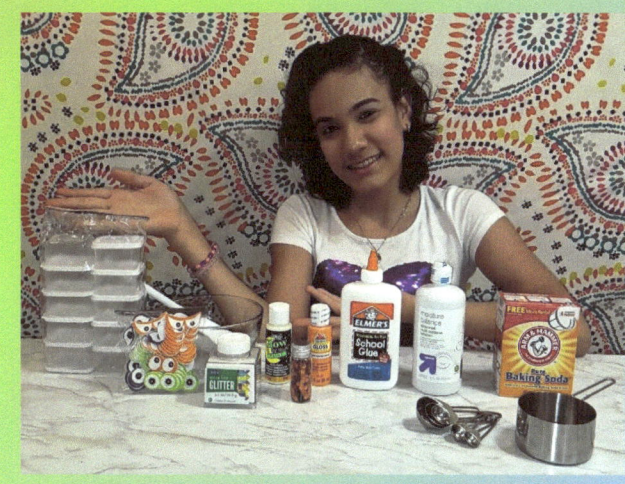

Ingredients

- 1 Cup White PVA Glue
- 2 Tablespoons Pumpkin Orange Acrylic Paint
- 3 Teaspoons Extra Fine Crystal Glitter
- 1 Tablespoon Orange Circle Sequins
- 3 Tablespoons Glow in the Dark Paint.
- 1 Teaspoon Baking Soda
- 4 Tablespoons Contact Lens Solution

Directions

1) Pour **White Glue** into your mixing bowl.

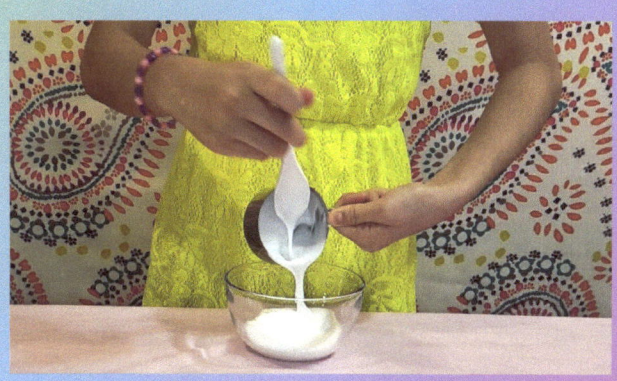

HOW TO MAKE SLIME

2) Add **Orange** **Paint** and mix well.

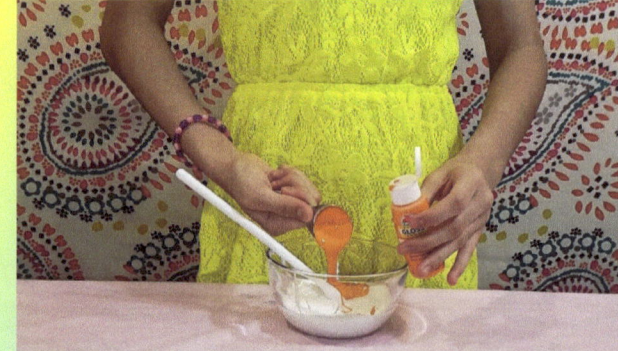

3) Add **Glow** **in** **the** **Dark** **Paint** mix well.

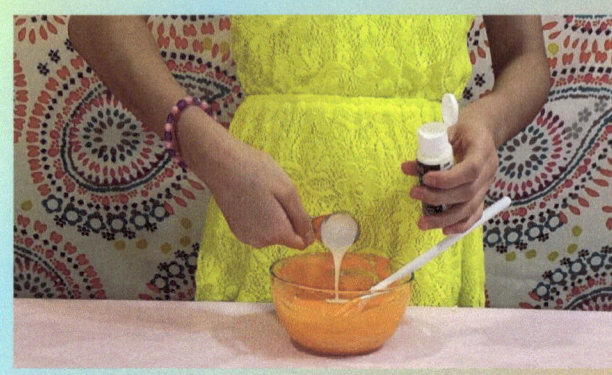

4) Add **Extra** **Fine** **Crystal** **Glitter** and mix well.

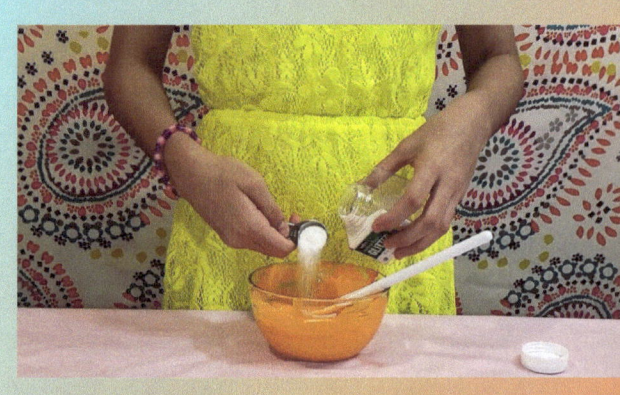

5) Add **Orange** **Circle** **Sequins** and mix well.

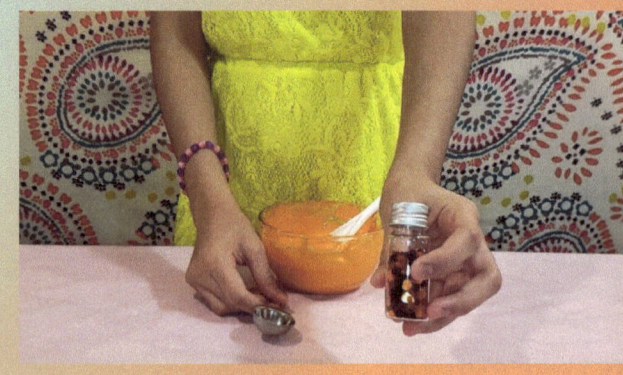

6) Add **Baking Soda** and mix well until dissolved.

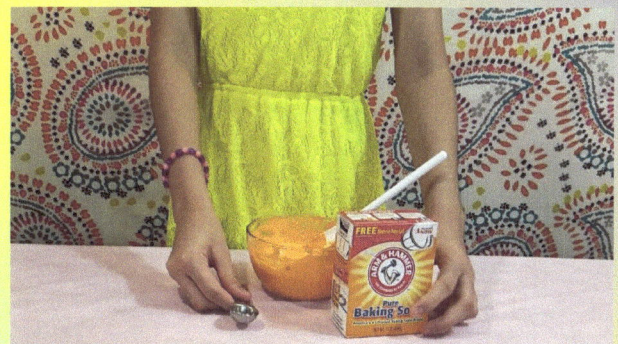

7) Add **Contact Lens Solution** slowly. Squirt directly from the bottle to mixing bowl. Don't over use contact lens solution or slime comes out hard like rubber. You need about 4 Tablespoons. No measuring spoons are being used, therefore, use your best judgement.

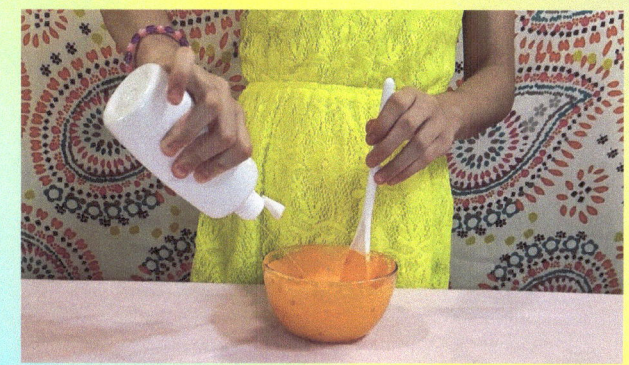

8) Use a **Spatula** to mix as you keep adding contact lens solution. Keep stirring until the slime doesn't stick to the bowl or your hands.

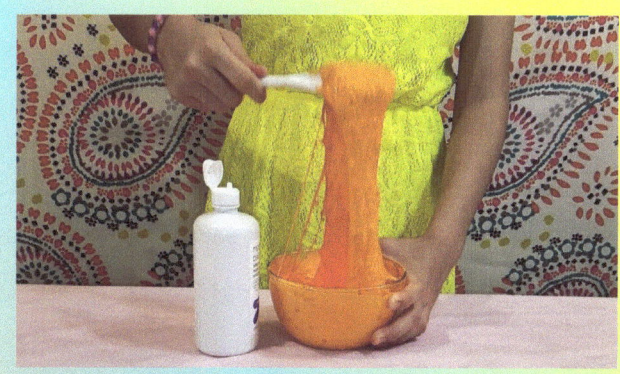

9) Once the glue starts to look like slime, **Knead** the mixture with your hands until you get the right slime consistency; smooth and soft enough to stretch with hands.

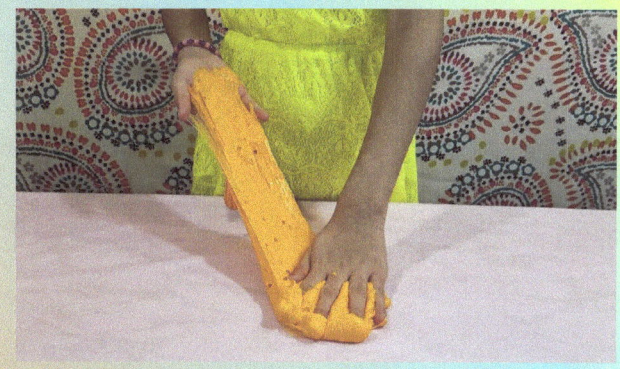

You can play with the slime now, but if you want to activate the glow in the dark properties you must let it sit under direct light for a few hours.

HOW TO MAKE SLIME

WHAT THE SLIME SHOULD LOOK LIKE

Stretched Jack O'Slime Jack O'Slime in a **Storage Container**

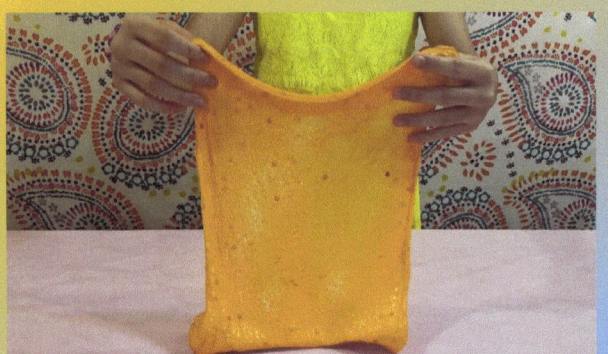 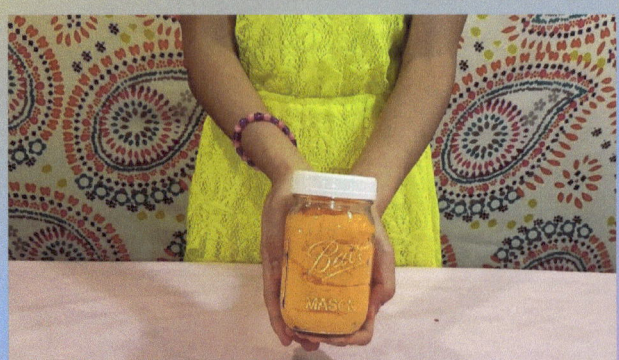

Now you have a spooky slime!

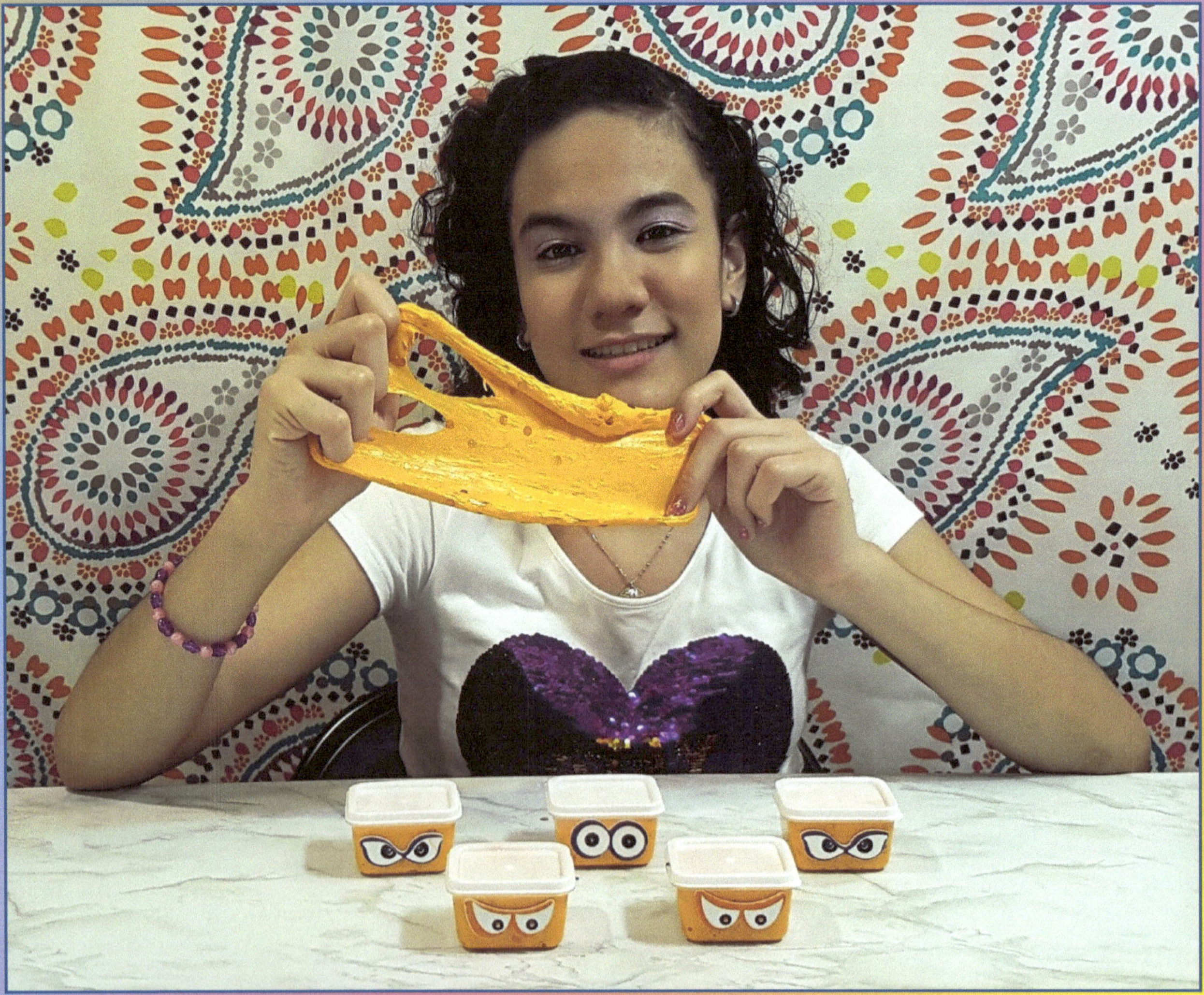

82

KUKI SHAMUS

HALLOWEEN TRICK OR TREAT GIFTS

Jack O'Slime recipe makes roughly 6 Halloween treats in 2.5 Ounce containers.

Supplies

- 6 Sealable Small Containers (2-3 Ounces)
- 6 Spooky Eye Stickers

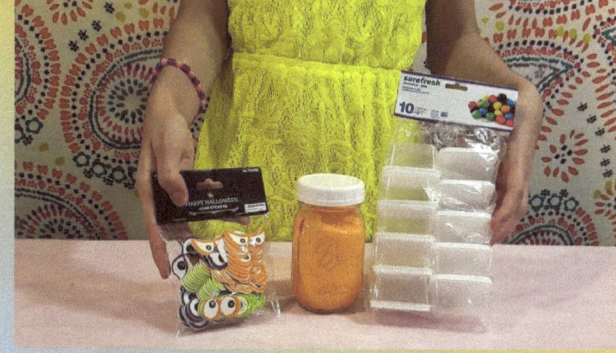

Directions

Apply 1 Sticker to each container.

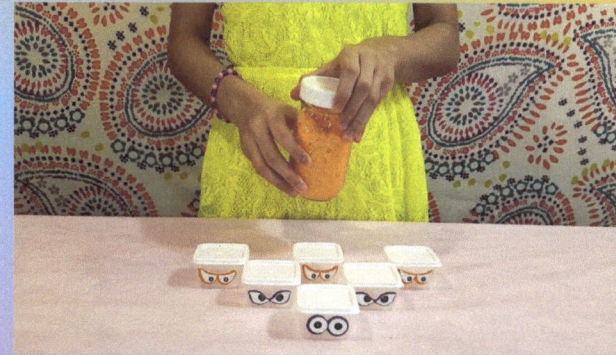

Fill Up each Container with Jack O'Slime

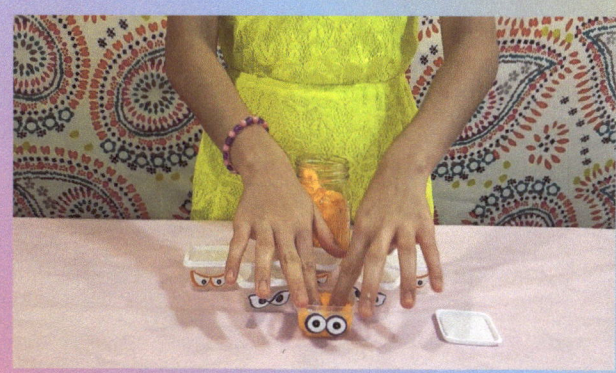

Jack O'Slime Halloween Treats **Ready to Give Out**. Happy Halloween!

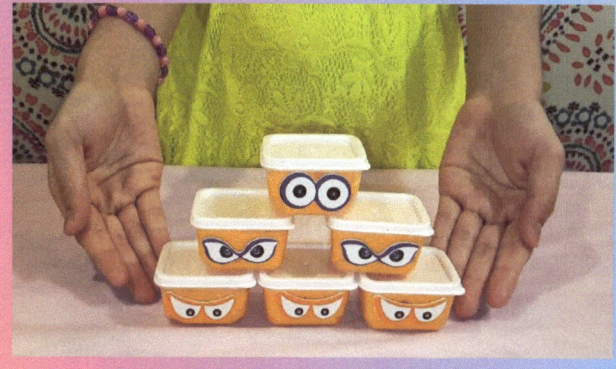

HOW TO MAKE SLIME

RECIPE 20. SNOWY CHRISTMAS SLIME

Christmas is one of the happiest of times for kids. I have a Christmas slime recipe for you. You can make a lasting memory with this activity which you can do at home on Christmas eve.

It is called Snowy Christmas Slime because it is fluffy white and frosty like that early Christmas snow. Who knows, maybe Santa Clause will play with your slime when he comes to your house.

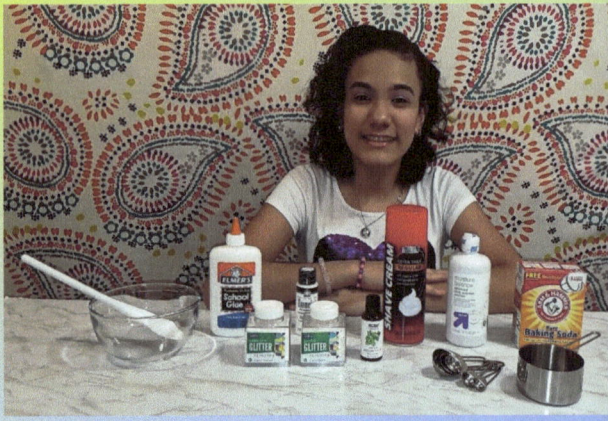

Note: this recipe calls for peppermint oil. I love using this because it brings aromatherapy and gives a little tingle to your hands. The oil is optional and does not take away from quality of the slime.

Ingredients

- 1 Cup White PVA Glue
- 2 Tablespoons White Acrylic Paint
- 2 Teaspoons Jumbo Crystal Glitter
- 2 Teaspoons Extra Fine Crystal Glitter
- 3 Cups Unscented Shaving Cream
- $1/2$ Teaspoon or 20 Drops peppermint Essential Oil
- 1 Teaspoon Baking Soda
- 4 Tablespoons Contact Lens Solution

KUKI SHAMUS

Directions

1) Pour **White Glue** into your mixing bowl.

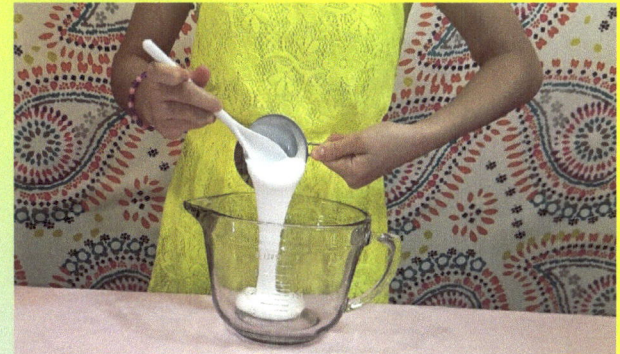

2) Add **White Paint** and mix well.

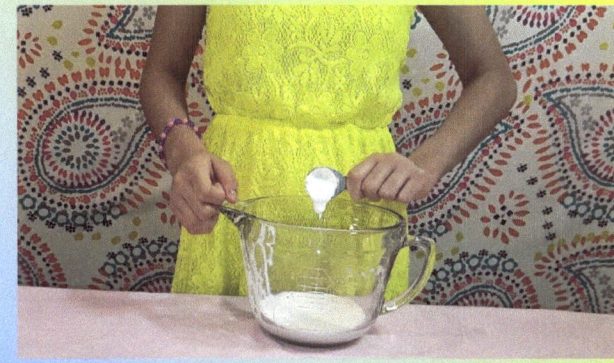

3) Add **Jumbo Glitter** and mix well

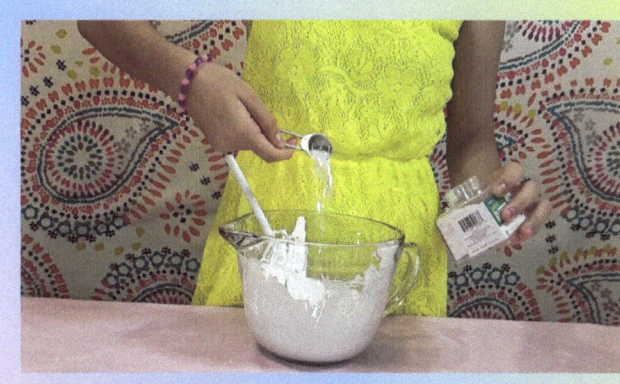

4) Add **Fine Glitter** and mix well

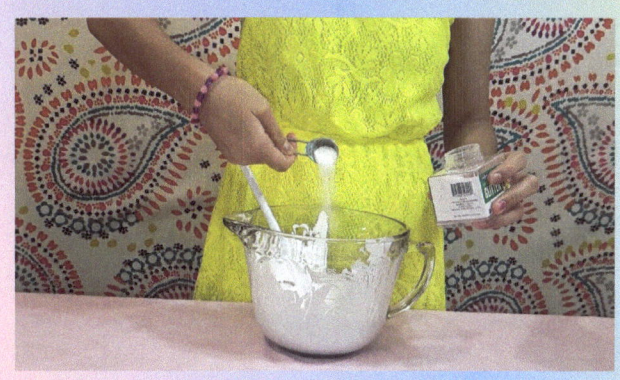

HOW TO MAKE SLIME

5) Add **Baking Soda** and mix well until dissolved.

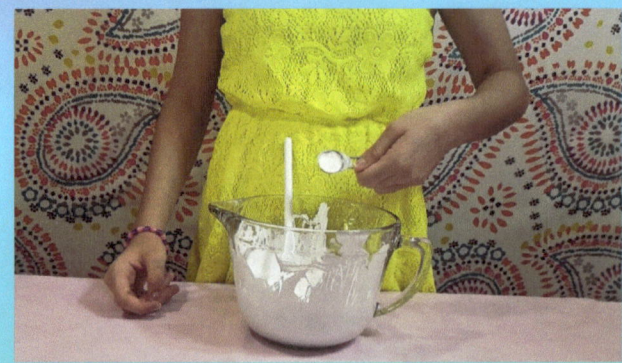

6) Add **Shaving Cream** with help of a spatula. Slowly add one cup at a time to make sure it mixes well.

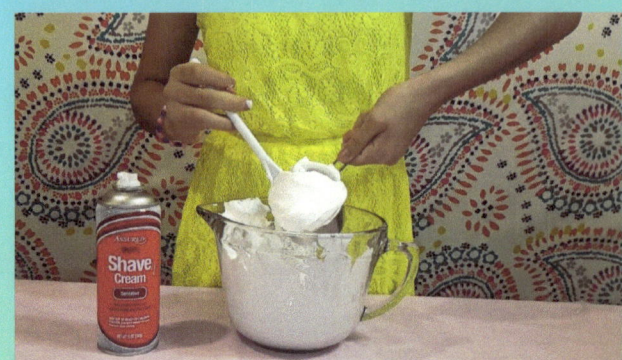

7) Add **Peppermint Essential Oil Scent** and mix well.

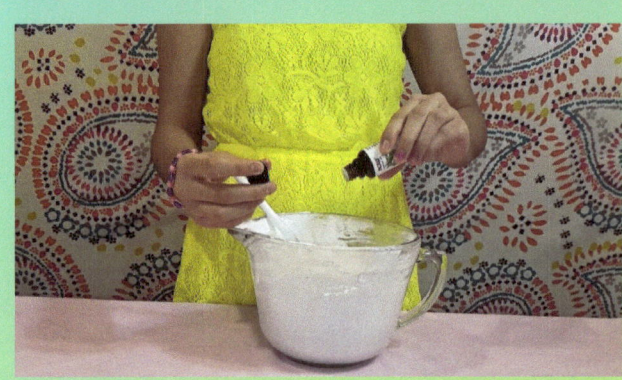

8) Add **Contact Lens Solution** slowly. Squirt directly from the bottle to mixing bowl. Don't over use contact lens solution or slime comes out hard like rubber. You need about 4 Tablespoons. No measuring spoons are being used, therefore, use your best judgement.

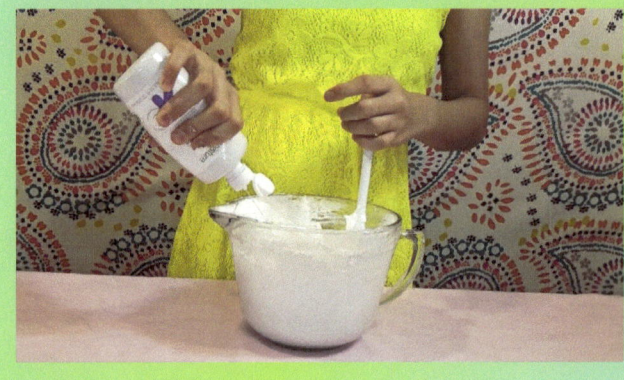

9) Use a **Spatula** to mix as you keep adding contact lens solution. Keep stirring until the slime doesn't stick to the bowl or your hands.

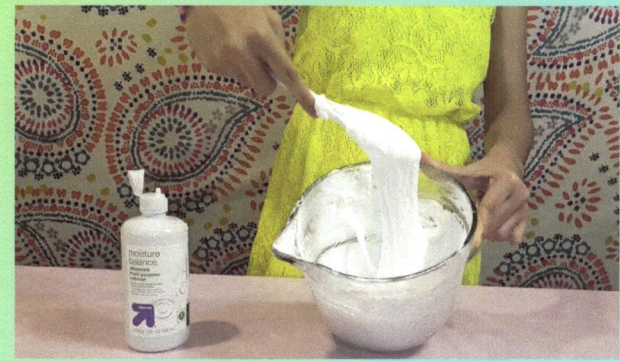

10) Once the glue starts to look like slime, **Knead** the mixture with your hands until you get the right slime consistency; smooth and soft enough to stretch with hands.

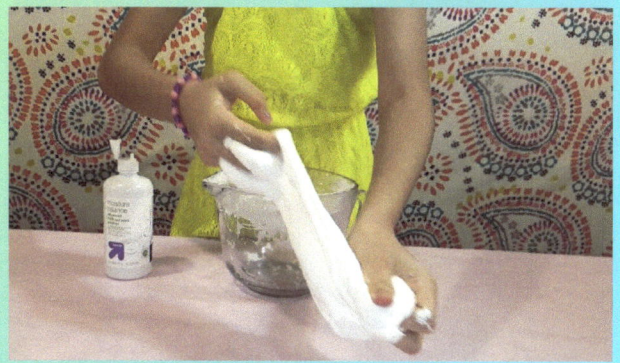

WHAT THE SLIME SHOULD LOOK LIKE

Stretched Snowy Christmas Slime

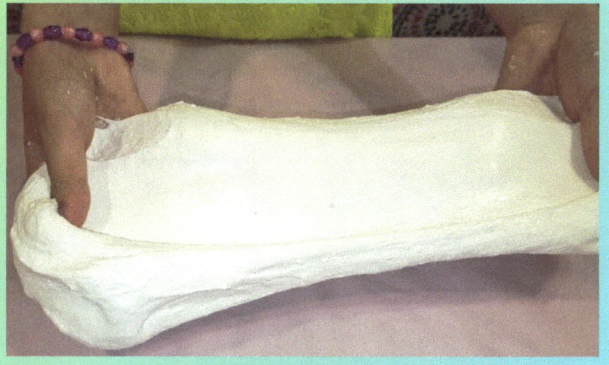

Snowy Christmas Slime in a **Storage Container**

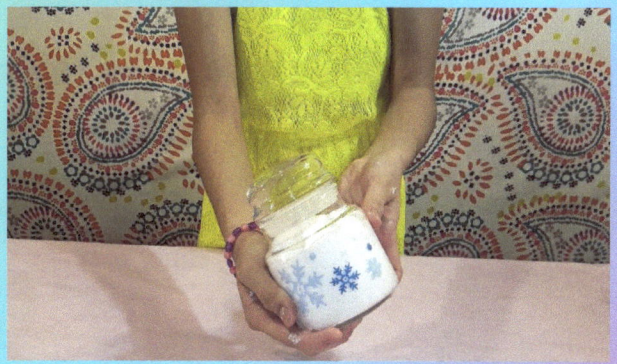

Now you have a minty jolly slime!

HOW TO MAKE SLIME

My "TESTING TEAM" aka sisters

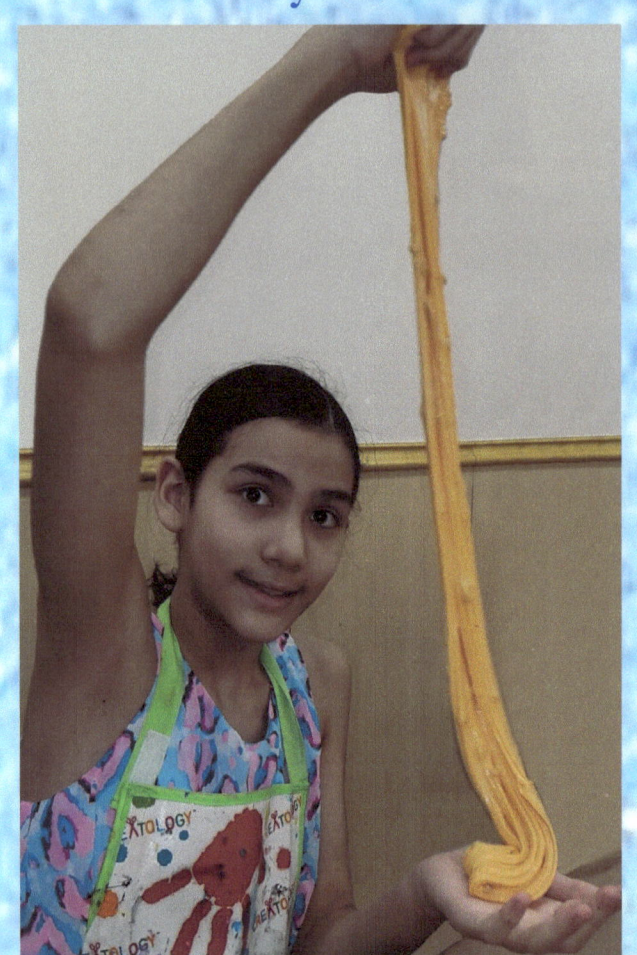
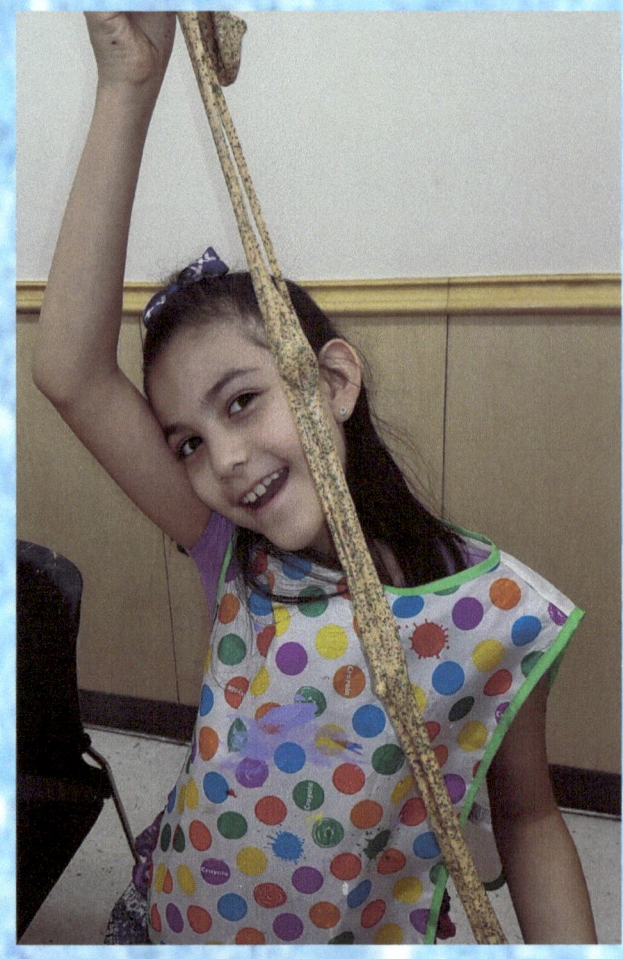
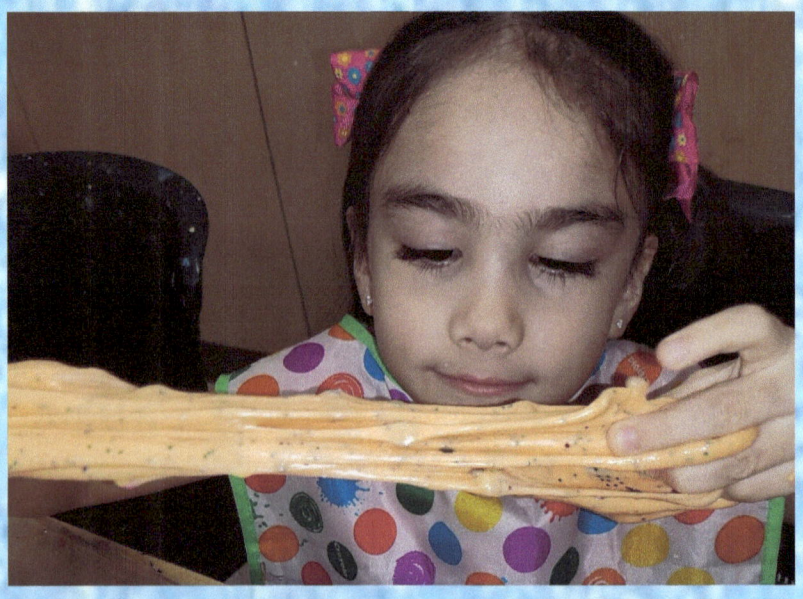

KUKI SHAMUS

SECTION III
BORAX SLIME RECIPES

All of the recipes in this section contain borax.

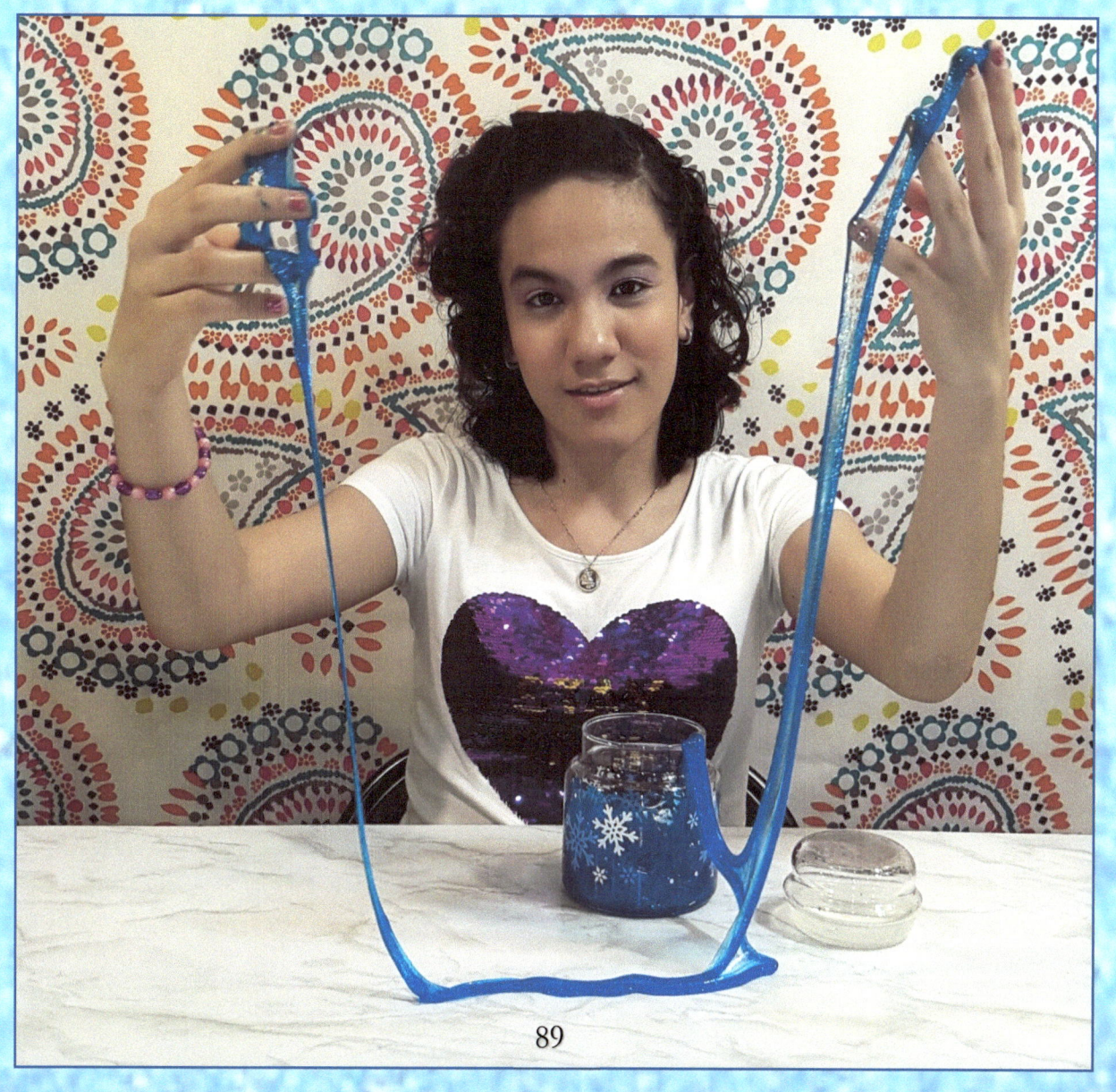

Recipe 21. Glitzy Slime

Diamonds are a girl's best friend, right? Well, we all love sparkles and gems. This slime is called Glitzy Slime because one of the ingredients used are small Rhine stone crystals.

I just love how beautiful this slime turns out. When making this recipe, please keep in mind to pick small size stones. Otherwise, they will fall out too easy from the slime.

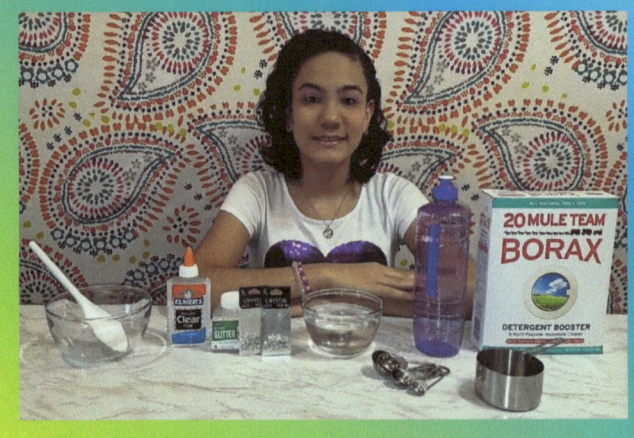

Ingredients

- 1/2 Cup Clear PVA Glue
- 1/2 Cup Cold Water
- 1 Teaspoon Small Crystals
- 1 Teaspoon Jumbo Glitter
- 1 Cup Borax Solution

Directions

1) Pour **Clear Glue** into your mixing bowl.

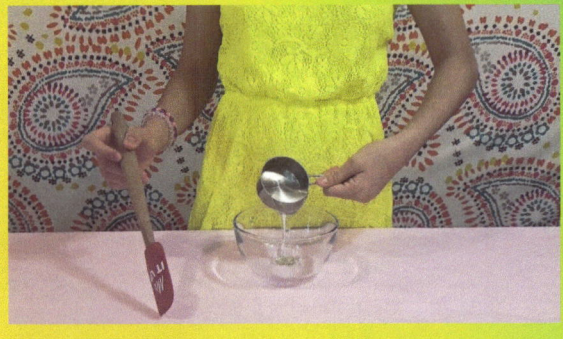

2) Add **Cold Water** to bowl and mix well.

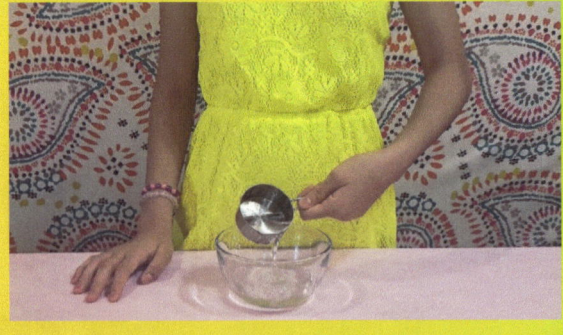

3) Add **Crystals** and mix well

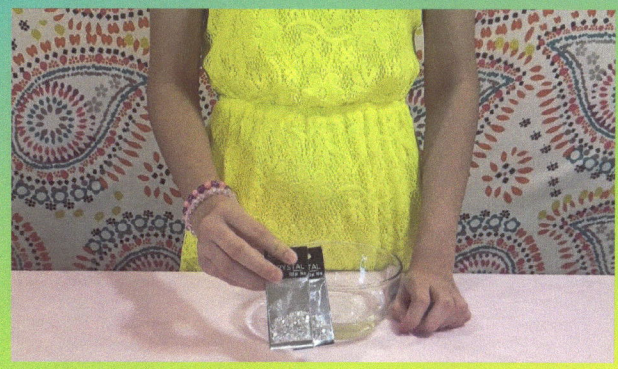

4) Add **Jumbo Glitter** and mix well

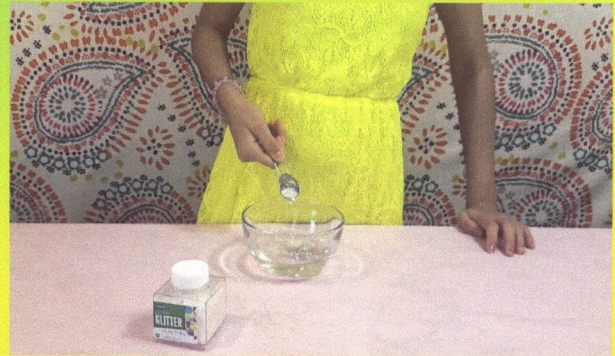

5) Add **Borax Solution** slowly. Squirt directly from the bottle to mixing bowl. Don't over use contact lens solution or slime comes out hard like rubber. You need about 1 Cup (16 Tablespoons). No measuring spoons are being used, therefore, use your best judgement.

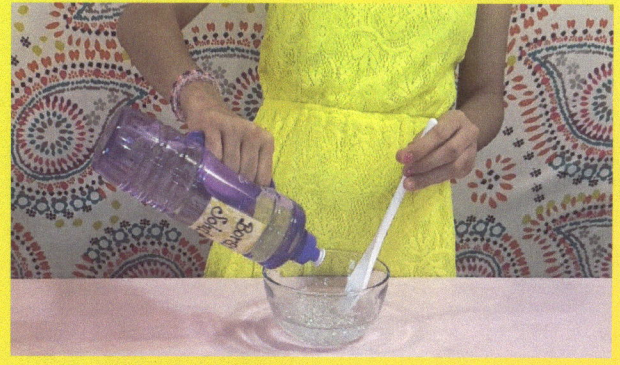

6) Use a **Spatula** to mix as you keep adding borax solution. Keep stirring until the slime doesn't stick to the bowl or your hands.

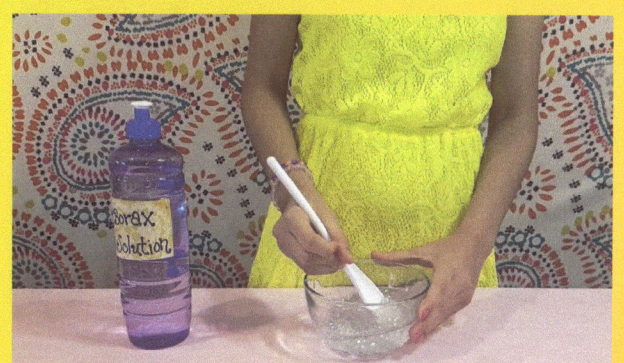

HOW TO MAKE SLIME

7) Once the glue starts to look like slime, **Knead** the mixture with your hands until you get the right slime consistency; smooth and soft enough to stretch with hands.

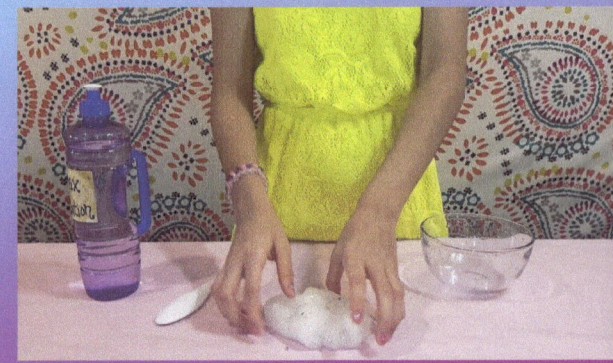

WHAT THE SLIME SHOULD LOOK LIKE

Stretched Glitzy Slime

Glitzy Slime in a **Storage Container**

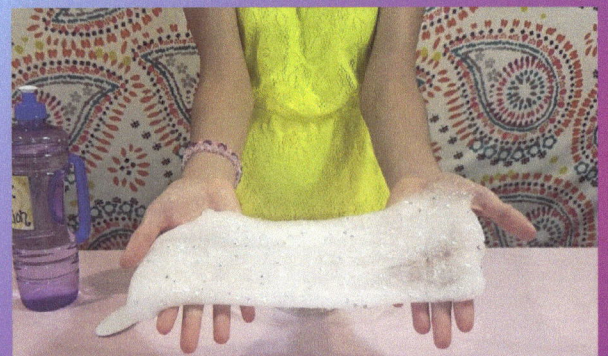
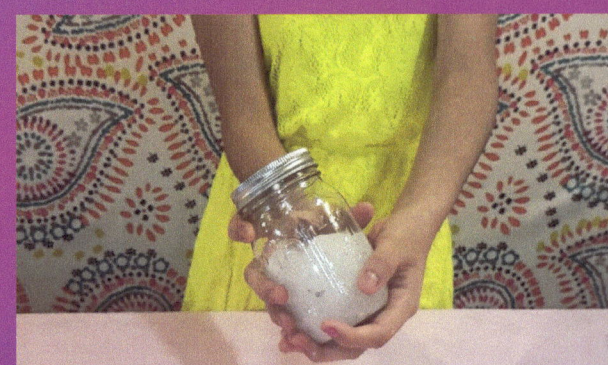

Now you have a glamorous slime!

RECIPE 22. EASY GLITTER SLIME

Glitter, glitter everywhere! This slime is so easy to make. I really love the way it sparkles! This is the easy, quick version of glittery slime because we cheat by buying already made sparkly glue, so you get to choose the color and glitter already pre-mixed in the glue you buy from the store

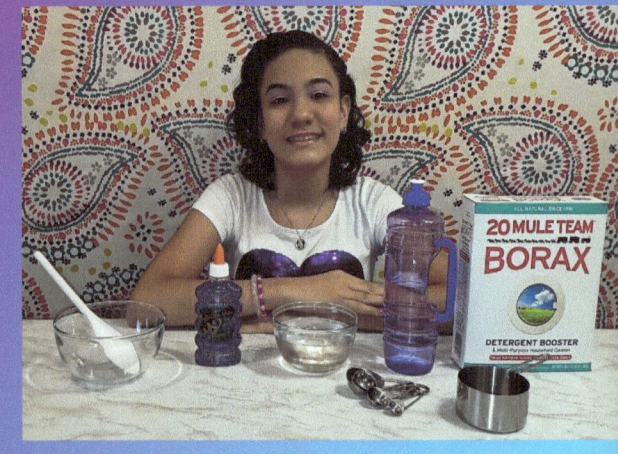

Ingredients

- ½ Cup Glittery PVA Glue
- ½ Cup Cold Water
- 1 Cup Borax Solution

Directions

1) Pour **Glittery Glue** into your mixing bowl.

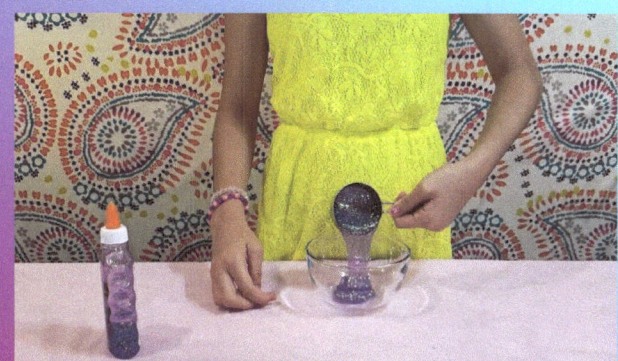

2) Add **Cold Water** to bowl and mix well.

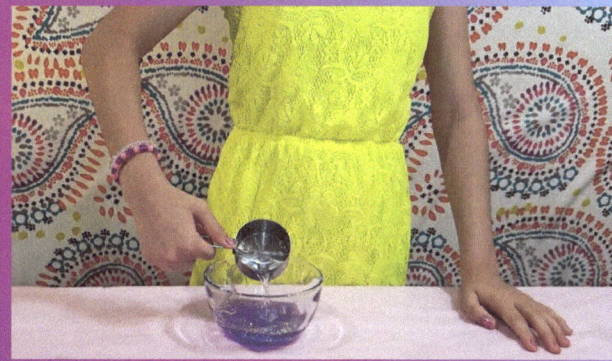

3) Add **Borax Solution** slowly. Squirt directly from the bottle to mixing bowl. Don't over use contact lens solution or slime comes out hard like rubber. You need about 1 Cup (16 Tablespoons). No measuring spoons are being used, therefore, use your best judgement.

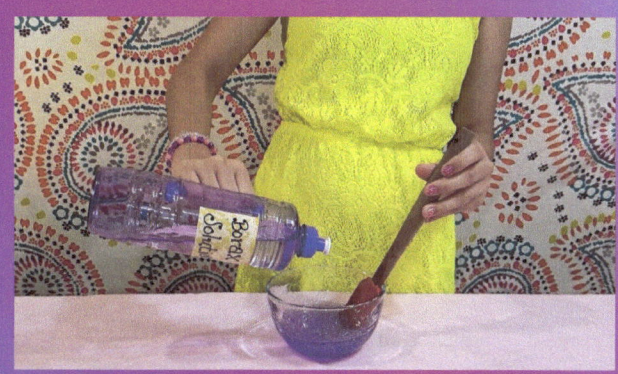

HOW TO MAKE SLIME

4) Use a **Spatula** to mix as you keep adding borax solution. Keep stirring until the slime doesn't stick to the bowl or your hands.

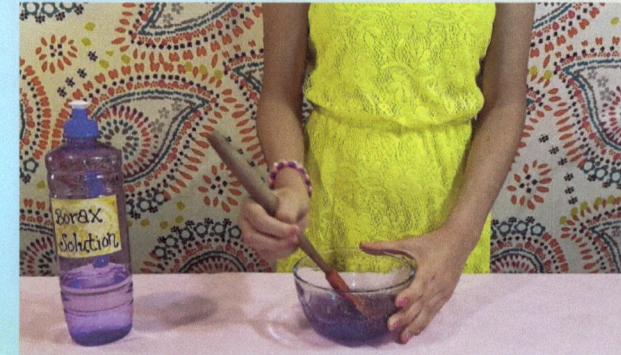

5) Once the glue starts to look like slime, **Knead** the mixture with your hands until you get the right slime consistency; smooth and soft enough to stretch with hands.

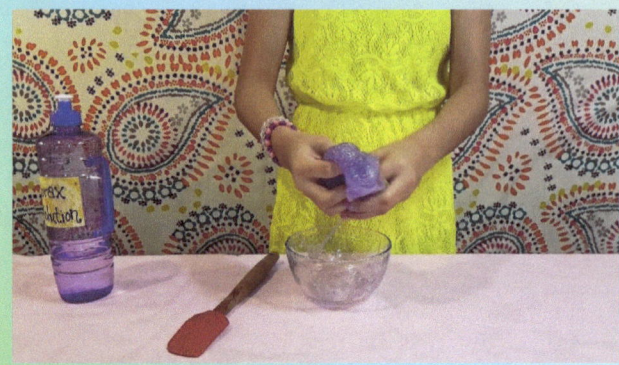

WHAT THE SLIME SHOULD LOOK LIKE

Stretched Easy Glitter Slime

Easy Glitter Slime in a **Storage Container**

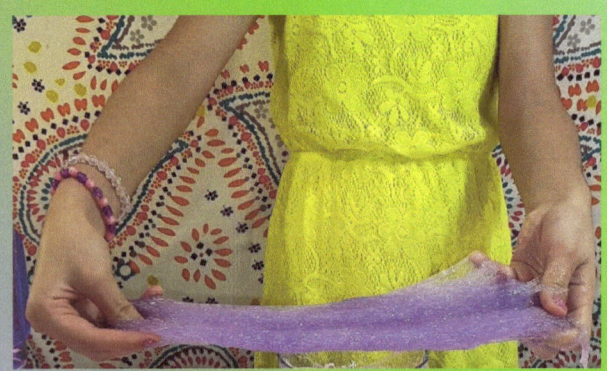
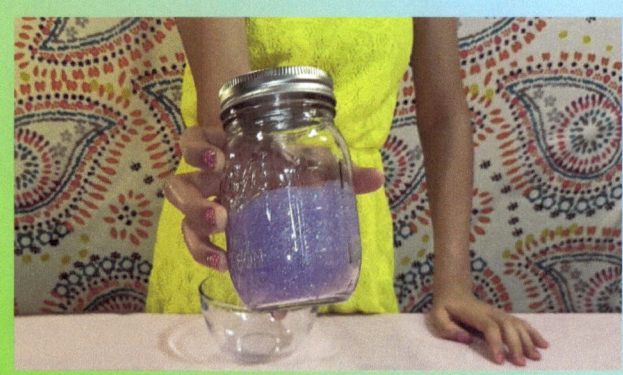

Now you have a glittery slime!

RECIPE 23. CHERRY JIGGLY SLIME

Jiggly slime is so popular because of how it jiggles. The reason it's called Jiggly Slime is because it wiggles like Jell-O. It feels and looks amazing! The most fun thing about it is that you can add scent into the slime and make it look and smell like your favorite Jell-O. My personal favorite is Cherry Jell-O, YUMM.

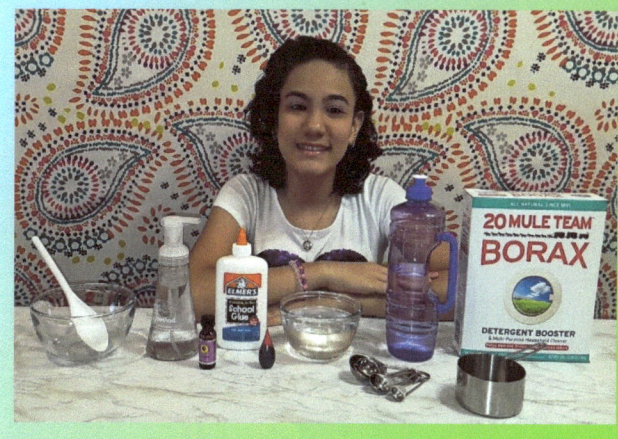

Ingredients

- 1 Cup White PVA Glue
- $1/2$ Cup Cold Water
- 10 Drops Red Food Coloring
- 5 Tablespoons Foaming Hand Wash
- $1/4$ Teaspoon or 40 Drops Cherry Scent
- 1 Cup Hot Water
- 1 Cup Borax Solution

Directions

1) Pour **White Glue** into your mixing bowl.

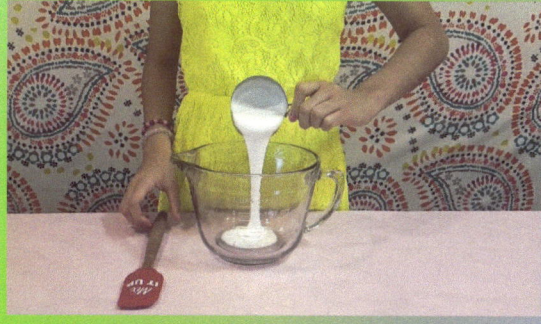

2) Add **Cold Water** to bowl and mix well.

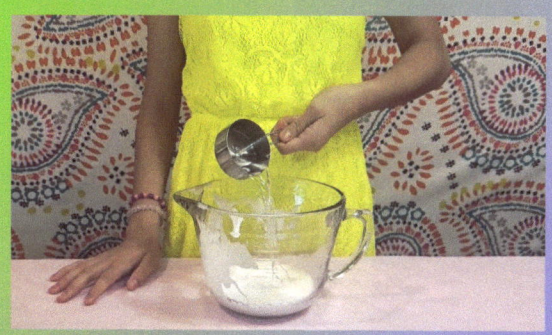

HOW TO MAKE SLIME

3) Add **Red Food Coloring** and mix well.

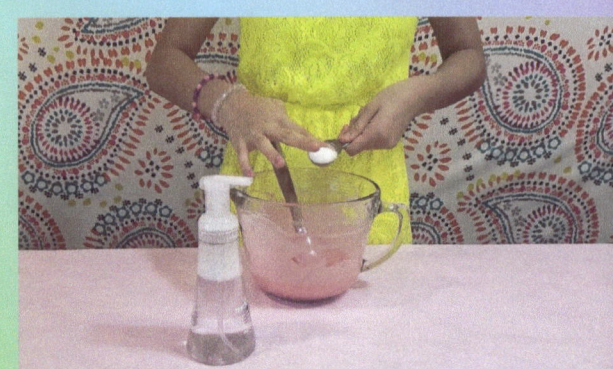

4) Add **Foaming Hand Soap** and mix well

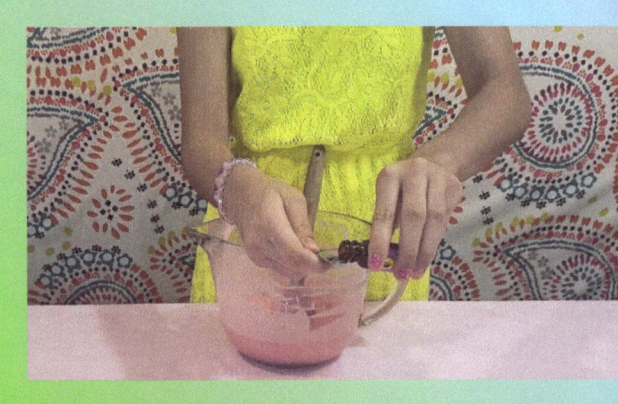

5) Add **Cherry Scent** and mix well.

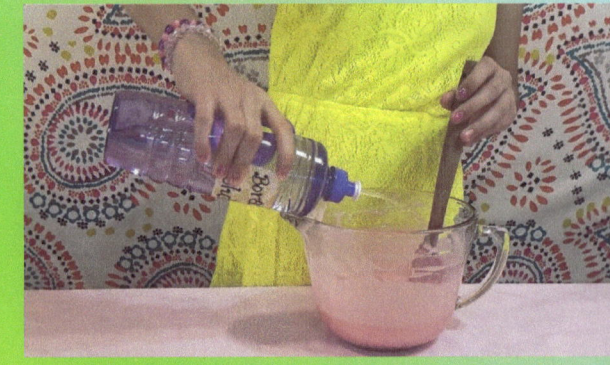

6) Add **Borax Solution** slowly. Squirt directly from the bottle to mixing bowl. Don't over use contact lens solution or slime comes out hard like rubber. You need about 1 Cup (16 Tablespoons). No measuring spoons are being used, therefore, use your best judgement.

7) Use a **Spatula** to mix as you keep adding borax solution. Keep stirring until the slime doesn't stick to the bowl or your hands.

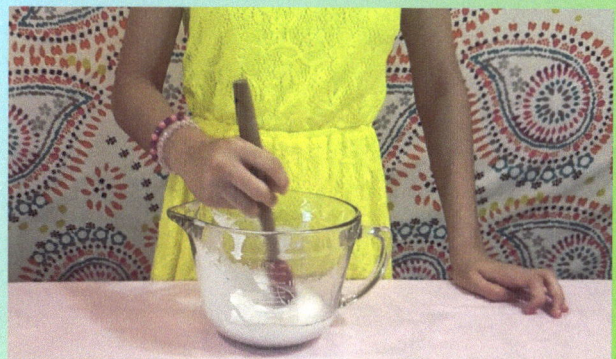

8) Once the glue starts to look like slime, **Knead** the mixture with your hands until you get the right slime consistency; smooth and soft enough to stretch with hands.

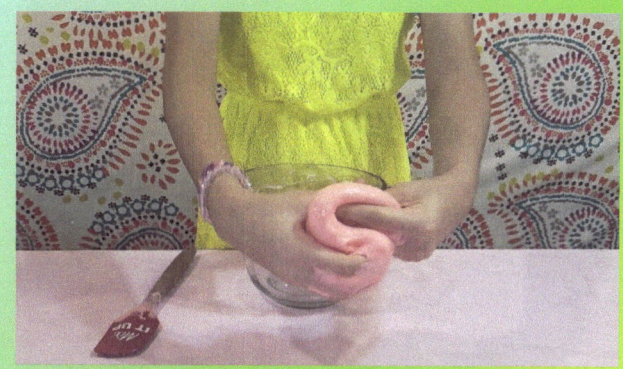

9) Add **Hot Water**. Please use a spatula and DO NOT BURN YOURSELF. Allow for slime to absorb all the water.

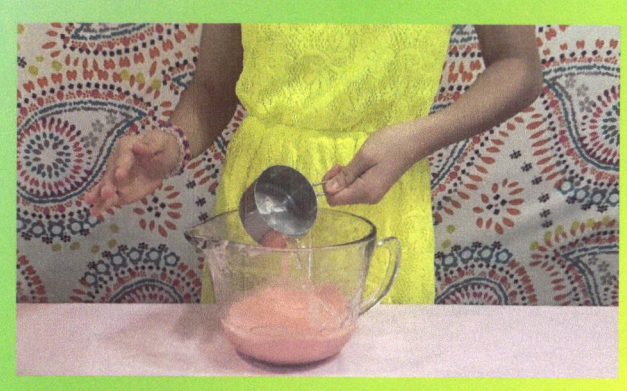

10) Pour into an **Airtight Container**. The slime will be sticky and runny.

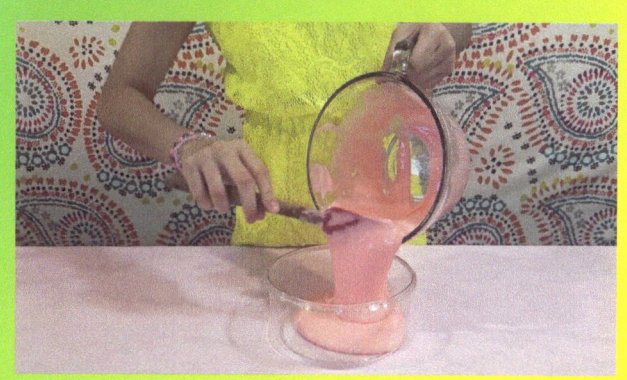

HOW TO MAKE SLIME

11) Let it cool and set for 2 hours in the **Fridge**. Come back and it will be ready.

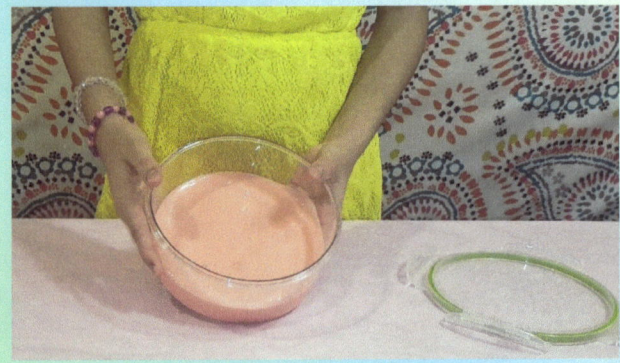

WHAT THE SLIME SHOULD LOOK LIKE

Stretched Cherry Jiggly Slime

Cherry Jiggly Slime in a **Storage Container**

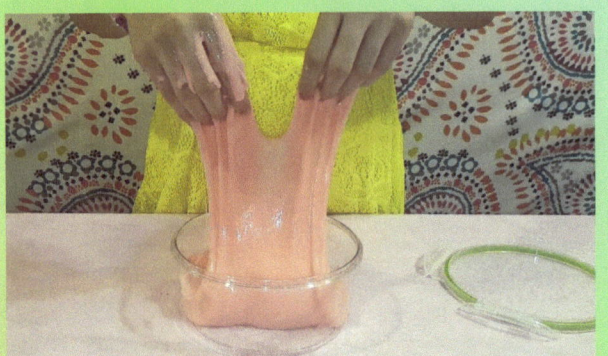
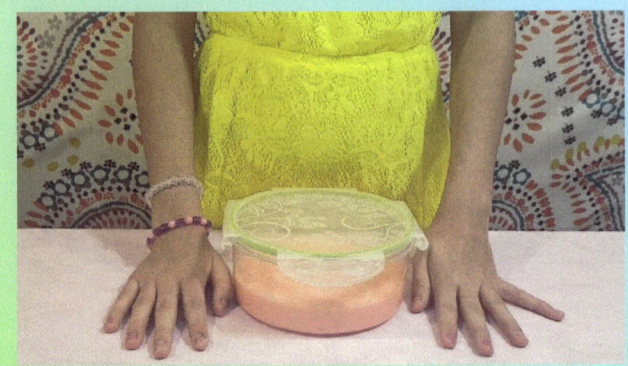

Now you have a jiggly slime!

RECIPE 24. SIMPLE CRUNCH SLIME

This slime is very satisfying. I like crunchy slime because it adds a different texture and sound to the slime. The reason this slime is called Simple Crunch is because it is simple to make and we just add rubber bands to make it crunch. Rubber bands are a very cheap and an easy topping to find.

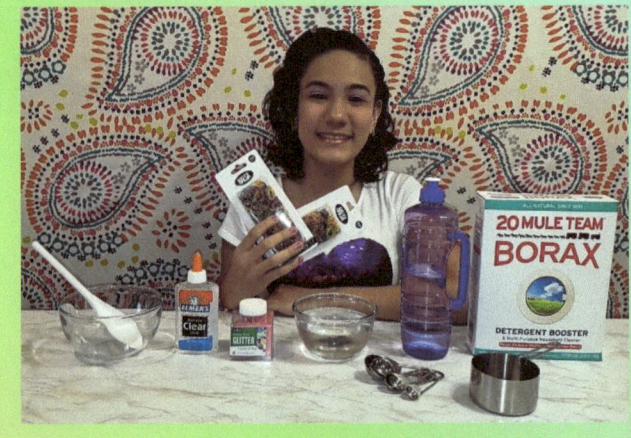

KUKI SHAMUS

Ingredients

- ½ Cup Clear PVA Glue
- ½ Cup Cold Water
- ½ Cup Colorful Rubber Hair bands
- 2 Teaspoons Pink Glitter
- 1 Cup Borax Solution

Directions

1) Pour **Clear Glue** into your mixing bowl.

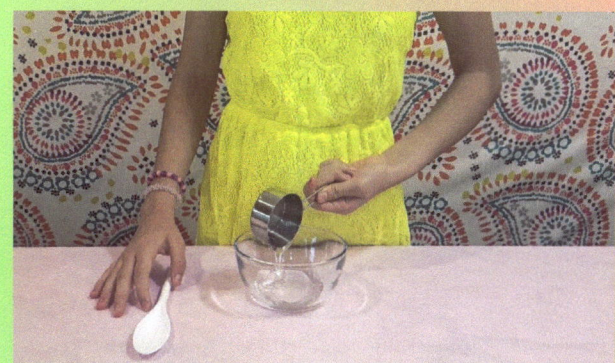

2) Add **Cold Water** to bowl and mix well

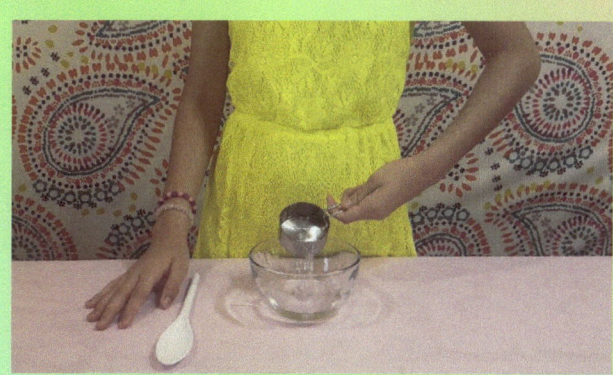

3) Add **Pink Glitter** and mix well.

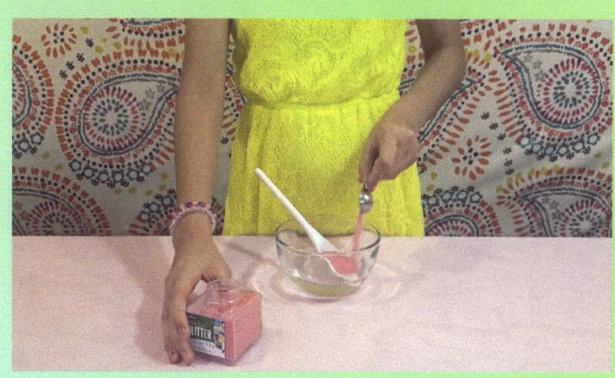

HOW TO MAKE SLIME

4) Add **Rubber Hair Bands** and mix in well.

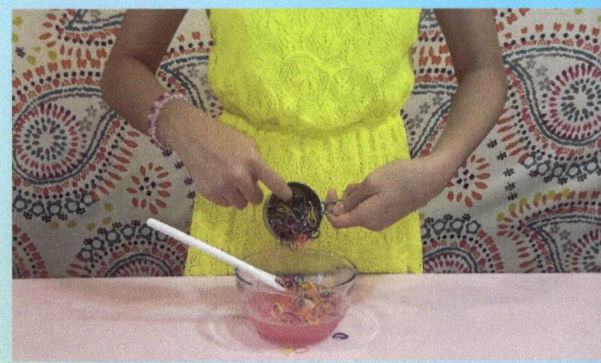

5) Add **Borax Solution** slowly. Squirt directly from the bottle to mixing bowl. Don't over use contact lens solution or slime comes out hard like rubber. You need about 1 Cup (16 Tablespoons). No measuring spoons are being used, therefore, use your best judgement.

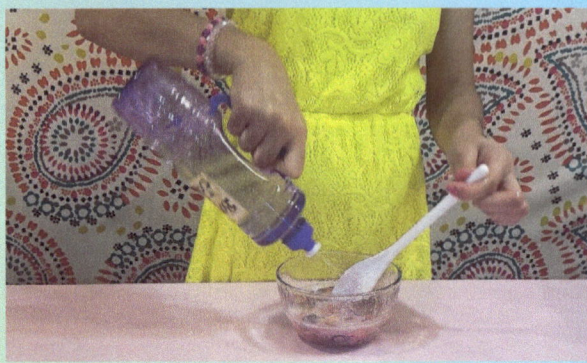

6) Once the glue starts to look like slime, **Knead** the mixture with your hands until you get the right slime consistency; smooth and soft enough to stretch with hands.

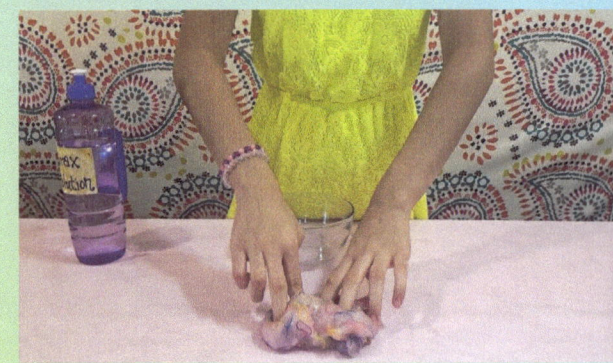

WHAT THE SLIME SHOULD LOOK LIKE

Stretched Simple Crunch Slime

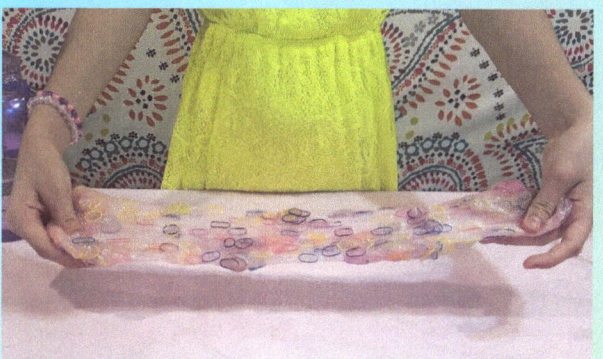

Simple Crunch Slime in a **Storage Container**

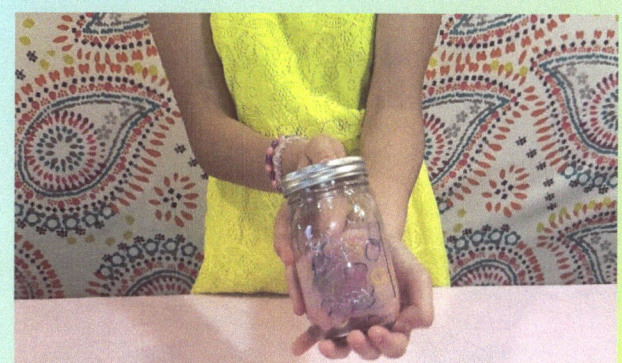

Now you have a fun, stretchy slime!

RECIPE 25. TIE DYE BUBBLY SLIME

This slime will leave you wanting to play with it all day. It's called Tie Dye Bubbly Slime because it gets bubbles at the top after we let it sit. You will use yellow, green and orange colors to make that amazing tie dye finish

You will be making three different color batches, so I recommend doing all three at the same time as it is much easier. The ingredient list is for each of the color, so multiple by 3.

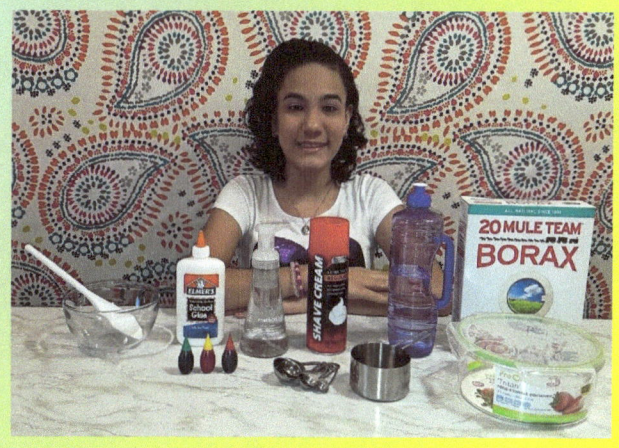

Ingredients

- $1/2$ Cup White PVA Glue
- 9 Drops Yellow Food Coloring
- 9 Drops Green Food Coloring
- 9 Drops Orange Food Coloring
- $1/2$ Cup Shaving Cream
- 5 Tablespoons Foaming Hand Wash
- 1 Cup Borax Solution

HOW TO MAKE SLIME

Directions

1) Pour **White Glue** into your mixing bowl.

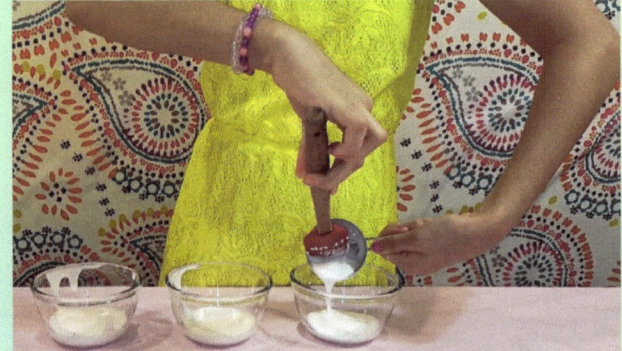

2) Add 6 Drops **Food Coloring** to each bowl (1 different color per bowl) and mix well.

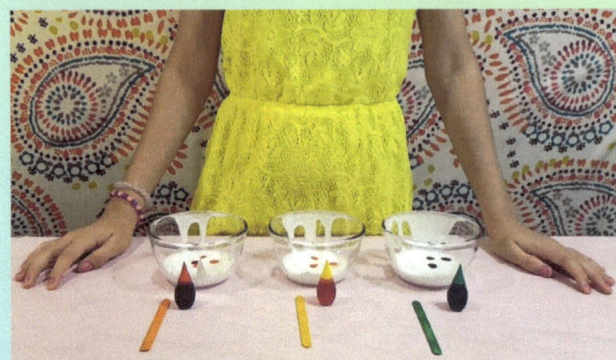

3) Add 3 Tablespoons of **Foaming Hand Soap** to each bowl and mix well

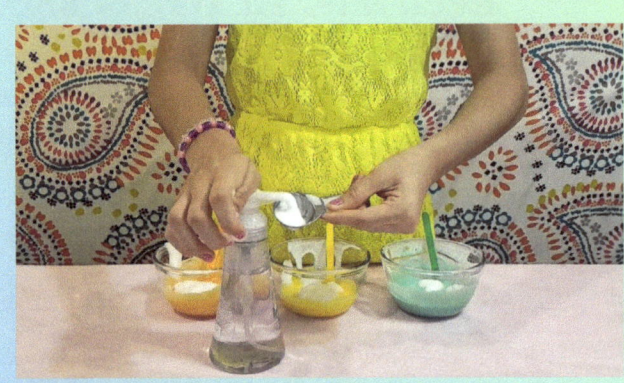

4) Add **Shaving Cream** to each bowl with help of a spatula and mix well.

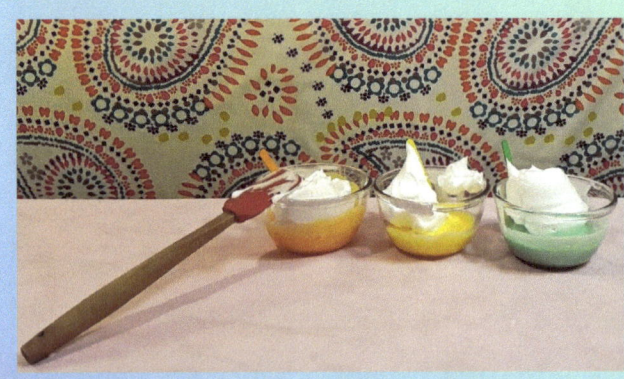

5) Add 3 more Drops of **Food Coloring** to each bowl (Same color as before for each bowl) and mix well.

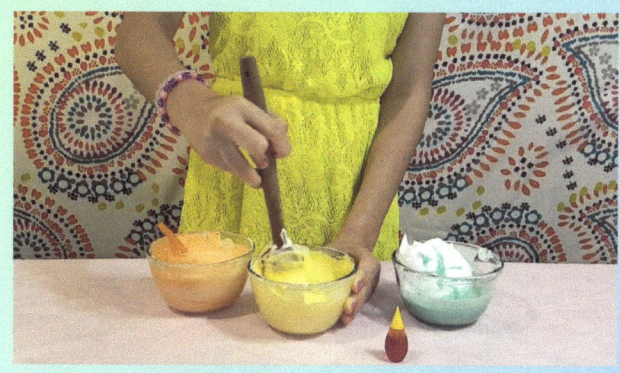

6) Add **Borax Solution** slowly. Squirt directly from the bottle to mixing bowl. Don't over use contact lens solution or slime comes out hard like rubber. You need about 1 Cup (16 Tablespoons). No measuring spoons are being used, therefore, use your best judgement.

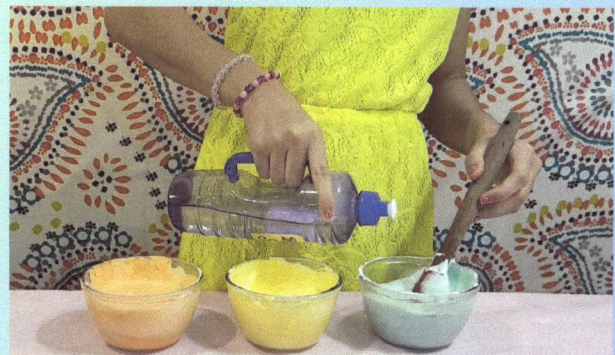

7) Use a **Spatula** to mix as you keep adding borax solution. Keep stirring until the slime doesn't stick to the bowls or your hands.

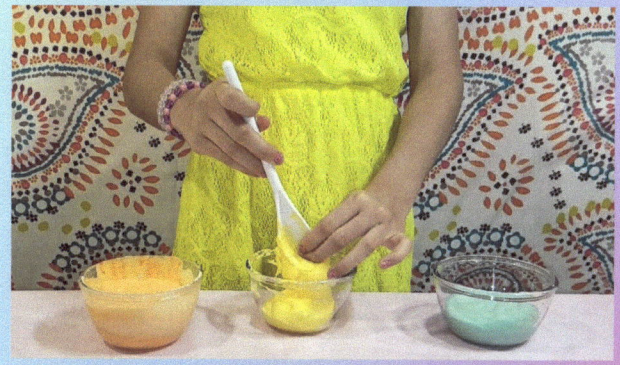

8) Once the glue starts to look like slime, **Knead** the mixture with your hands until you get the right slime consistency; smooth and soft enough to stretch with hands.

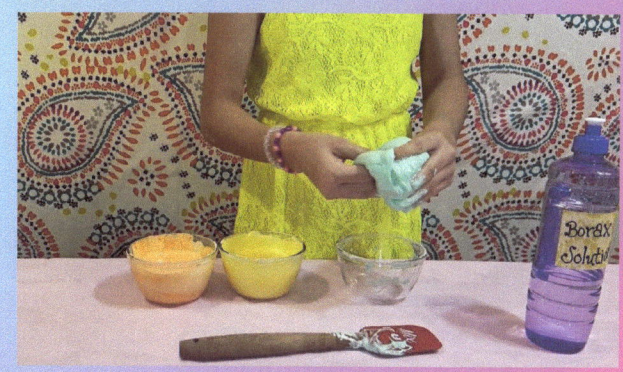

HOW TO MAKE SLIME

9) Now you have three separate slimes. Put them side to side in an **Airtight Container**.

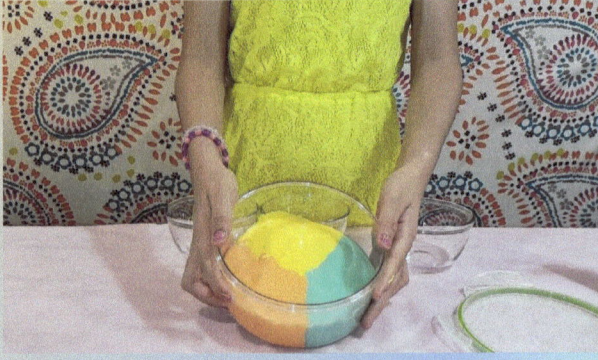

10) Top slime with 2 Tablespoons of **Foaming Hand Soap** on each color and spread it well with your hands. Cover container and let slime sit for 48 hours.

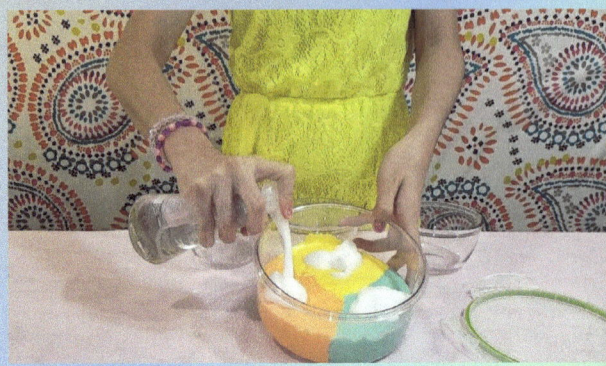

11) After 48 hours has passed, the **Slime is Ready**

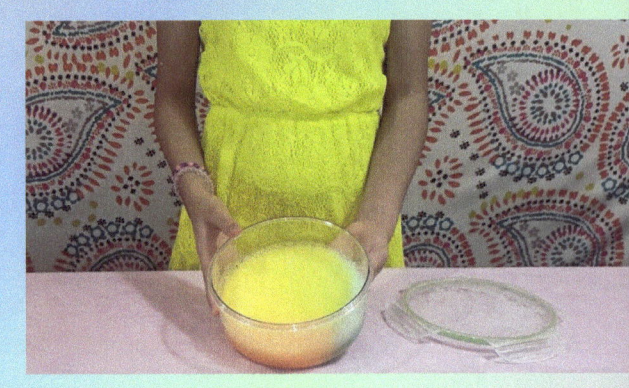

WHAT THE SLIME SHOULD LOOK LIKE

Stretched Tie Dye Bubbly Slime

Tie Dye Bubbly Slime in a **Storage Container**

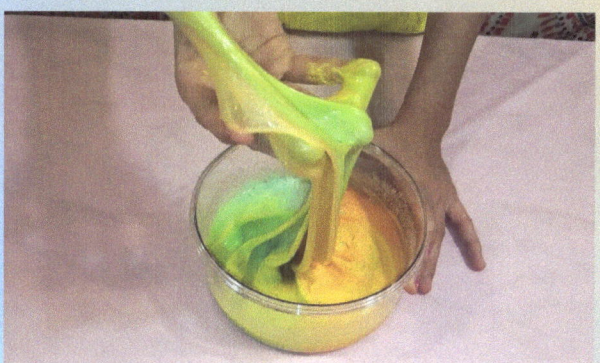
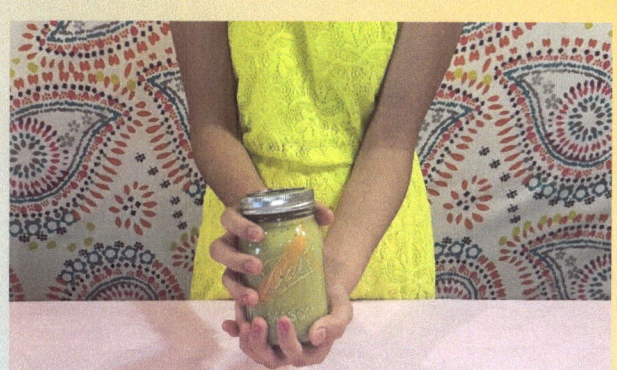

Now you have a crispy crunchy slime!

RECIPE 26. CHOCO NUTELLA SLIME

Nutella slime is so simple. The reason it's called Nutella is because the color looks just like the real stuff you buy at the food store. When you put this brown slime in an empty jar of Nutella, it looks just like Nutella. Just make sure you don't eat it!

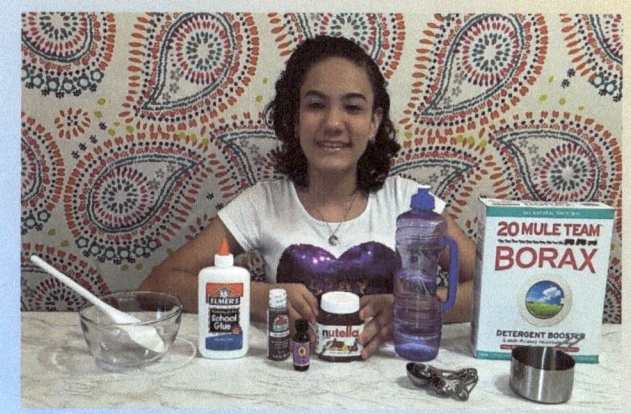

Ingredients

- $1/2$ Cup White PVA Glue
- 2 Tablespoons Brown Acrylic Paint
- $1/4$ Teaspoon or 20 Drops Chocolate Scent
- 1 Cup Borax Solution

HOW TO MAKE SLIME

Directions

1) Pour **White Glue** into your mixing bowl.

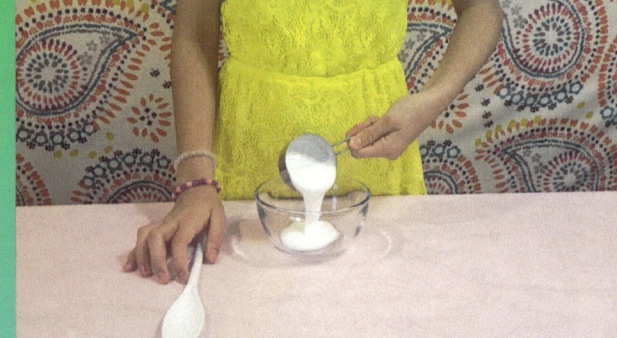

2) Add **Brown Paint** and mix well

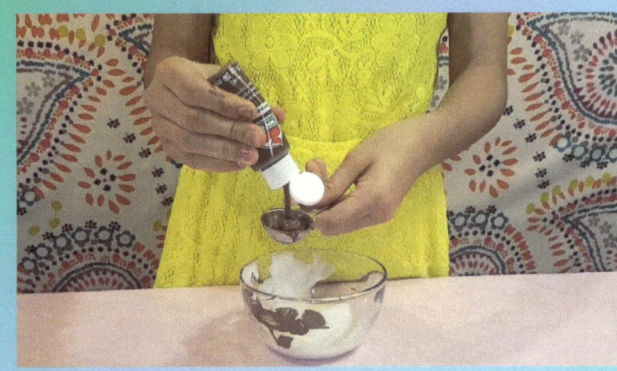

3) Add **Chocolate Scent** and mix well.

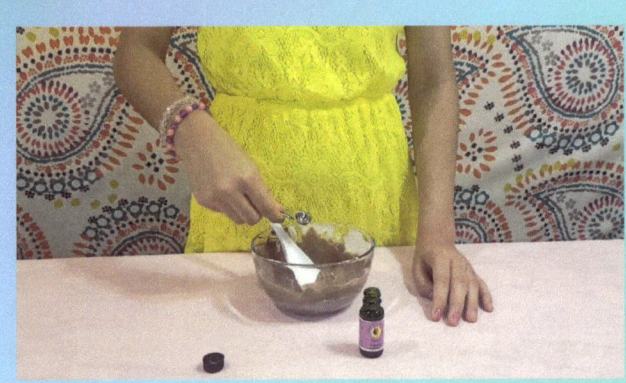

4) Add **Borax Solution** slowly. Squirt directly from the bottle to mixing bowl. Don't over use contact lens solution or slime comes out hard like rubber. You need about 1 Cup (16 Tablespoons). No measuring spoons are being used, therefore, use your best judgement.

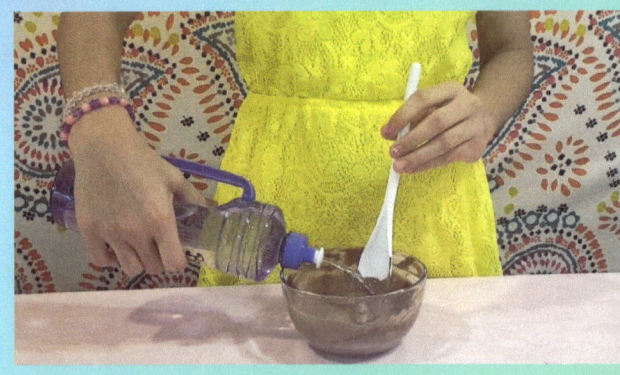

5) Use a **Spatula** to mix as you keep adding borax solution. Keep stirring until the slime doesn't stick to the bowl or your hands.

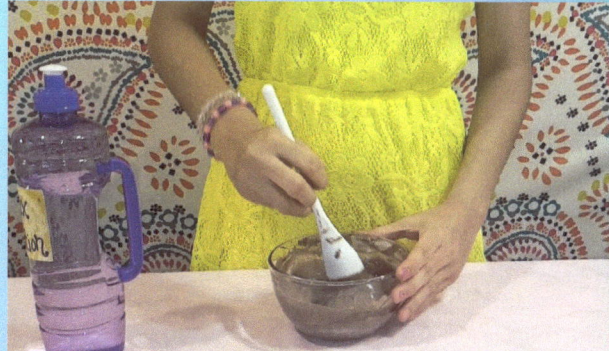

6) Once the glue starts to look like slime, **Knead** the mixture with your hands until you get the right slime consistency; smooth and soft enough to stretch with hands.

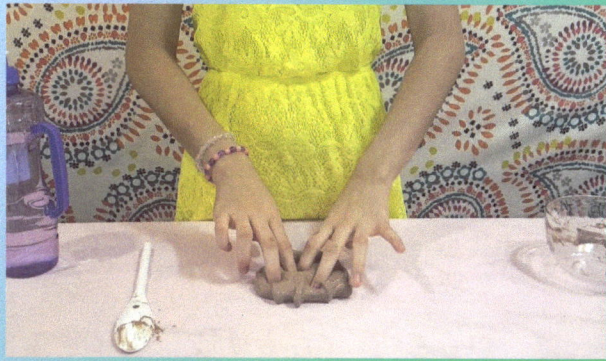

7) Once ready add your slime into a **Nutella Bottle**.

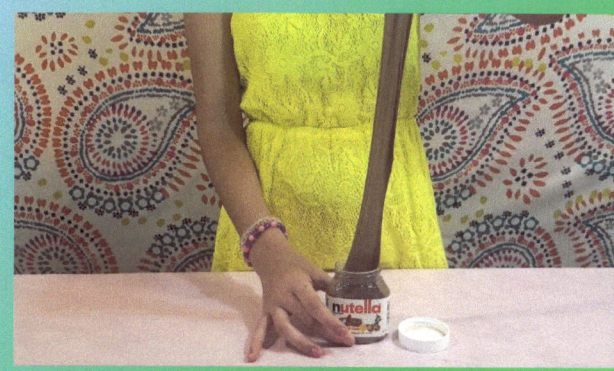

HOW TO MAKE SLIME

WHAT THE SLIME SHOULD LOOK LIKE

<u>Stretched</u> Choco Nutella Slime

Choco Nutella Slime in a **<u>Nutella Storage Container</u>**

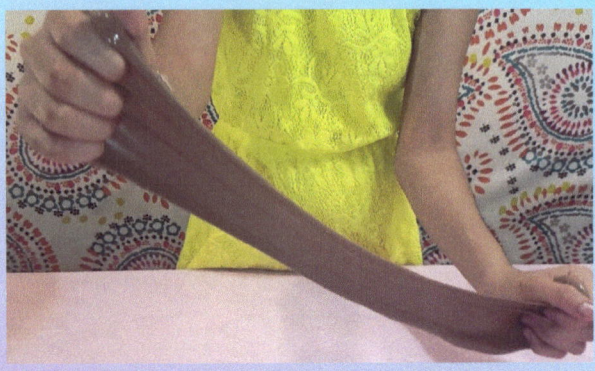
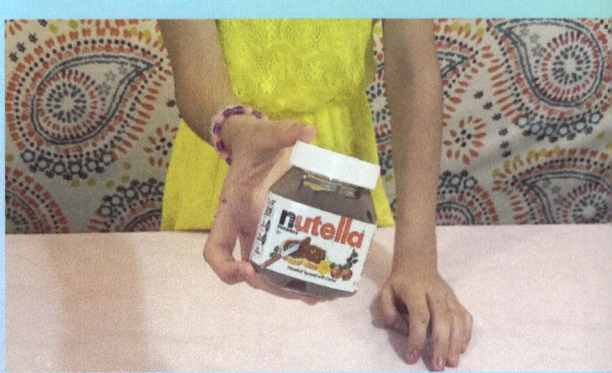

Now you have a chocolate scented slime!

RECIPE 27. PURPLELICIOUS SLIME

This is also one of my favorite slimes because of how it looks. It's called Purplelicious Slime is because the purple color it has is simply delicious. It has hologram powder and glitter combined, thus it gives off a beautiful finish and shimmer. The key to making this slime even better is to let your slime sit for 48 hours in an airtight container.

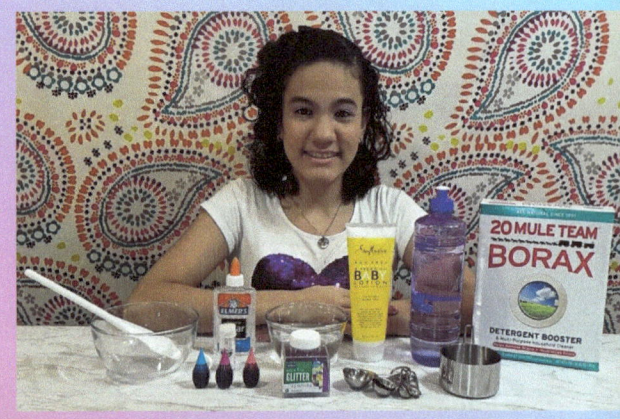

<u>Ingredients</u>

- 1 Cup Clear PVA Glue
- $\frac{1}{2}$ Cup Cold Water
- 8 Drops Neon Purple Food Coloring
- 4 Drops Neon Blue Food Coloring
- 4 Drops Neon Pink Food Coloring

- 1 Tablespoon Extra Fine Purple Glitter
- 1 Teaspoon Hologram Powder
- 3 Tablespoons Hand Lotion
- 1 Cup Borax Solution

Directions

1) Pour **Clear Glue** into your mixing bowl.

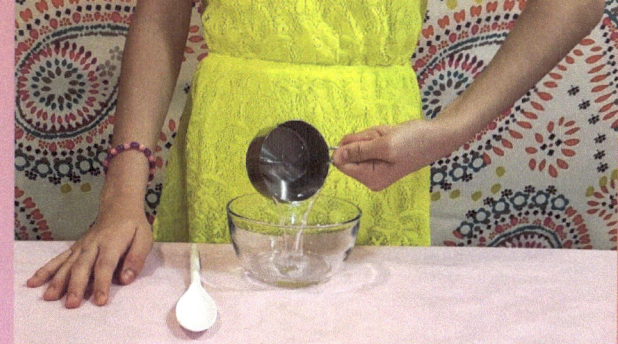

2) Add **Cold Water** to bowl and mix well

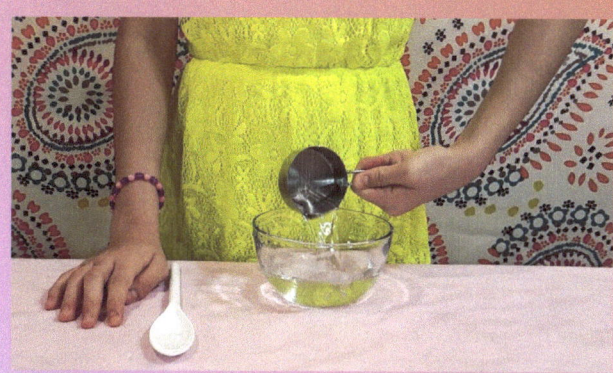

3) Add 8 Drops **Neon Purple Food Coloring** followed immediately by 4 Drops **Neon Blue Food Coloring** followed immediately by 4 Drops **Neon Pink Food Coloring** and mix well.

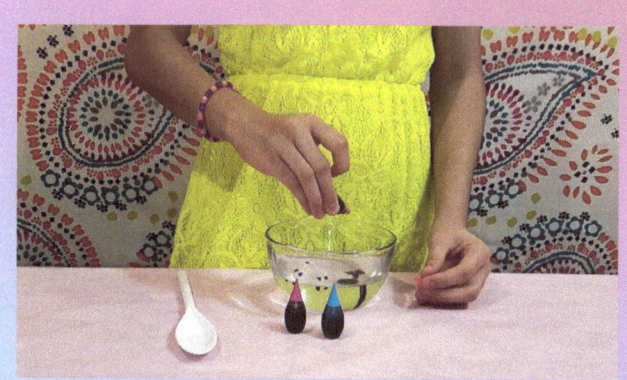

4) Add **Extra Fine Purple Glitter** and mix well.

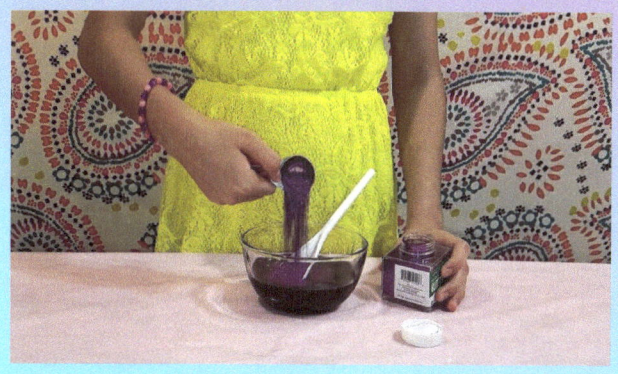

HOW TO MAKE SLIME

5) Add **Hand Lotion** and mix well.

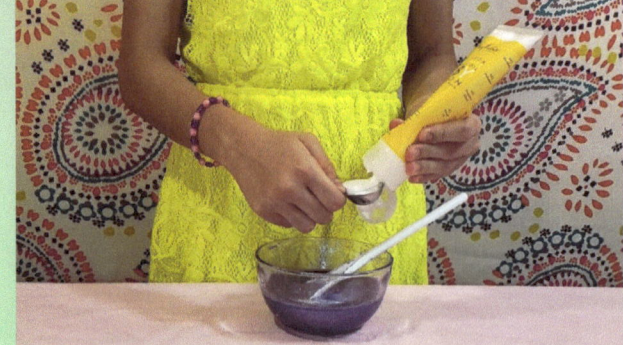

6) Add **Hologram Powder** to bowl and mix well

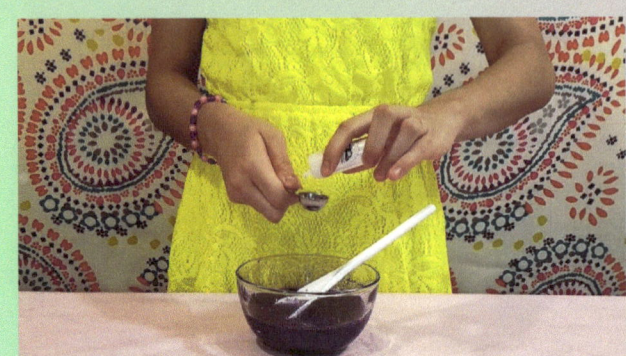

7) Add **Borax Solution** slowly. Squirt directly from the bottle to mixing bowl. Don't over use contact lens solution or slime comes out hard like rubber. You need about 1 Cup (16 Tablespoons). No measuring spoons are being used, therefore, use your best judgement.

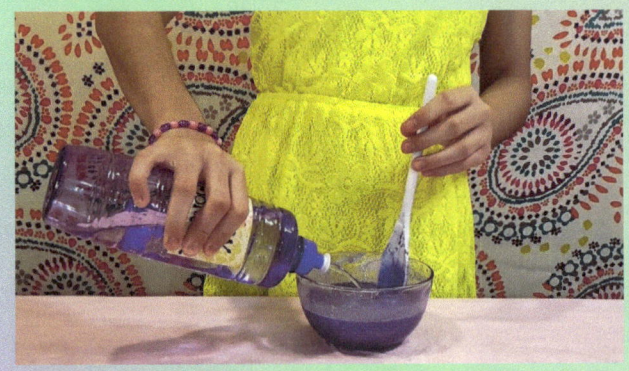

8) Use a **Spatula** to mix as you keep adding borax solution. Keep stirring until the slime doesn't stick to the bowl or your hands.

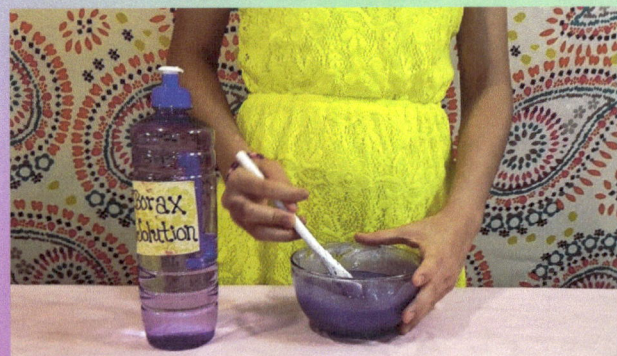

9) Once the glue starts to look like slime, **Knead** the mixture with your hands until you get the right slime consistency; smooth and soft enough to stretch with hands.

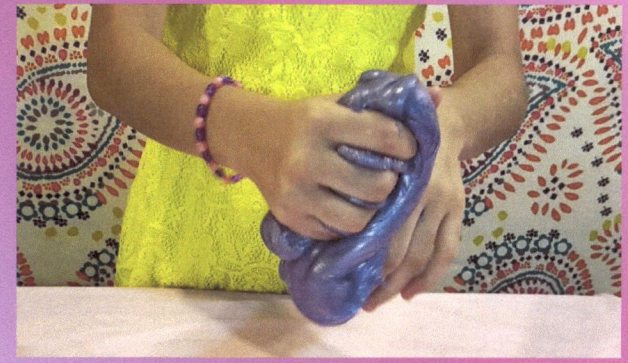

WHAT THE SLIME SHOULD LOOK LIKE

Stretched Purplelicious Slime

Purplelicious Slime in a **Storage Container**

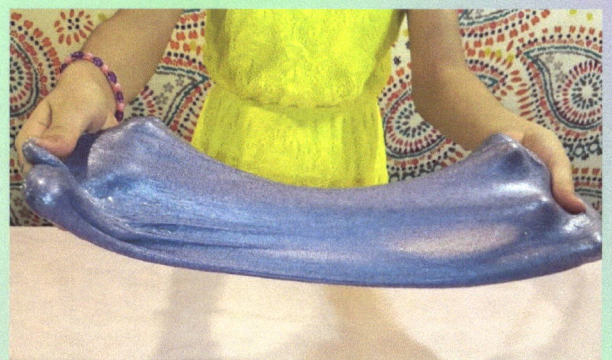
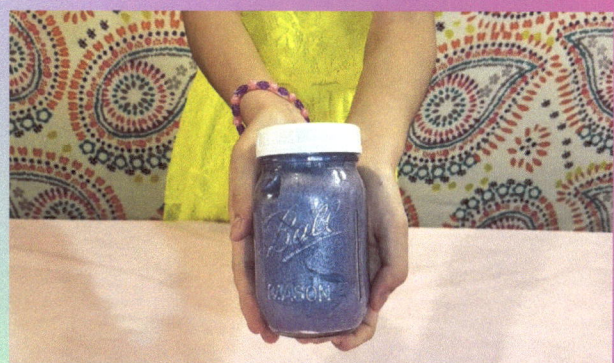

Now you have a pretty purple slime!

RECIPE 28. SASSY GLOSSY SLIME

This slime is so unique. The reason it is called Glossy Slime is because it actually looks very glossy, just like the kind of gloss you get when you use nail polish. The top of it reflects light and is very sleek.

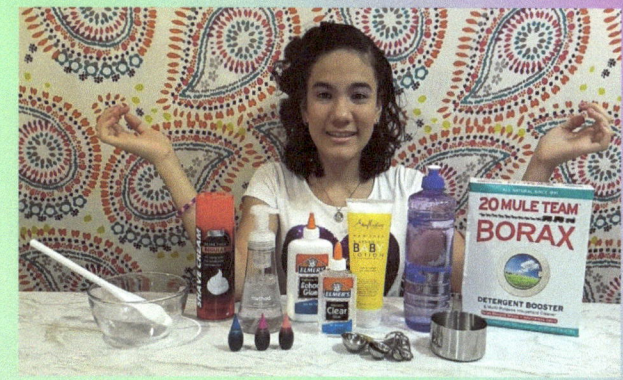

HOW TO MAKE SLIME

Ingredients

- 1 Cup of White PVA Glue
- $\frac{1}{4}$ Cup Clear PVA Glue
- 6 Drops Neon Pink Food Coloring
- 3 Drops Neon Purple Food Coloring
- 4 Drops Blue Food Coloring
- 1 Cup Shaving Cream
- 4 Tablespoons Foaming Hand Soap
- 4 Tablespoons Hand Lotion
- 1 Cup Borax Solution

Directions

1) Pour **White Glue** into your mixing bowl.

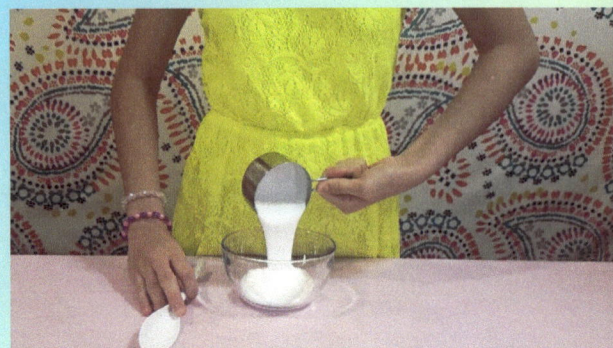

2) Pour **Clear Glue** and mix well.

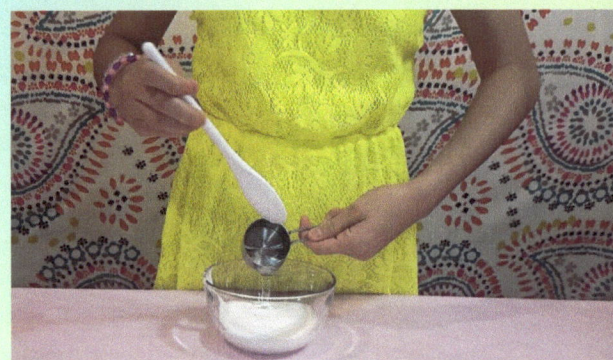

3) Add **Shaving Cream** with help of a spatula and mix well.

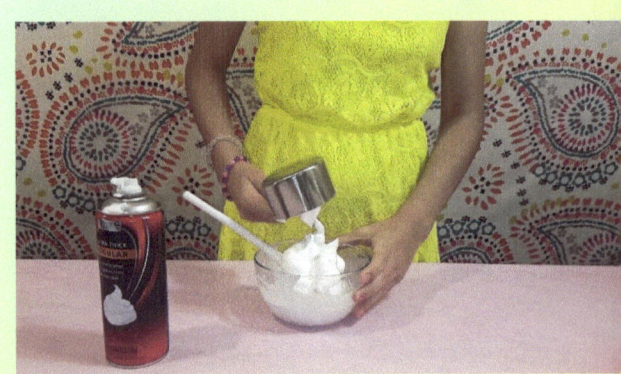

4) Add the **Foaming** **Hand** **Soap** and mix well

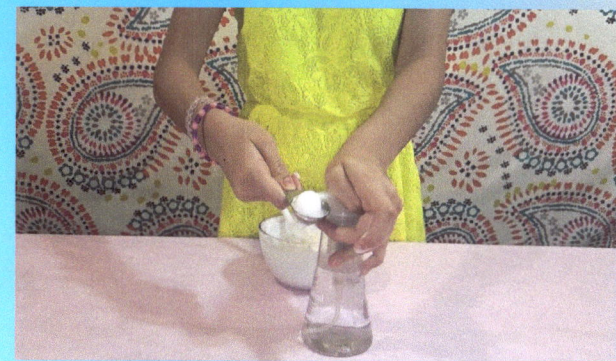

5) Add **Hand** **Lotion** and mix well

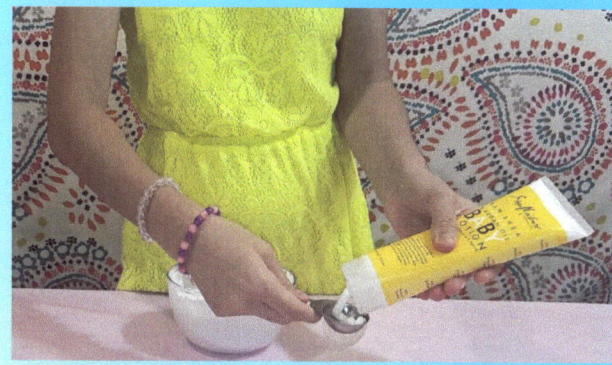

6) Add 6 Drops **Pink** **Food** **Coloring** followed immediately by 3 Drops **Purple** **Food** **Coloring** and mix well.

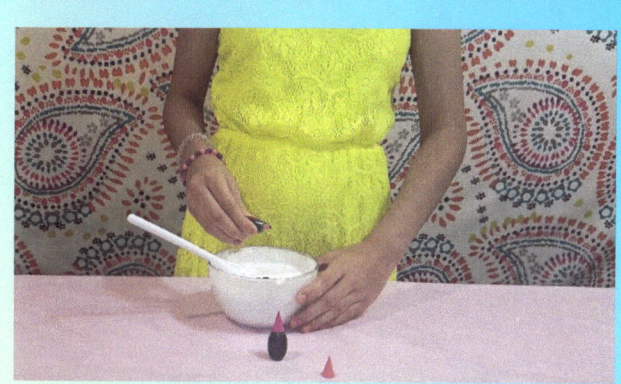

7) Add 4 Drops **Blue** **Food** **Coloring** and mix well.

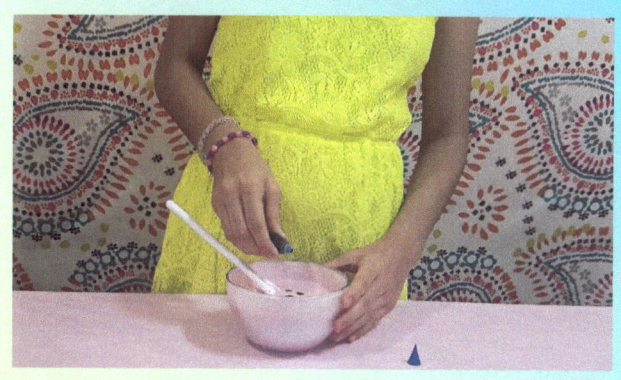

HOW TO MAKE SLIME

8) Add **Borax** **Solution** slowly. Squirt directly from the bottle to mixing bowl. Don't over use contact lens solution or slime comes out hard like rubber. You need about 1 Cup (16 Tablespoons). No measuring spoons are being used, therefore, use your best judgement.

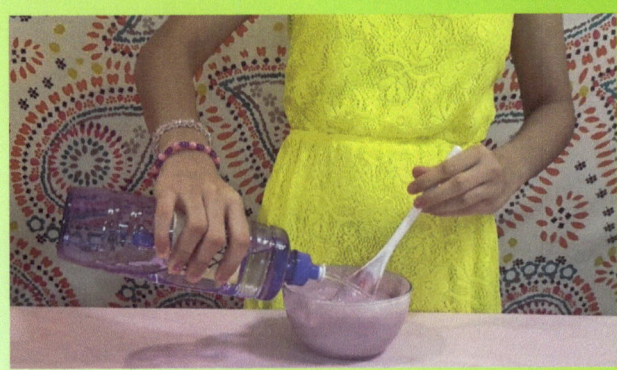

9) Use a **Spatula** to mix as you keep adding borax solution. Keep stirring until the slime doesn't stick to the bowl or your hands.

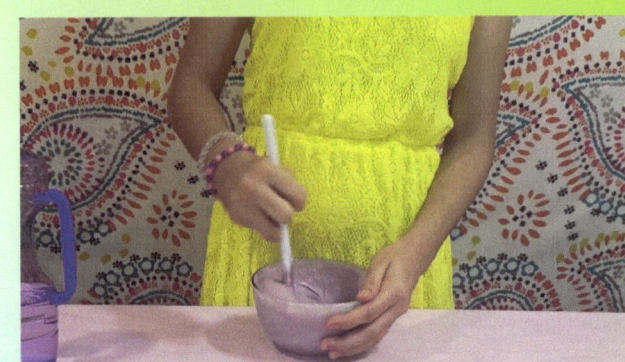

10) Once the glue starts to look like slime, **Knead** the mixture with your hands until you get the right slime consistency; smooth and soft enough to stretch with hands.

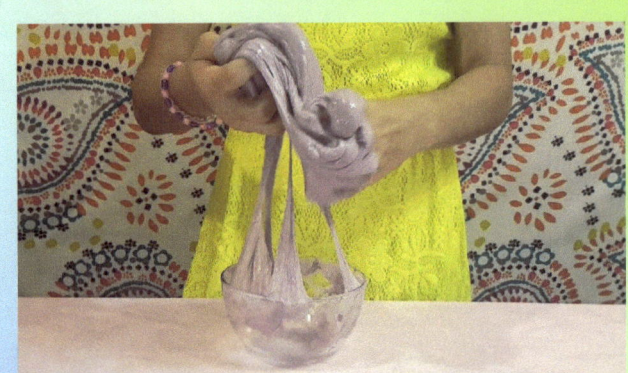

11) Let it sit in an **Airtight** **Container** for 1 hour so the chemicals can combine together and activate that glossy finish. Then the slime will be ready.

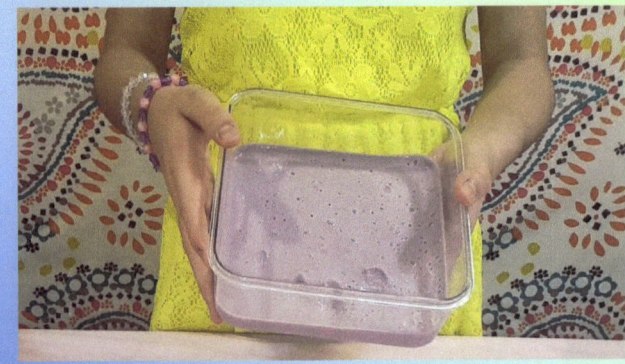

WHAT THE SLIME SHOULD LOOK LIKE

Stretched Sassy Glossy Slim**e**

Sassy Glossy Slime in a **Storage Container**

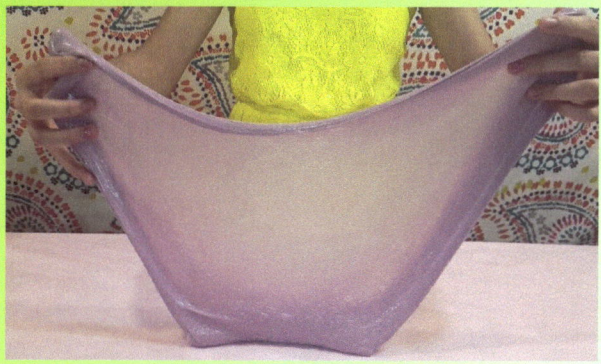
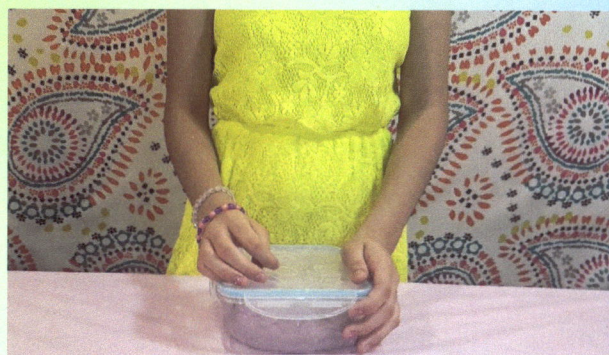

Now you have a super stretchy slime!

RECIPE 29. DARK MATTER SLIME

All I can say is WOW. Magnetic slime comes from using fine iron oxide powder. This is a specialty ingredient and usually only found online. I STRONGLY suggest you try this. My mom and I love it because no other slime screams science than this one.

You can stretch it and poke it, but because of its magnetic properties, you can see it eat up magnets We decided to call it Dark Matter Slime because it is black in color and it comes alive as it eats up magnets in its path.

Basic fridge magnets are too weak in magnetic charge to get a big attraction of the iron oxide filings. Use **Neodymium Magnets** with this slime to get the most

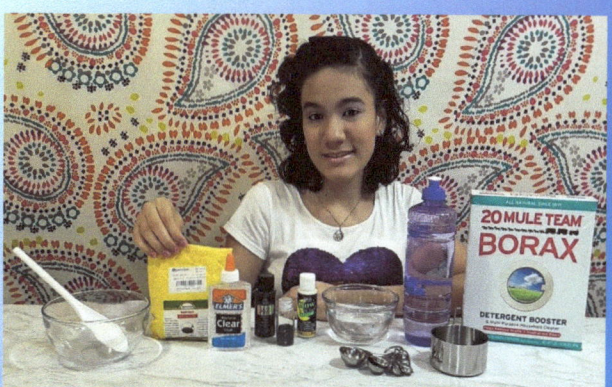

impressive affect. These type of magnets are the strongest and safest magnets to use; thus producing the result we show you.

Note: This slime is quiet messy, so you need to be careful and only play with it in areas where you can easily wash slime off.

HOW TO MAKE SLIME

Ingredients

- ¹/₂ Cup Clear PVA Glue
- ¹/₂ Cup Cold Water
- 4 Tablespoons Black Iron Oxide Filings
- 2 Tablespoons Black Sequins
- 3 Tablespoons Glow in the Dark Paint
- 1 Tablespoon Black Metallic Acrylic Paint
- 1 Cup Borax Solution

Directions

1) Pour **Clear Glue** into your mixing bowl.

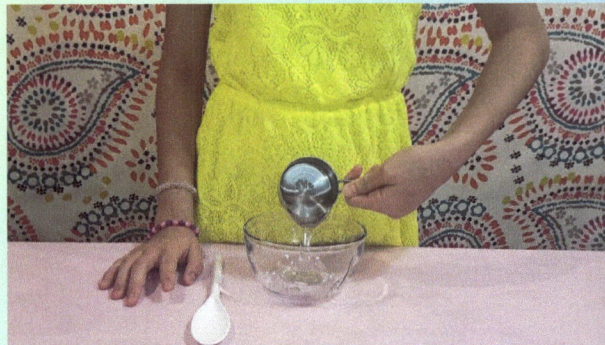

2) Add **Cold Water** to bowl and mix well

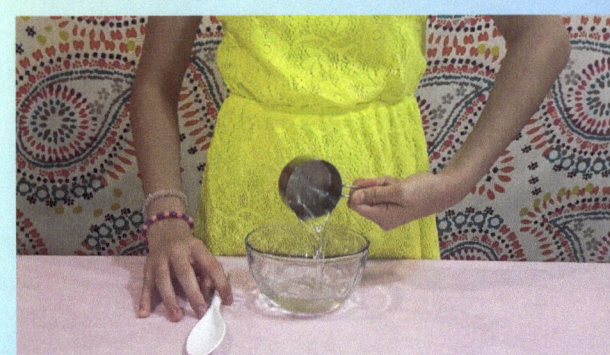

3) Add **Iron Oxide**, one Tablespoon at a time and mix it well. I advise wearing eye protection as well as gloves. You will need to sufficiently work the iron powder into slime and is always advice to protect your hand when you first mix compounds together.

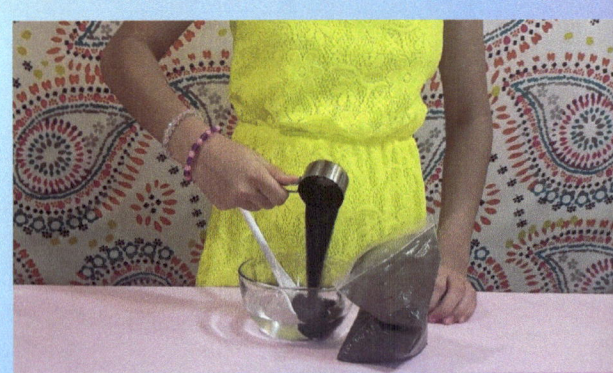

4) Add **Black Sequins** and mix well.

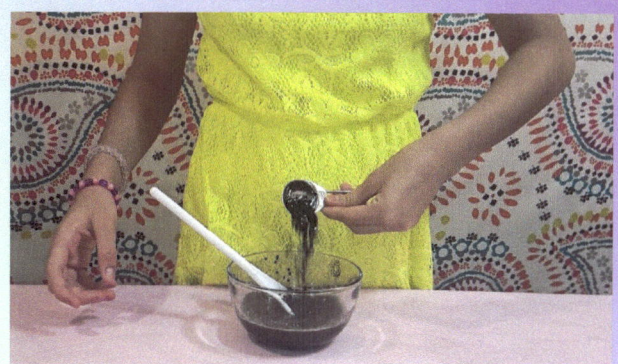

5) Add **Glow in the Dark Paint** and mix well

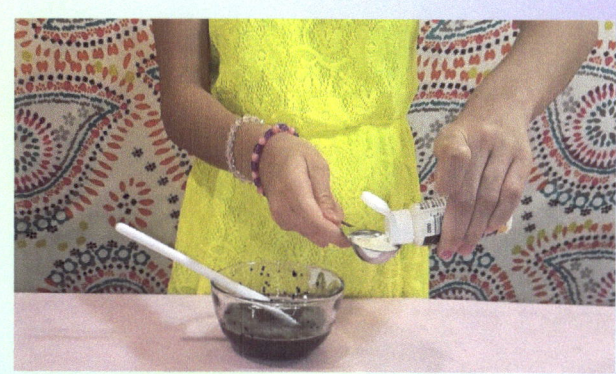

6) Add **Black Paint** and mix well

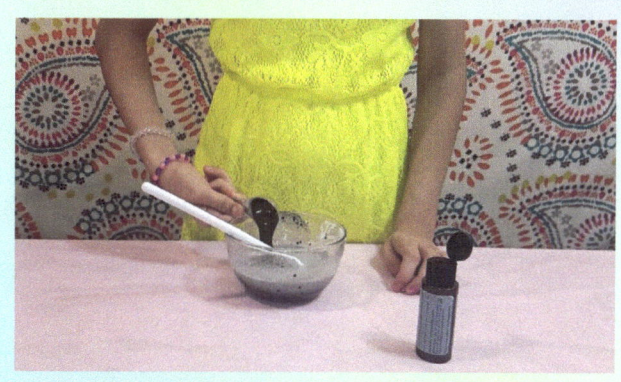

7) Add **Borax Solution** slowly. Squirt directly from the bottle to mixing bowl. Don't over use contact lens solution or slime comes out hard like rubber. You need about 1 Cup (16 Tablespoons). No measuring spoons are being used, therefore, use your best judgement.

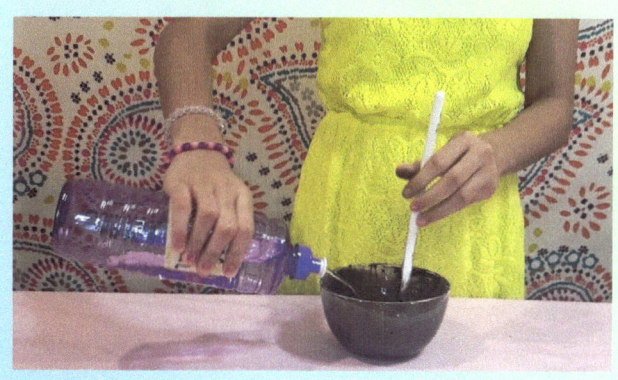

HOW TO MAKE SLIME

8) Use a **Spatula** to mix as you keep adding borax solution. Keep stirring until the slime doesn't stick to the bowl or your hands.

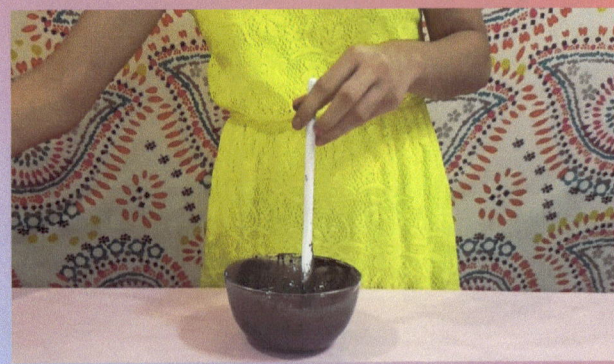

9) Once the glue starts to look like slime, **Knead** the mixture with your hands until you get the right slime consistency; smooth and soft enough to stretch with hands.

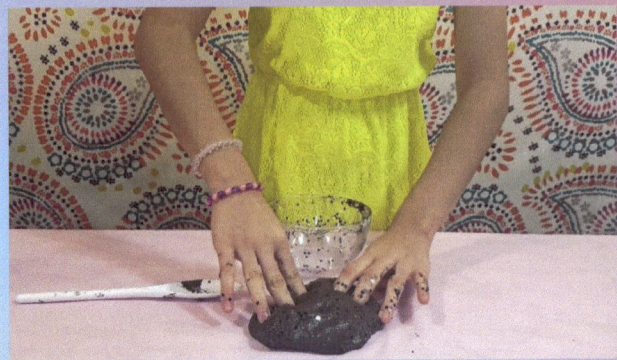

WHAT THE SLIME SHOULD LOOK LIKE

Stretched Dark Matter Slime

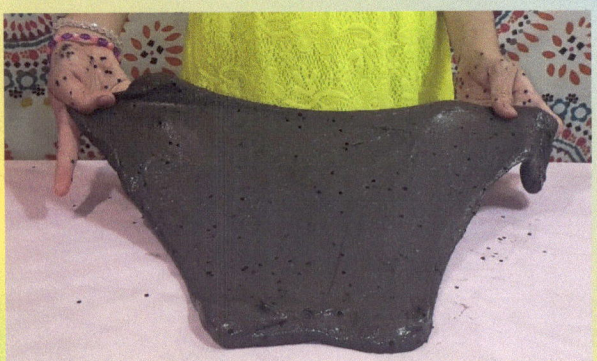

Dark Matter Slime in a **Storage Container**

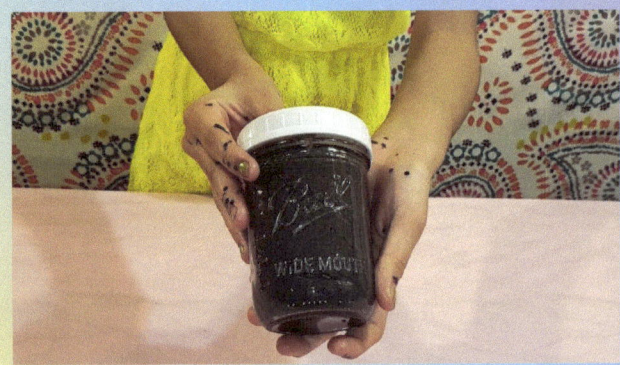

Dark Matter Slime is **Magnetic**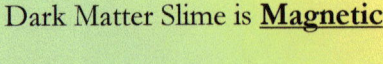

Now you have a magnetic slime!

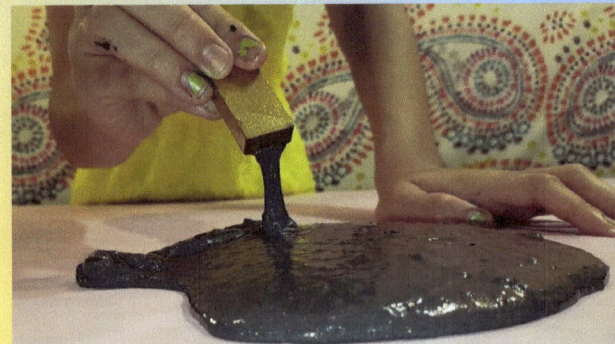

Recipe 30. Blue Jelly Slime

This is called Blue Jelly Slime because it is blue and jelly kind of like Jolly Rancher candies, where you can see through them. Make this amazing recipe in various colors is fun.

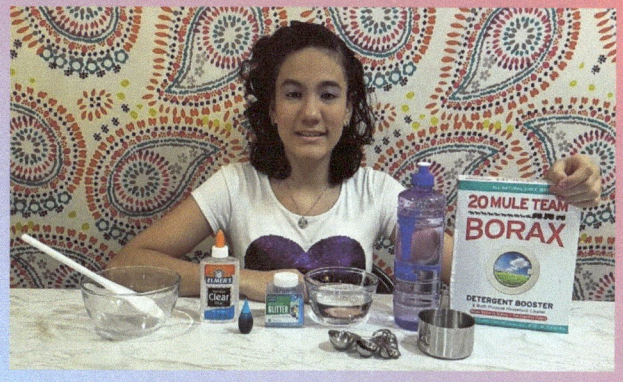

Ingredients

- $1/2$ Cup Clear PVA Glue
- $1/2$ Cup Cold Water
- 10 Drops Neon Blue Food Coloring
- 1 Teaspoon Extra Fine Blue Glitter
- 1 Cup Borax Solution

Directions

1) Pour **Clear Glue** into your mixing bowl.

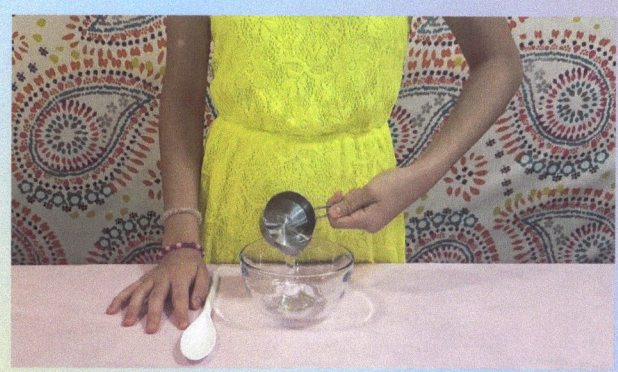

2) Add **Cold Water** and mix well

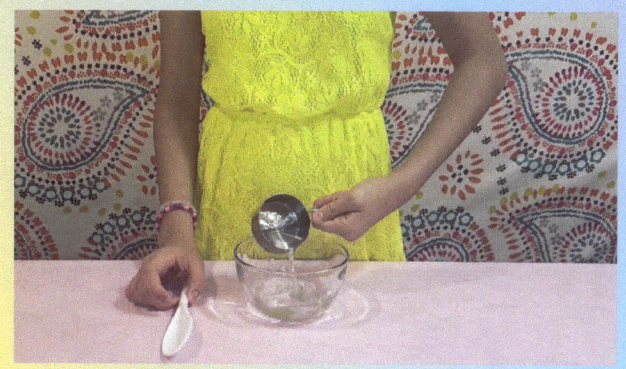

HOW TO MAKE SLIME

3) Add <u>**Neon Blue Food Coloring**</u> and mix well.

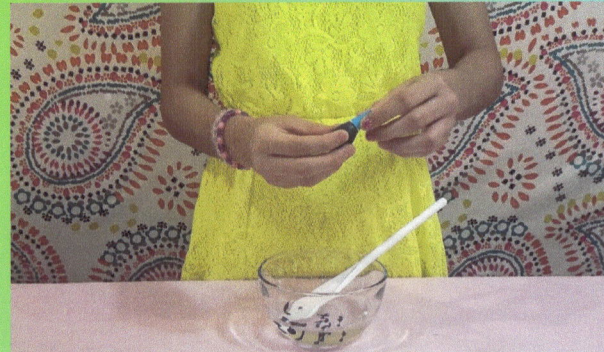

4) Add <u>**Extra Fine Blue Glitter**</u> and mix well

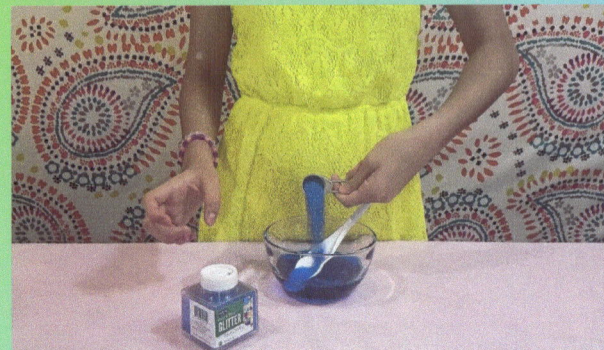

5) Add <u>**Borax Solution**</u> slowly. Squirt directly from the bottle to mixing bowl. Don't over use contact lens solution or slime comes out hard like rubber. You need about 1 Cup (16 Tablespoons). No measuring spoons are being used, therefore, use your best judgement.

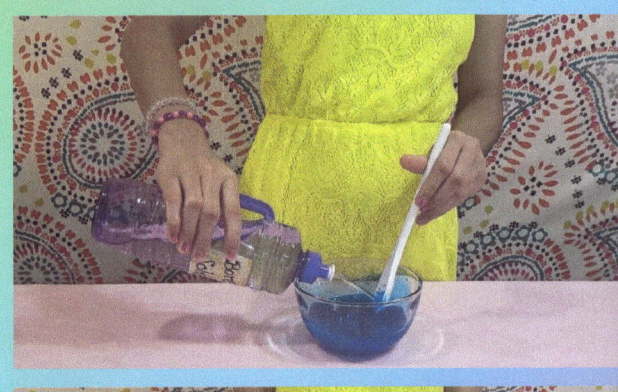

6) Use a <u>**Spatula**</u> to mix as you keep adding borax solution. Keep stirring until the slime doesn't stick to the bowl or your hands.

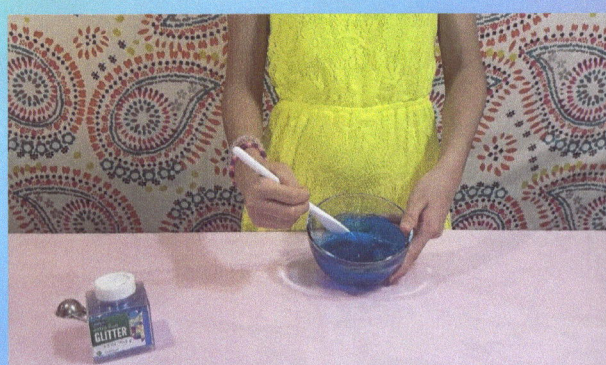

7) Once the glue starts to look like slime, **Knead** the mixture with your hands until you get the right slime consistency; smooth and soft enough to stretch with hands.

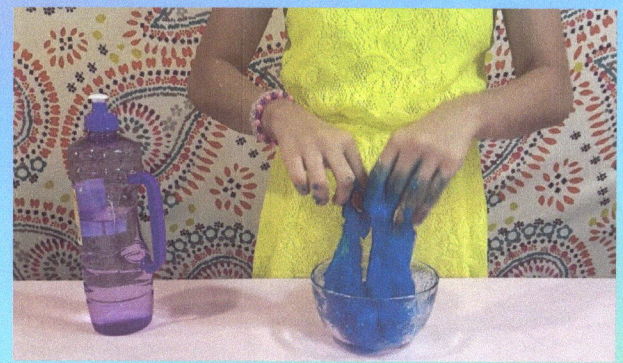

WHAT THE SLIME SHOULD LOOK LIKE

Stretched Blue Jelly Slime

Blue Jelly Slime in a **Storage Container**

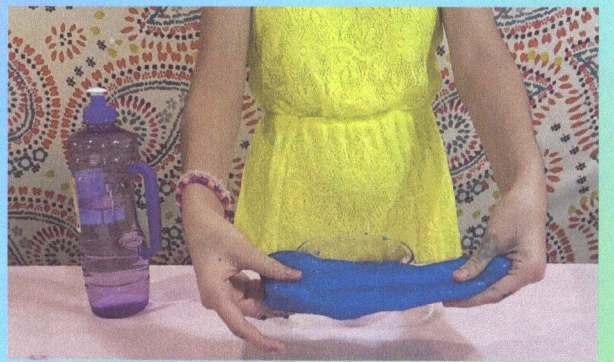
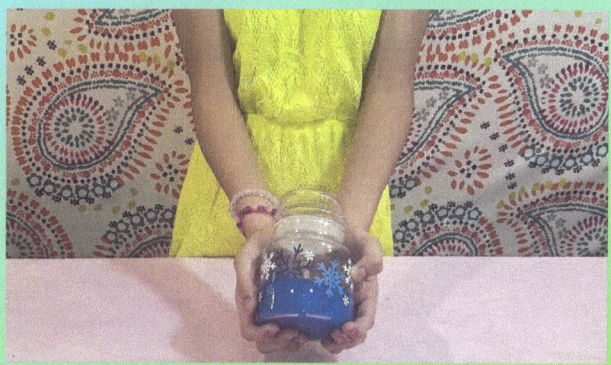

Now you have a peaceful, glittery slime!

RECIPE 31. CHERRY SLUSHY SLIME

The consistency of this slime is like no other. My sisters just love this This recipe is called Cherry Slushy Slime because it looks just like a Slushy you buy on a hot summer day.

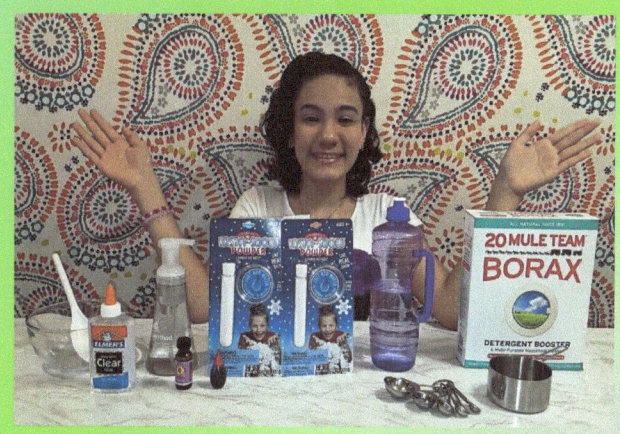

HOW TO MAKE SLIME

Ingredients

- 1 Cup Clear PVA Glue
- 16 Drops Red Food Coloring
- $1/2$ Teaspoon or 20 Drops Cherry Scent
- 4 Tablespoons Foaming Hand Soap
- 1 Cup Borax Solution
- 1 Cup Insta-Snow

Directions

1) Pour **Clear Glue** into your mixing bowl.

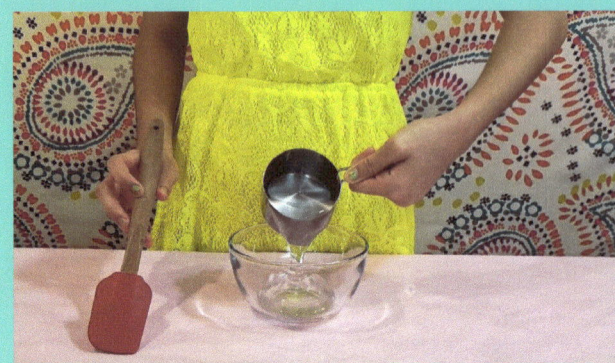

2) Add 8 drops of **Red Food Coloring** and mix well.

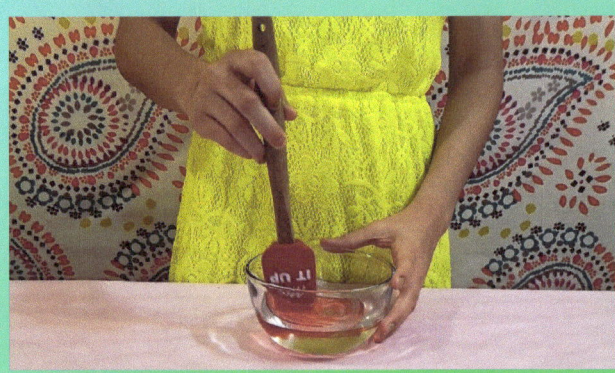

3) Add **Foaming Hand Soap** and mix well

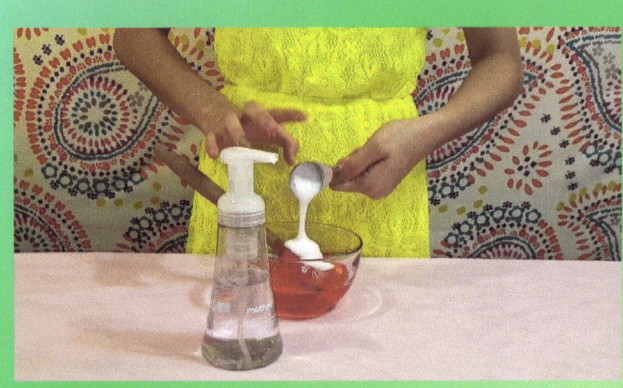

4) Add **Cherry** **Scent** and mix well.

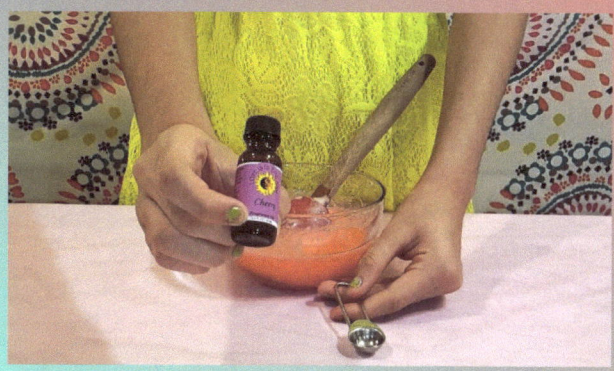

5) Add **Borax Solution** slowly. Squirt directly from the bottle to mixing bowl. Don't over use contact lens solution or slime comes out hard like rubber. You need about 1 Cup (16 Tablespoons). No measuring spoons are being used, therefore, use your best judgement.

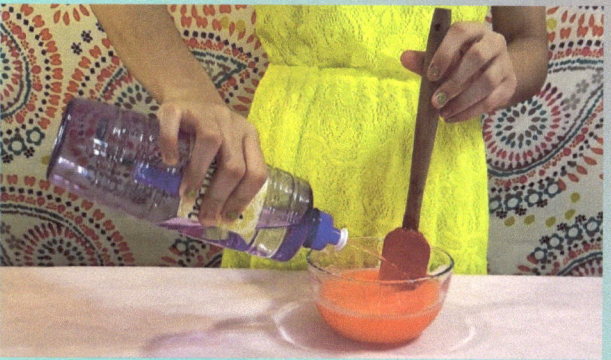

6) Use a **Spatula** to mix as you keep adding borax solution. Keep stirring until the slime doesn't stick to the bowl or your hands.

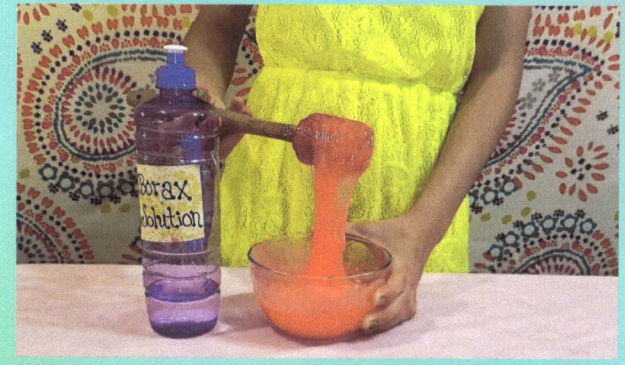

7) Once the glue starts to look like slime, **Knead** the mixture with your hands until you get the right slime consistency; smooth and soft enough to stretch with hands.

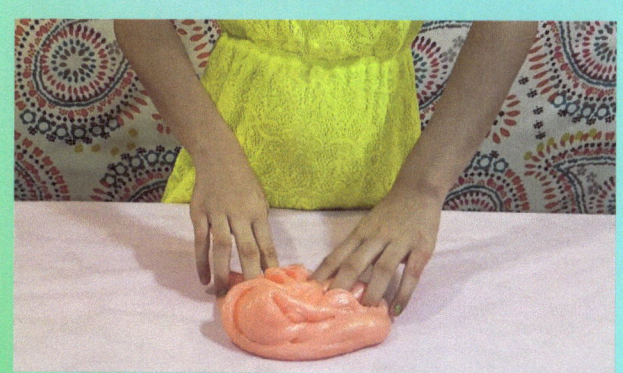

HOW TO MAKE SLIME

8) Add **Cold** **Water** to bowl

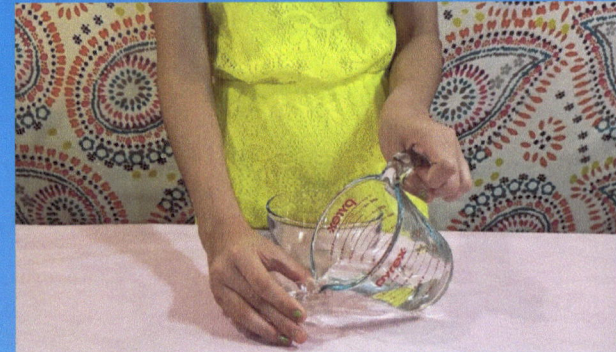

9) Add **Fake** **Snow** **Powder** and mixed well

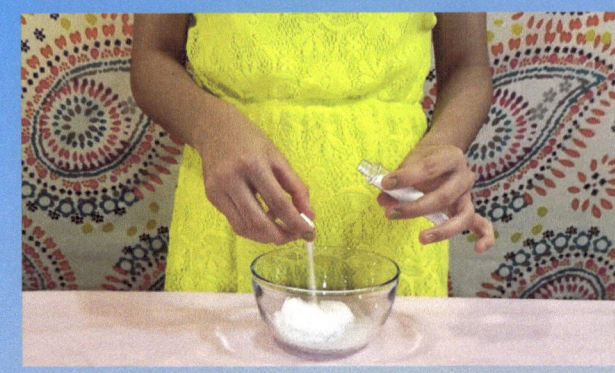

10) Add 8 drops of **Red** **Food** **Coloring** and mix well.

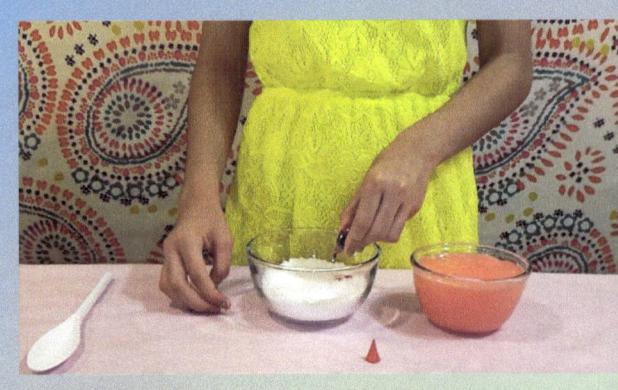

11) **Combine** your slime to the Insta-Snow.

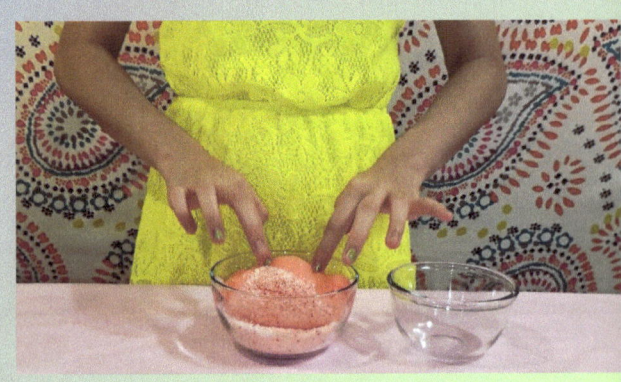

12) **Knead** with your hands until it's combined.

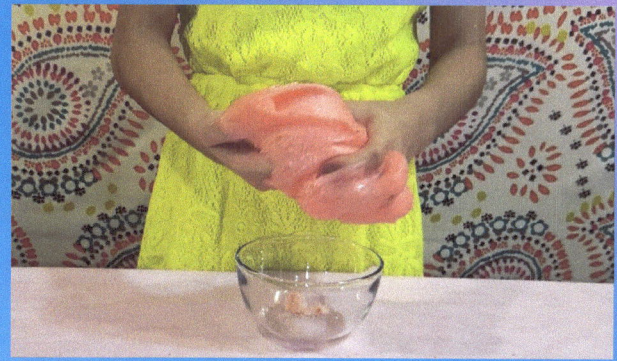

WHAT THE SLIME SHOULD LOOK LIKE

Stretched Cherry Slushy Slime

Cherry Slushy Slime in a **Storage Container**

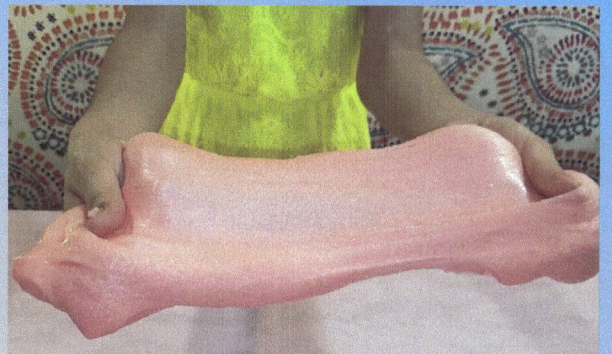
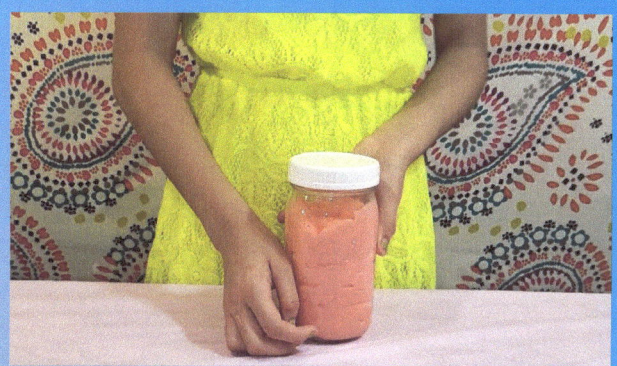

Now you have a soft, light slime!

RECIPE 32. HOLOGRAPHIC SLIME

Holographic powder gives an amazing futuristic finish to any craft. I love playing and mixing this amazing pigment. This recipe is called Holographic Slime because we use real holographic pigment to give it its amazing color effect.

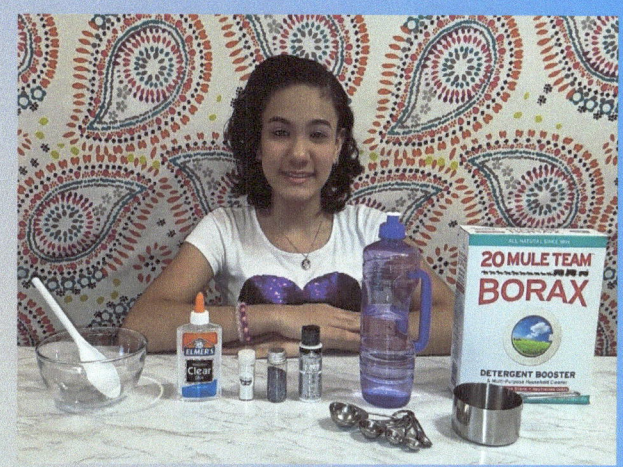

HOW TO MAKE SLIME

Ingredients

- $\frac{1}{2}$ Cup Clear PVA Glue
- 1 Teaspoon Hologram Sequins
- 1 Teaspoon or 2 Teaspoons Holographic Acrylic Paint
- 2 Teaspoons Extra Fine Glitters
- 1 Cup Borax Solution

Directions

1) Pour **Clear Glue** into your mixing bowl.

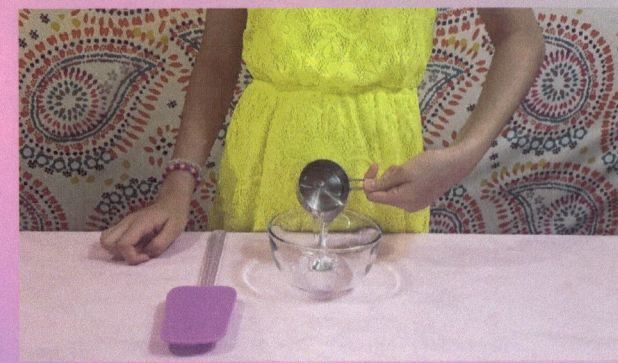

2) Add the **Extra Fine Glitter** and mix well

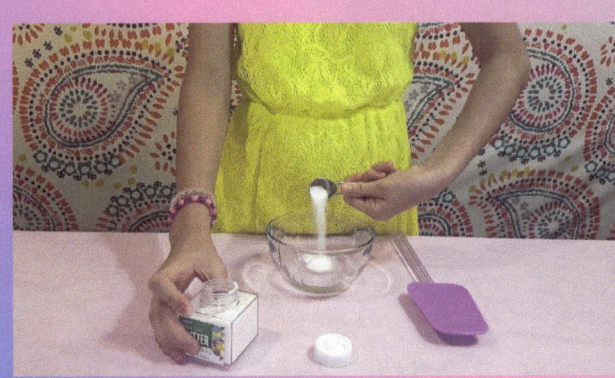

3) Add **Hologram Powder** and mix well. Use acrylic paint if u cannot find powder.

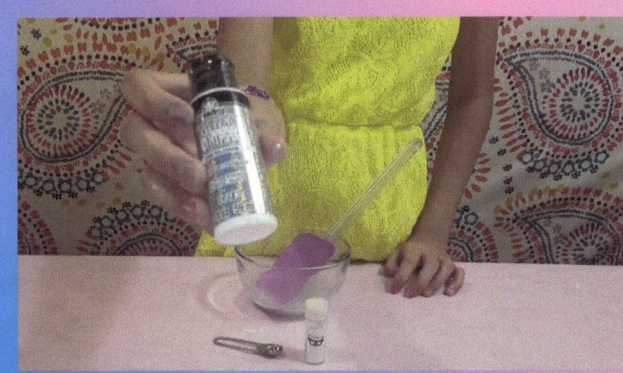

4) Add **Hologram Sequins** and mix well

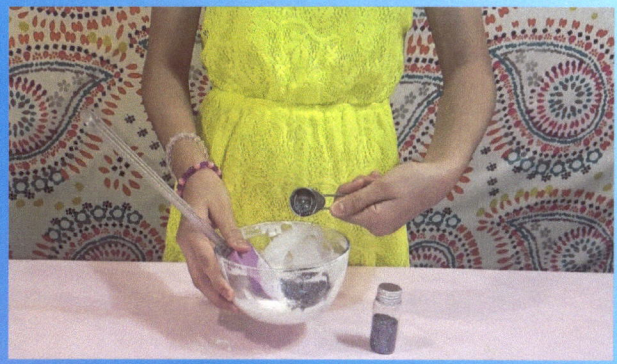

5) Add **Borax Solution** slowly. Squirt directly from the bottle to mixing bowl. Don't over use contact lens solution or slime comes out hard like rubber. You need about 1 Cup (16 Tablespoons). No measuring spoons are being used, therefore, use your best judgement.

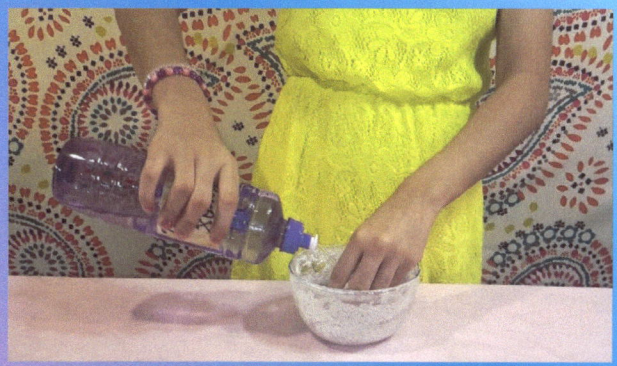

6) Use a **Spatula** to mix as you keep adding borax solution. Keep stirring until the slime doesn't stick to the bowl or your hands.

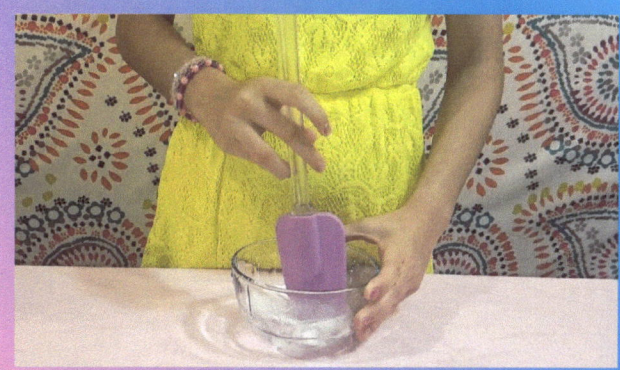

7) Once the glue starts to look like slime, **Knead** the mixture with your hands until you get the right slime consistency; smooth and soft enough to stretch with hands.

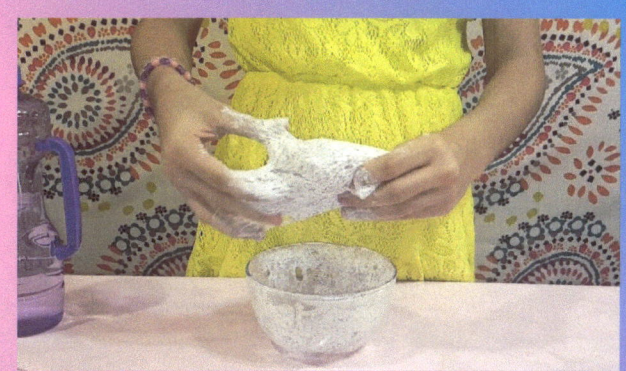

HOW TO MAKE SLIME

HAT THE SLIME SHOULD LOOK LIKE

<u>Stretched</u> Holographic Slime

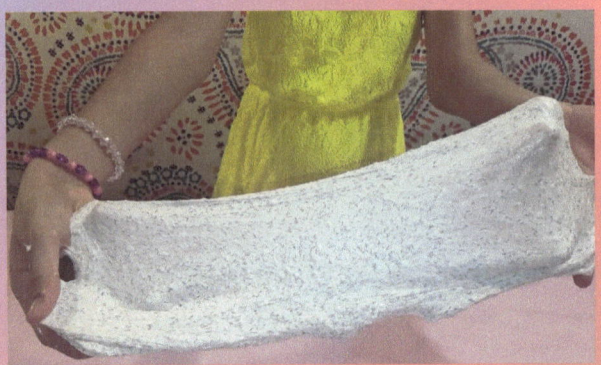

Holographic Slime in a <u>Storage Container</u>

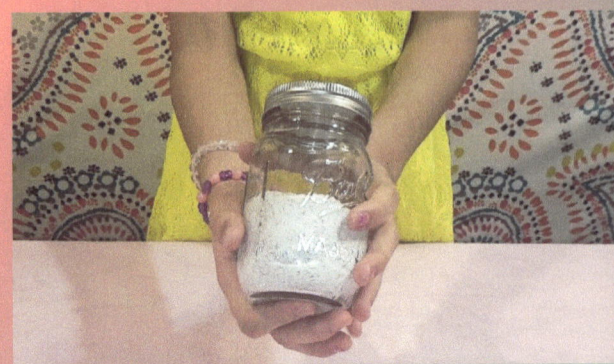

Now you have a cool futuristic slime!

RECIPE 33. YIN YANG SLIME

This slime is Yin Yang because it represents the dark and the light. It is super stretchy and super smooth. You will enjoy seeing the two different colors clash together.

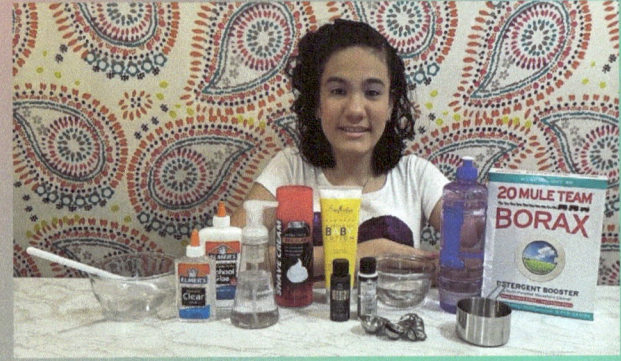

<u>Ingredients</u>

- 1 Cup White PVA Glue
- 1/2 Cup Clear PVA Glue
- 1/2 Cup Cold Water
- 2 Tablespoons Hologram Acrylic Paint
- 2 Tablespoons Metallic Black Acrylic Paint
- 1 Cup Shaving Cream
- 4 Tablespoons Foaming Hand Soap
- 3 Tablespoons Hand Lotion
- 1 Cup Borax Solution

KUKI SHAMUS

Directions

1) Pour **White Glue** into your mixing bowl.

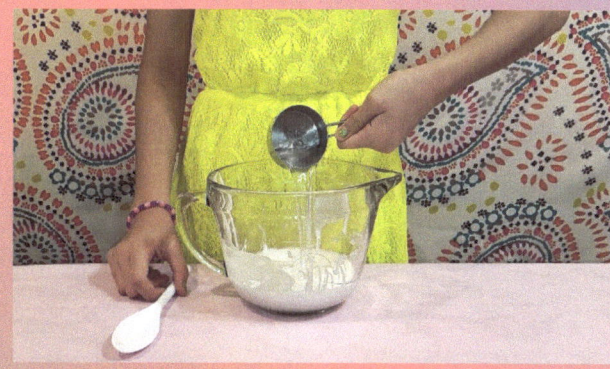

2) Pour **Clear Glue** and mix well.

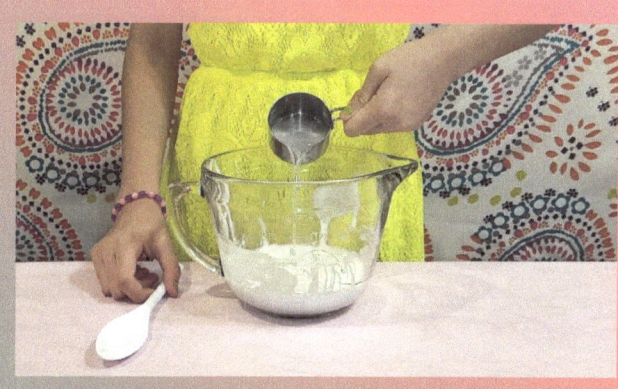

3) Pour **Cold Water** and mix well.

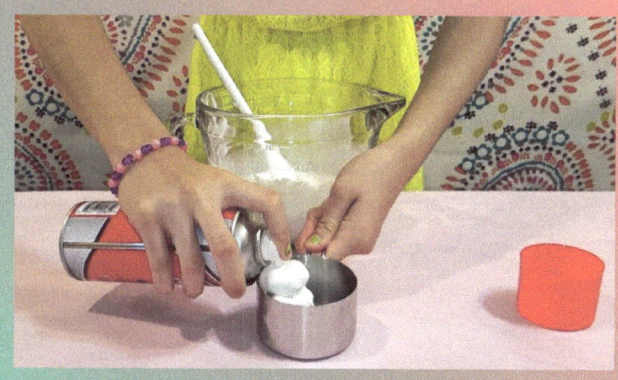

4) Add **Shaving Cream** with help of a spatula and mix well

HOW TO MAKE SLIME

5) Add **<u>Foaming Hand Soap</u>** and mix well

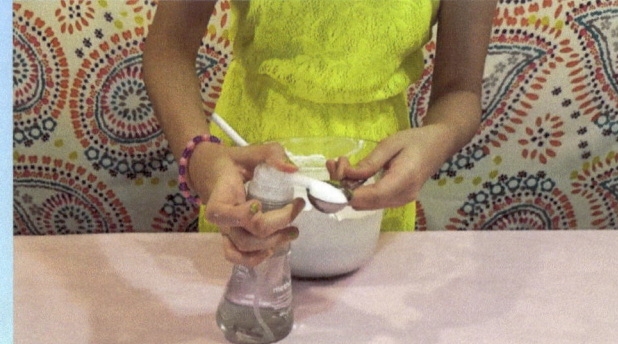

6) Add **<u>Hand Lotion</u>** and mix well

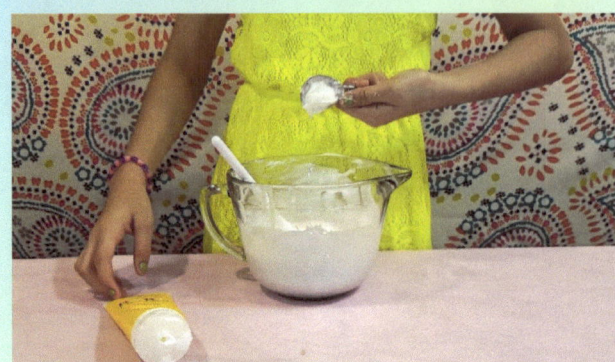

7) Add **<u>Borax Solution</u>** slowly. Squirt directly from the bottle to mixing bowl. Don't over use contact lens solution or slime comes out hard like rubber. You need about 1 Cup (16 Tablespoons). No measuring spoons are being used, therefore, use your best judgement.

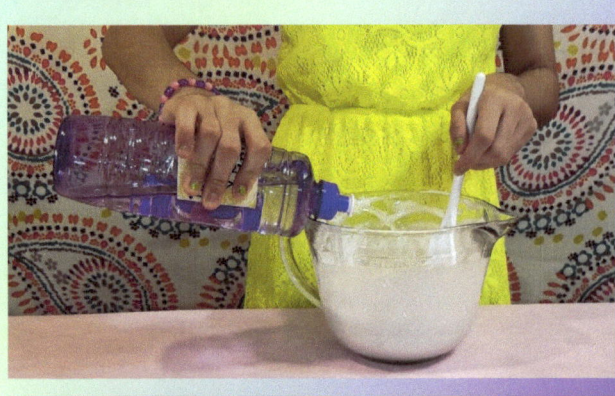

8) Use a **<u>Spatula</u>** to mix as you keep adding borax solution. Keep stirring until the slime doesn't stick to the bowl or your hands.

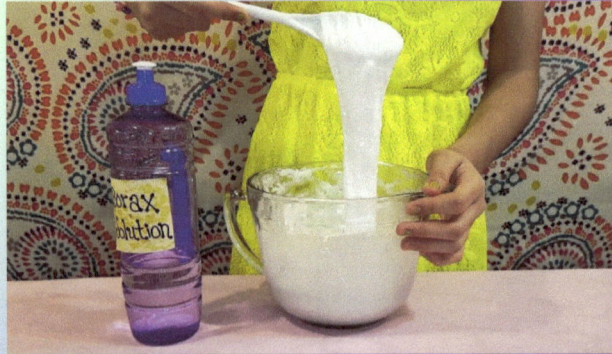

9) Once the glue starts to look like slime, **<u>Knead</u>** the mixture with your hands until you get the right slime consistency; smooth and soft enough to stretch with hands.

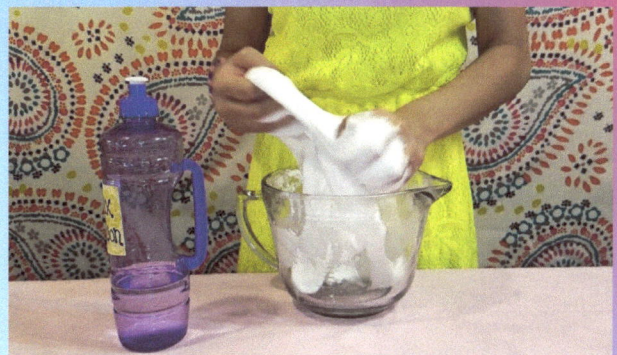

10) **<u>Divide</u> <u>the</u> <u>Slime</u>** into two equal parts. Put both parts of slime into separate bowls.

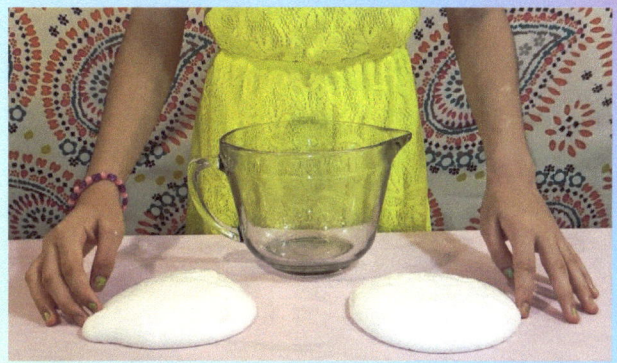

11) Add **<u>Hologram</u> <u>Paint</u>** to the first part of slime. Mix well to make the white yang.

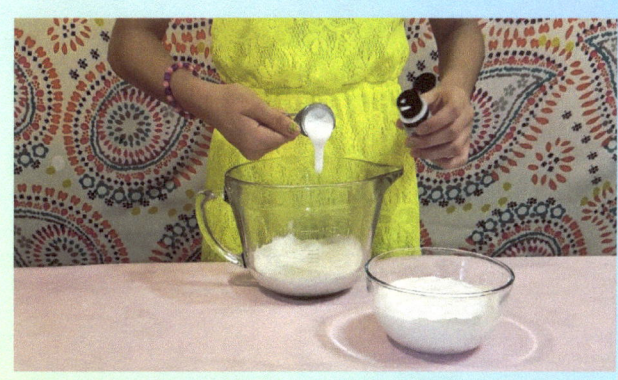

12) Add **<u>Metallic</u> <u>Black</u> <u>Paint</u>** to the second part of slime. Mix well to make the black yin.

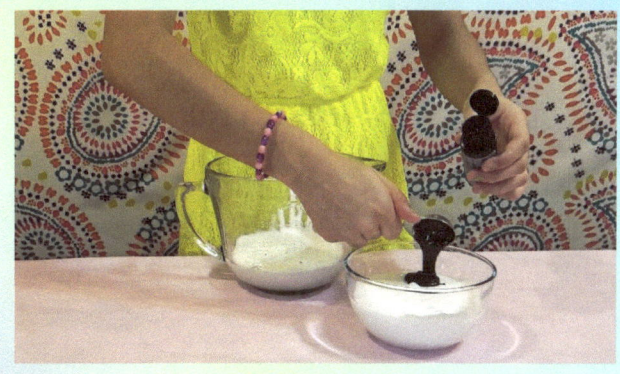

HOW TO MAKE SLIME

13) Lay both slimes next to each other in a **Yin Yang** design.

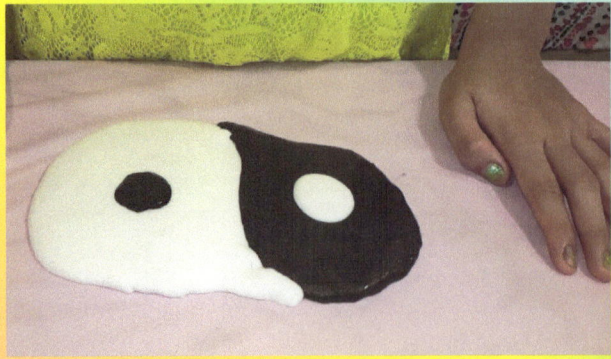

WHAT THE SLIME SHOULD LOOK LIKE

Stretched Yin-Yang Slime

Yin-Yang Slime in a **Storage Container**

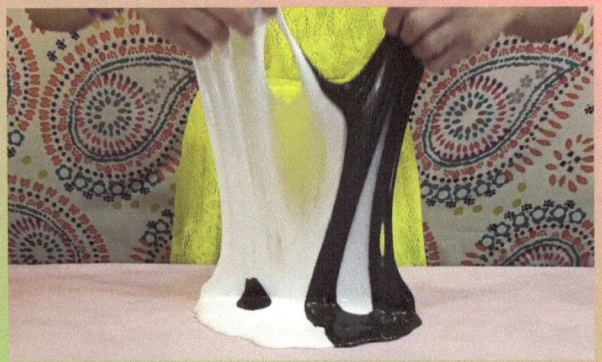
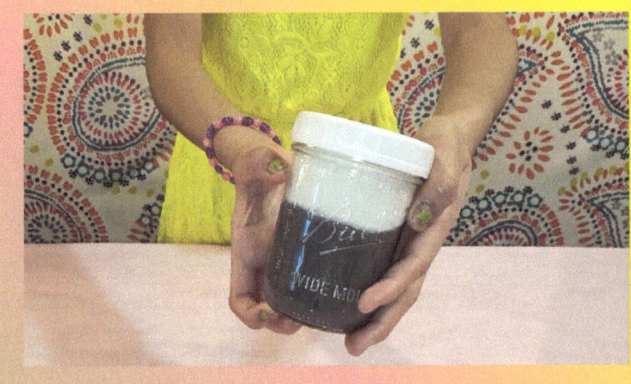

Now you have a Zen energy slime!

RECIPE 34. POTTY POOPY SLIME

Two things are for sure. Kids love slime and kids love emojis. Besides the happy face we all love, there a new emoji that made a big statement and that is "The Poop Emoji" KIDS seem to really find this emoji pretty funny. The fact is that they really do love it. So, in honor of the poop emoji I decided to

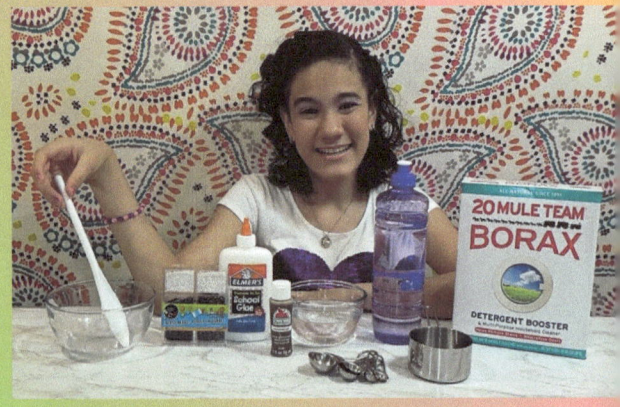

include it in the book via the slime I named Potty Poopy Slime.

KUKI SHAMUS

Ingredients

- ½ Cup White PVA Glue
- ½ Cup Cold Water
- 1 Cup Borax Solution
- 2 Tablespoons Dark Brown Acrylic Paint
- 1 Tablespoon Small White Beads (optional)

Directions

1) Pour **White Glue** into your mixing bowl.

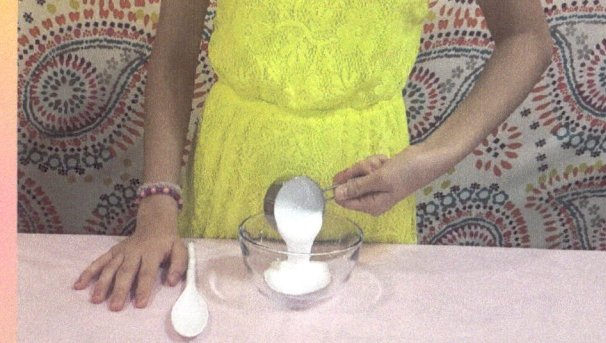

2) Add **Cold Water** to bowl and mix well.

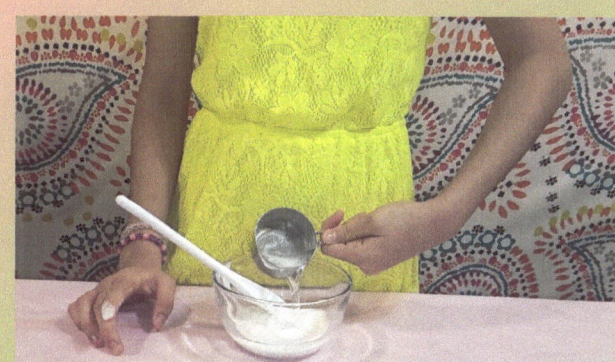

3) Add **Brown Paint** and mix well

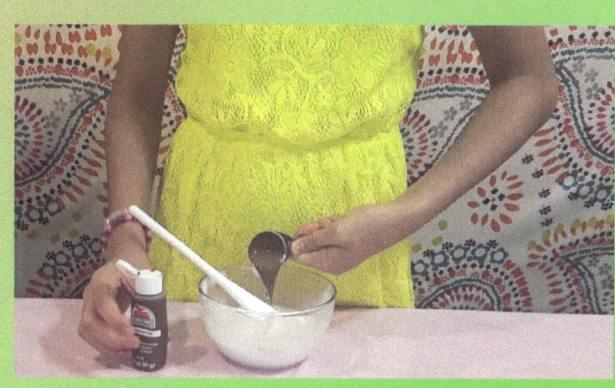

HOW TO MAKE SLIME

4) When the slime isn't form yet and still sticky add the **<u>Beads</u>** and blend in together.

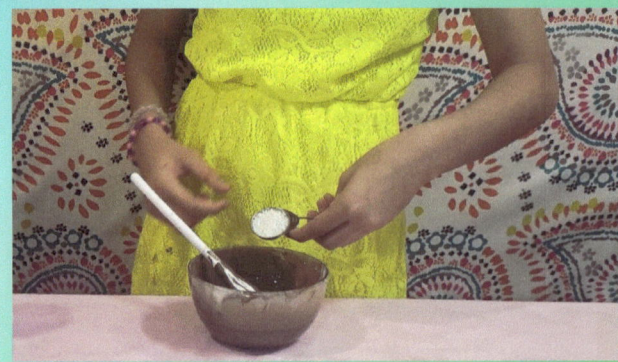

5) Add **<u>Borax Solution</u>** slowly. Squirt directly from the bottle to mixing bowl. Don't over use contact lens solution or slime comes out hard like rubber. You need about 1 Cup (16 Tablespoons). No measuring spoons are being used, therefore, use your best judgement.

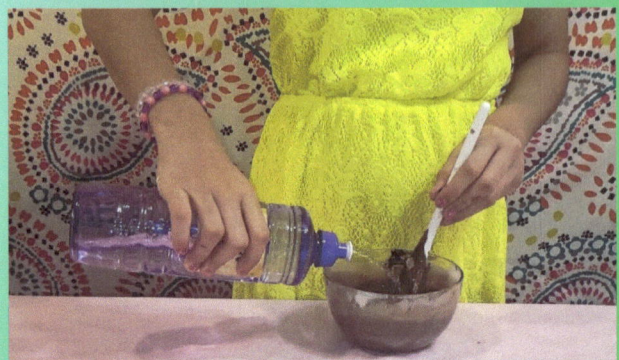

6) Use a **<u>Spatula</u>** to mix as you keep adding borax solution. Keep stirring until the slime doesn't stick to the bowl or your hands.

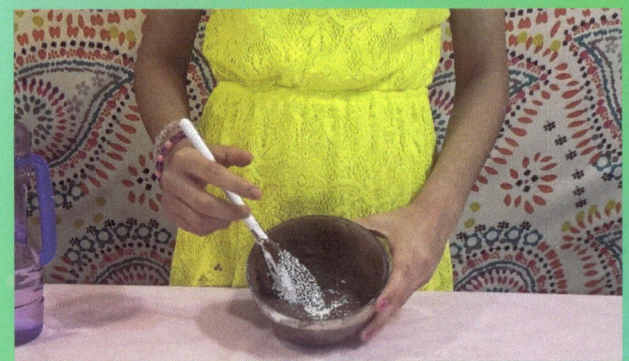

7) Once the glue starts to look like slime, **<u>Knead</u>** the mixture with your hands until you get the right slime consistency; smooth and soft enough to stretch with hands.

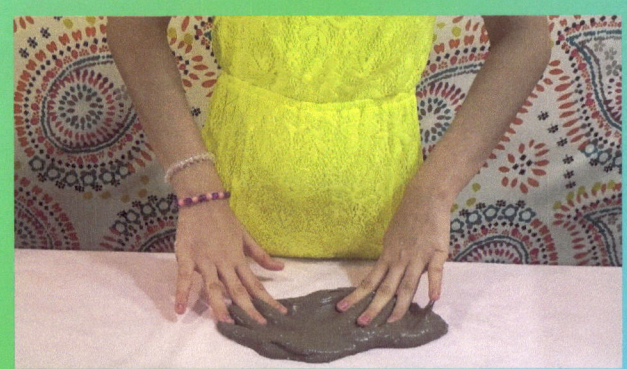

WHAT THE SLIME SHOULD LOOK LIKE

Stretched Potty Poopy Slime   Potty Poopy Slime in a **Storage** **Container**

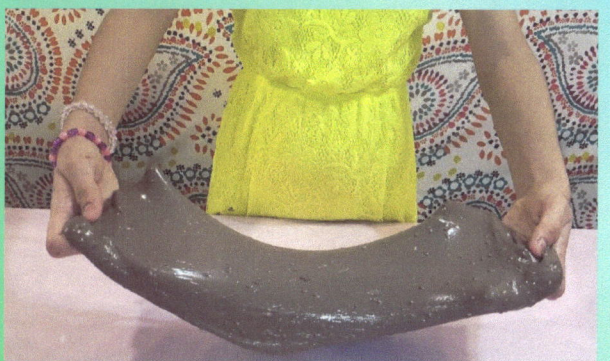 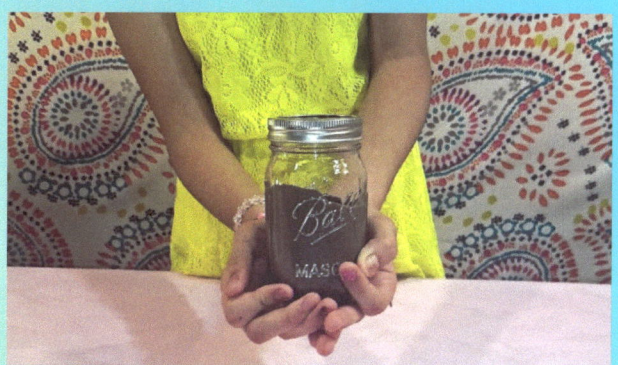

Now you have a poopylicious slime!

RECIPE 35. SURPRISE SLIME

Originally, I was going to call this left over slime because you may have some left over materials just being stored. This is the perfect way to use up any little left over toppings (dry ingredients) and just have fun with the outcome product. What I use in this recipe for materials is just what I had, so you can be creative and do your own blend.

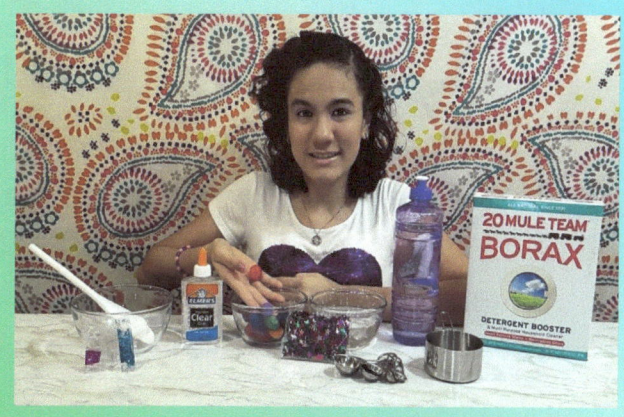

Note: Keep the ratio of dry to wet ingredients (slime) at a max of 1 to 1. Don't put more than 1 cup of overall toppings. Otherwise, the toppings will start falling out as you play with the slime.

Ingredients

- 1 Cup Clear PVA Glue
- $1/2$ Cup Cold Water
- $1/2$ Teaspoon Pink Glitter
- $1/2$ Teaspoon Blue Glitter
- $1/2$ Cup Sparkly Pom-Poms
- 1 Tablespoon Confetti
- 1 Cup Borax Solution

HOW TO MAKE SLIME

Directions

1) Pour **<u>Clear Glue</u>** into your mixing bowl.

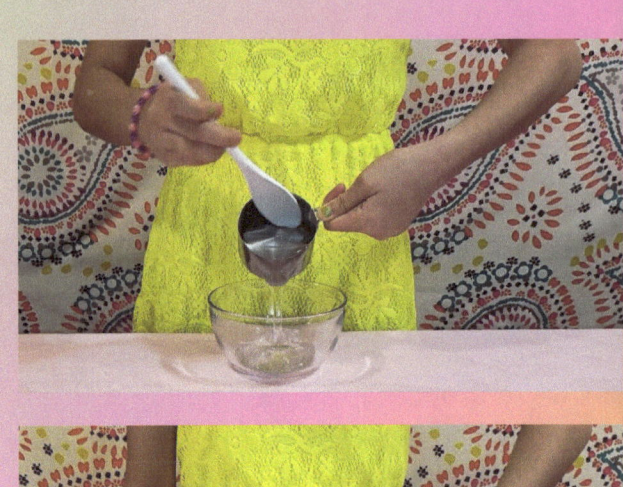

2) Add **<u>Cold Water</u>** and mix well.

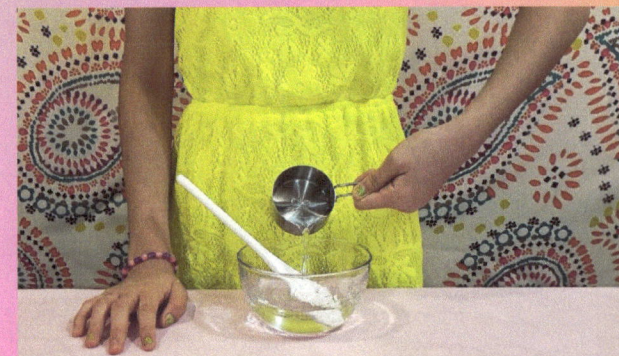

3) Add **<u>Borax Solution</u>** slowly. Squirt directly from the bottle to mixing bowl. Don't over use contact lens solution or slime comes out hard like rubber. You need about 1 Cup (16 Tablespoons). No measuring spoons are being used, therefore, use your best judgement.

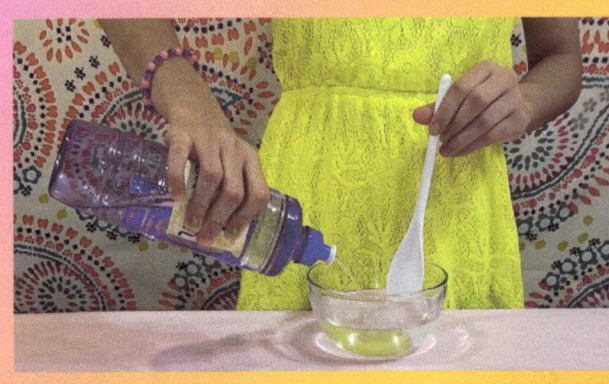

4) Use a **<u>Spatula</u>** to mix as you keep adding borax solution. Keep stirring until the slime doesn't stick to the bowl or your hands.

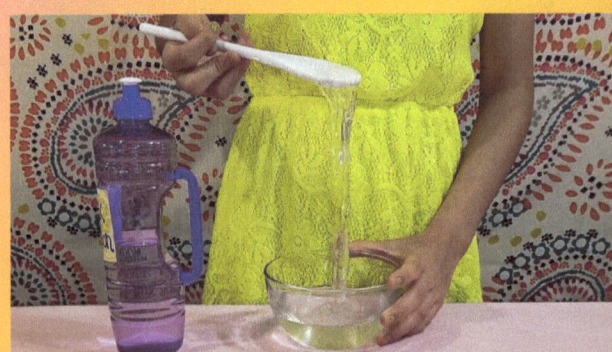

KUKI SHAMUS

5) Add **<u>Pink</u> <u>Glitter</u>** and mix well

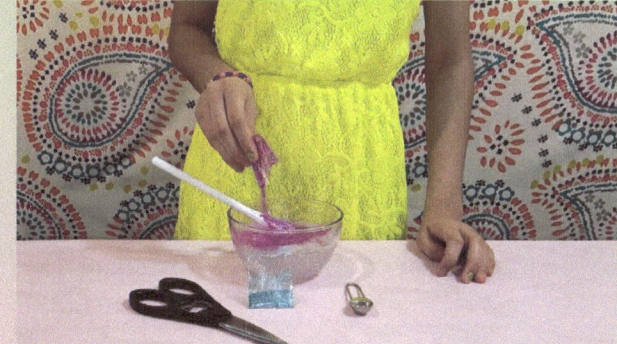

6) Add **<u>Blue</u> <u>Glitter</u>** and mix well

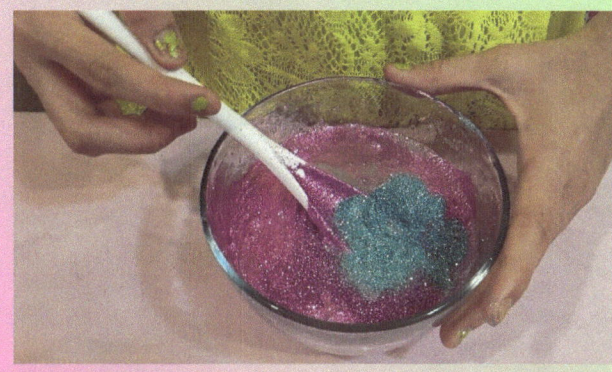

7) Add **<u>Confetti</u>** and mix well

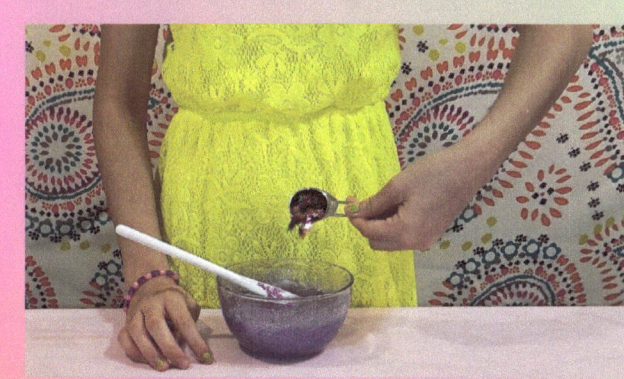

8) Add **<u>Pom-Poms</u>** and mix well

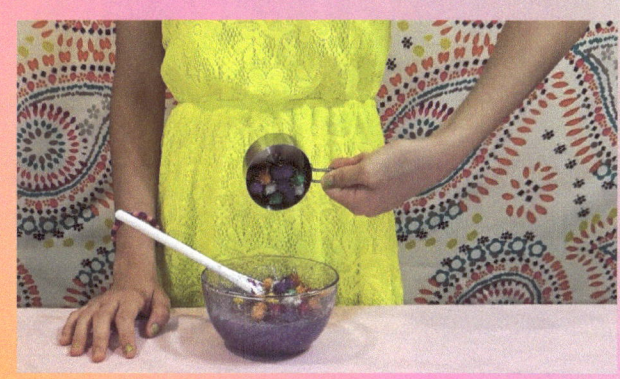

HOW TO MAKE SLIME

9) Add **Borax** **Solution** slowly with small squirts at a time. Squirt directly from the bottle to the mixing bowl and mix well.

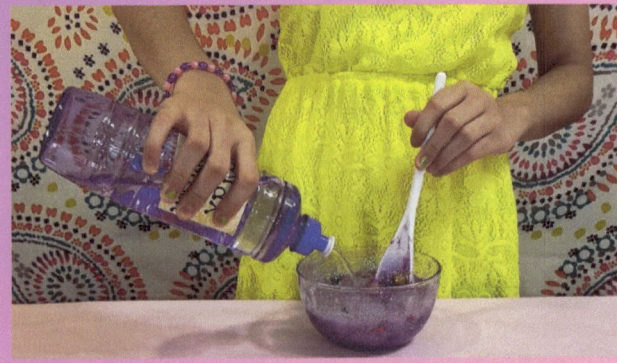

10) Once the glue starts to look like slime, **Knead** the mixture with your hands until you get the right slime consistency; smooth and soft enough to stretch with hands.

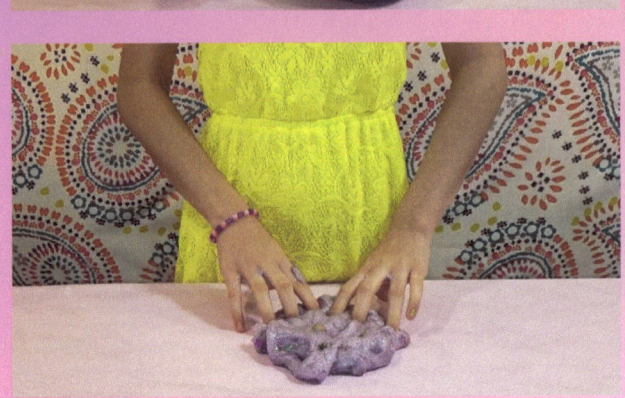

WHAT THE SLIME SHOULD LOOK LIKE

Stretched Surprise Slime

Surprise Slime in a **Storage Container**

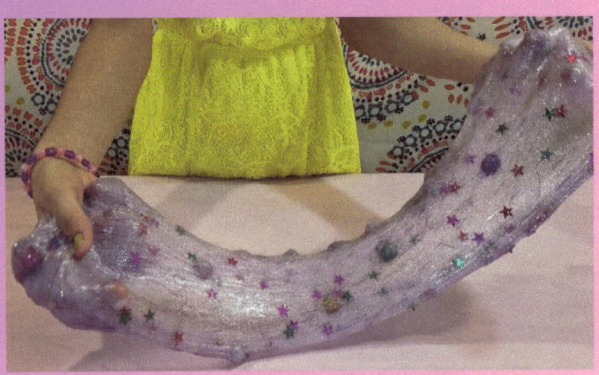
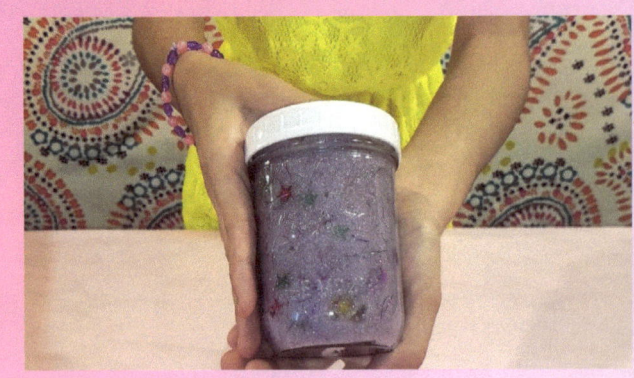

Now you have a very unique textured slime!

Closing

It's time to use what you learned in **How to Make Slime** to help guide you in creating your own batches of slime from home. No need to rely on someone else to make it for you or some store to sell you a certain type of overpriced slime. Now you can have countless hours of satisfying slime fun whenever you want.

Congrats for reading my whole book about slime. I want to give my gratitude to you one more time for getting a copy of my book. It brings me much joy to know other people will be creating beautiful slime and having lots of fun too. Make it a messy day and keep on sliming.

Thank You!

Kuki Shamus

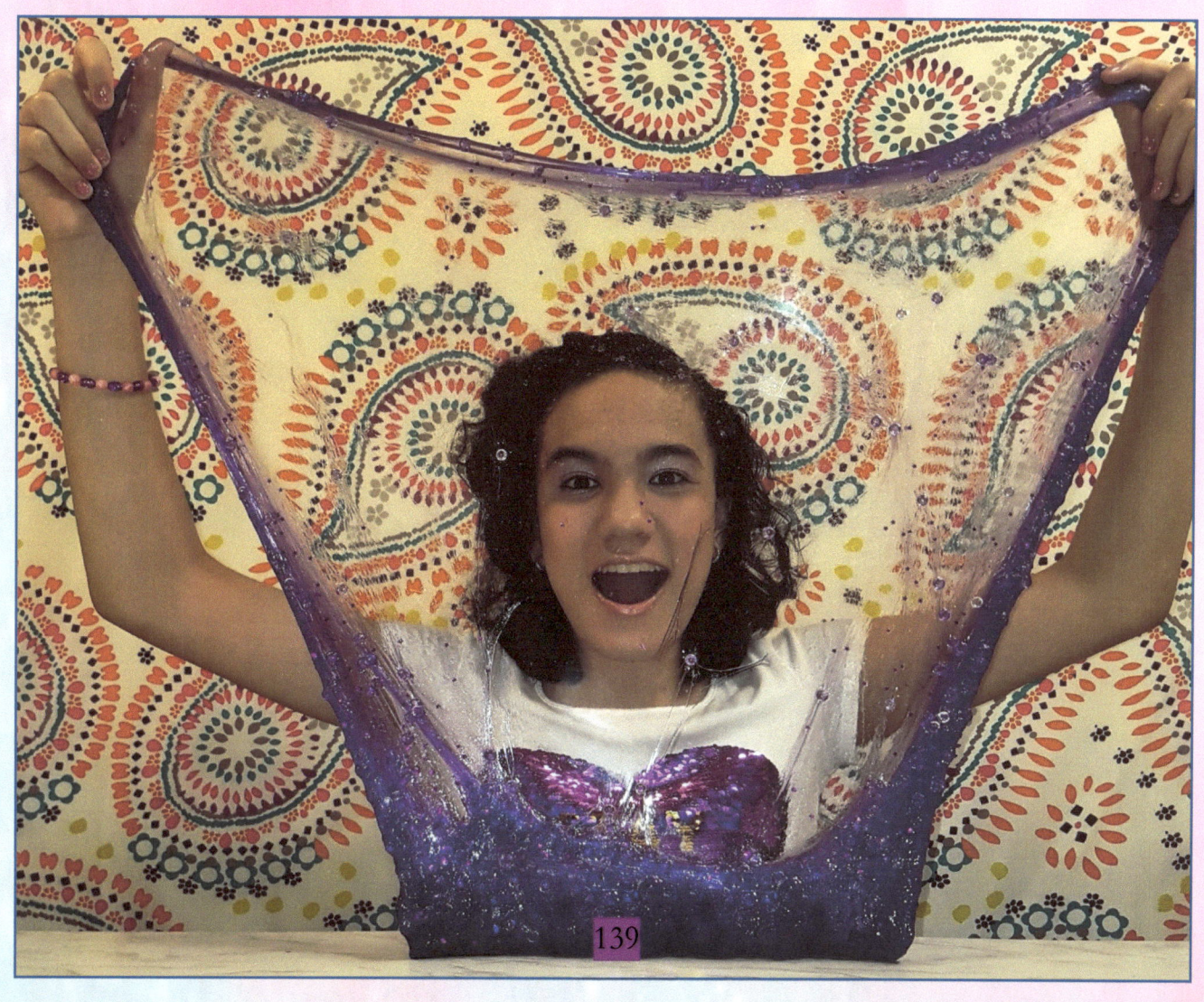

About the Author

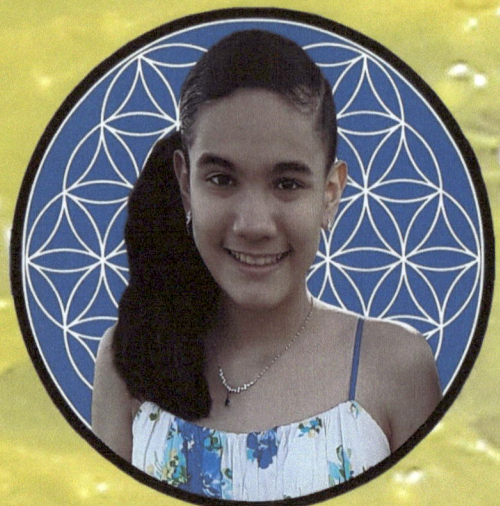

Kuki Shamus is the oldest daughter of Marc & Silvia Shamus. She is a lifelong lover of dogs, music and art. She is one of the Illustrators of the children's book, The Story of Goo.

She lives in Fontana, California with her Dad Marc, Mom Silvia and 4 siblings. Kuki has a background as being home-schooled and has had several successful entrepreneurial projects. She loves singing, social media and having fun with friends.

Learn more about Kuki at:

iMasterLife.com/KukiShamus

Personal Dedication

My parents are published authors who taught me to love reading and putting my own thoughts into words. Mom and dad have supported my dream to have my own published book and video course about slime. I love you deeply and appreciate all the things you did to make this dream a reality.

I also want to give thanks to my three sisters and one brother whose unique personalities keep life exciting. Your help with testing out the slime recipes made a big difference in getting this slime book and video course achieved. I love you all.

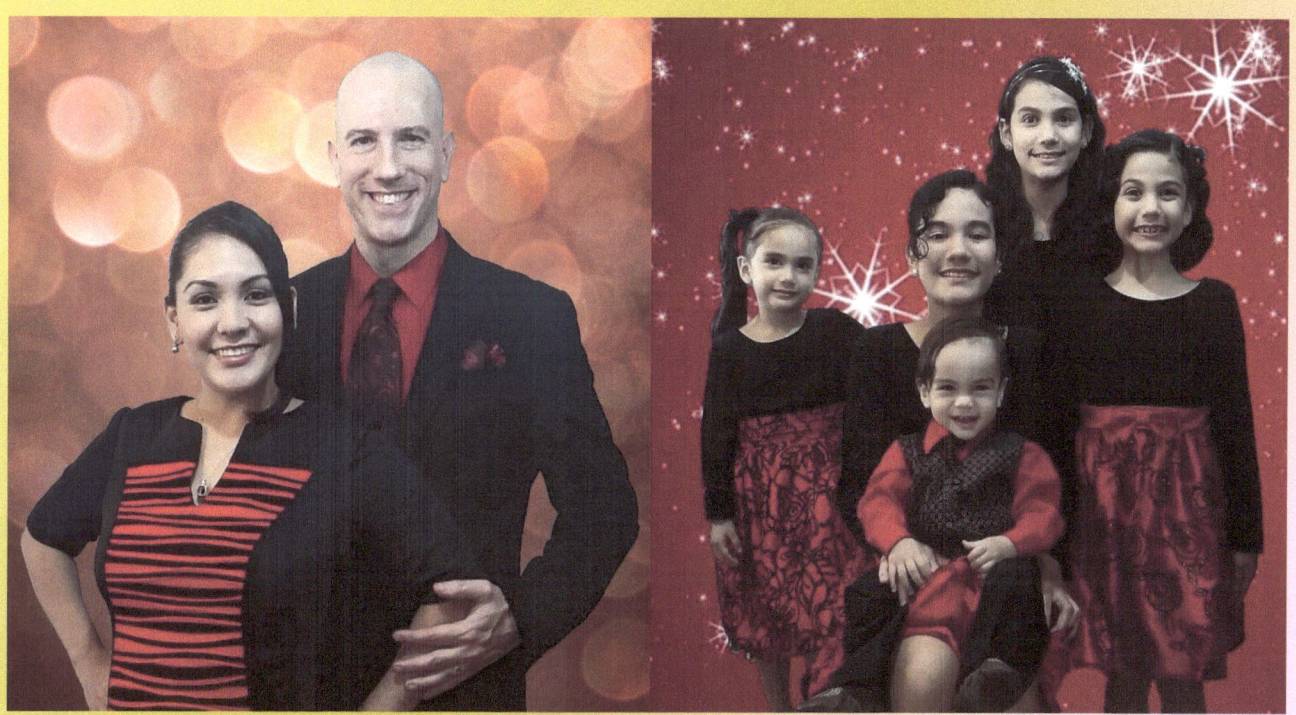

Silvia Shamus and Marc Shamus   Kimiko Shamus, Kuki Shamus, Zen Shamus, Kali Shamus & Zivena Shamus

Did You Love How to Make Slime?

Thank you for investing in yourself and in this book.

If you enjoyed this book, please let others know how much they can benefit from it by leaving a review here:

iMasterLife.com/Reviews/Kuki

If you have feedback on how to make this book even better, I'd love to hear it at kuki@imasterlife.com

Thanks!

Kuki Shamus

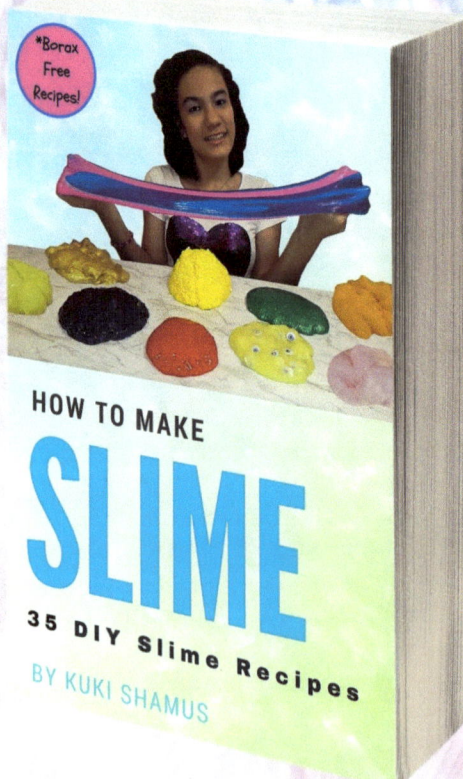

Thanks again for your support!

Watch "How To Make Slime" Video Course

Get access to the video course this slime book is based on by going to **iMasterLife.com/SlimeCourse**

Inside the course, you'll discover...

• What are the Basics of slime

• How to make 20 100% Borax Free Slime Recipes

• How to make 15 Borax Slime Recipes

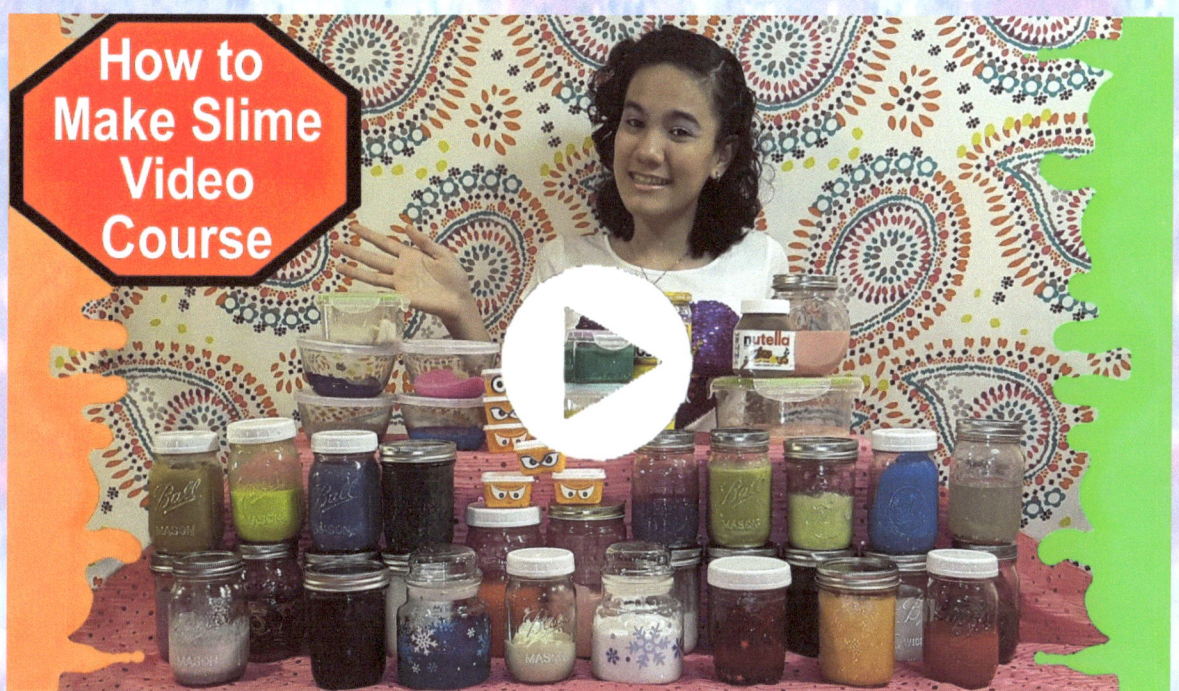

www.ingramcontent.com/pod-product-compliance
Lightning Source LLC
Chambersburg PA
CBHW051148220526
45473CB00003B/694